Contents

Table of Cases   vii
Acknowledgements   ix
Series Preface   xi

1   Introduction   1

2   Political Science and Sociology   25

3   Conservative Jurisprudence: The Natural Law Approach   51

4   Conservative Jurisprudence and the Rehnquist Justices: The Harlan Legacy v. Fainthearted Originalism   69

5   Privacy and Abortion   89

6   Disagreements Amongst the Conservatives: *Planned Parenthood of S.E. Pennsylvania v. Casey*   105

7   Dualist Jurisprudence: Ackerman, Meiklejohn and Ely   119

8   Ronald Dworkin v. Cass Sunstein: First- and Second-Wave Liberalism   145

9   Tribe and Dorf: On How to Read the Constitution   175

10   Bringing it all Together: The Affirmative Action Controversy   187

11   Conclusions   217

Bibliography   233
Index   239

Table of Cases

Akron v. *Akron Center for Reproductive Health*, 462 U.S. 416 (1983)
Baker v. *Carr*, 369 U.S. 186 (1962)
Bolling v. *Sharp*, 347 U.S. 497 (1954)
Bowers v. *Hardwick*, 478 U.S. 186 (1986)
Brown v. *Board of Education*, 347 U.S. 483 (1954)
City of Richmond v. *J.A. Croson Co.*, 488 U.S. 469 (1989)
DeFunis v. *Odegaard*, 416 U.S. 312 (1974)
Doe v. *Bolton*, 410 U.S. 179 (1973)
Eisenstadt v. *Baird*, 405 U.S. 438 (1972)
Employment Division, Oregon Department of Human Resources v. *Smith*, 494 U.S. 872 (1990)
Escobedo v. *Illinois*, 378 U.S. 478 (1964)
Fullilove v. *Klutznick*, 448 U.S. 448 (1980)
Furman v. *Georgia*, 408 U.S. 238 (1972)
Gault, In re, 387 U.S. 1 (1967)
Gregg v. *Georgia*, 428 U.S. 153 (1976)
Griggs v. *Duke Power Company*, 401 U.S. 424 (1971)
Griswold v. *Connecticut*, 381 U.S. 479 (1965)
Johnson v. *Transportation Agency, Santa Clara County, California*, 480 U.S. 616 (1987)
Korematsu v. *U.S.*, 323 U.S. 214 (1944)
Lau v. *Nichols*, 414 U.S. 563 (1974)
Lochner v. *New York*, 198 U.S. 45 (1905)
Mapp v. *Ohio*, 367 U.S. 643 (1961)
Marbury v. *Madison*, 5 U.S. (1 Cr.) 137 (1803)
McCulloch v. *Maryland*, 17 U.S. (4 Wheat.) 316 (1819)
Metro Broadcasting, Inc. v. *FCC*, 497 U.S. 547 (1990)
Miami Herald Publishing Co. v. *Tornillo*, 418 U.S. 241 (1974)
Michael H. v. *Gerald D.*, 491 U.S. 110 (1989)
Miller v. *California*, 413 U.S. 15 (1973)
Miranda v. *Arizona*, 384 U.S. 436 (1966)
New York Times Co. v. *Sullivan*, 376 U.S. 254 (1964)
New York Transit Authority v. *Beazer*, 440 U.S. 568 (1979)
Planned Parenthood of Central Missouri v. *Danforth*, 428 U.S. 52 (1976)

Planned Parenthood of South East Pennsylvania v. *Casey*, 112 S. Ct. 2791 (1992)

Plessy v. *Ferguson*, 163 U.S. 537 (1896)

Poe v. *Ullman*, 367 U.S. 497 (1961)

Regents of the University of California v. *Bakke*, 438 U.S. 265 (1978)

Roe v. *Wade*, 410 U.S. 113 (1973)

Stanley v. *Georgia*, 394 U.S. 557 (1969)

Tennessee Valley Authority v. *Hill*, 437 U.S. 153 (1978)

Thornburgh v. *American College of Obstetricians and Gynecologists*, 476 U.S. 747 (1986)

United Steelworkers of America v. *Weber*, 443 U.S. 193 (1979)

Wards Cove Packing Co. v. *Antonio*, 490 U.S. 642 (1989)

Washington v. *Davis*, 426 U.S. 229 (1976)

West Coast Hotel Co. v. *Parrish*, 300 U.S. 379 (1937)

Wygant v. *Jackson Board of Education*, 476 U.S. 267 (1986)

Acknowledgements

Some sections of this work have been presented at various times to conferences and seminars and I have enjoyed these opportunities to formulate my views and to benefit from criticisms. I am particularly grateful to David Luban who made clear, in the kindest possible way, how and why liberal Americans are likely to respond to my views about the Rehnquist Court. It is partly because of his stimulation that I felt obliged to address the work of liberal constitutional scholars such as Dworkin, Tribe and Ackerman in such detail. Tom Campbell, the editor of the Dartmouth Applied Legal Philosophy series, commented on a first draft of the manuscript and was sufficiently encouraging to keep me on track. I am also grateful to Viktor Vanberg and Richard Wagner, the editors of *Constitutional Political Economy*, for publishing an early statement of my position (vol. 3, no. 2), and for their useful comments and suggestions for revision. Finally I thank Nerida Hodgkins and Craig Lonsdale for their help.

I was assisted by grants from Melbourne University and from the Australian Research Council that enabled me to study in the United States. I must also thank Georgetown University and particularly Colin Campbell as the Director of the Public Policy Program for hospitality.

Series Preface

The objective of the Dartmouth Series in Applied Legal Philosophy is to publish work which adopts a theoretical approach to the study of particular areas or aspects of law or deals with general theories of law in a way which focuses on issues of practical moral and political concern in specific legal contexts.

In recent years there has been an encouraging tendency for legal philosophers to utilize detailed knowledge of the substance and practicalities of law and a noteworthy development in the theoretical sophistication of much legal research. The series seeks to encourage these trends and to make available studies in law which are both genuinely philosophical in approach and at the same time based on appropriate legal knowledge and directed towards issues in the criticism and reform of actual laws and legal systems.

The series will include studies of all the main areas of law, presented in a manner which relates to the concerns of specialist legal academics and practitioners. Each book makes an original contribution to an area of legal study while being comprehensible to those engaged in a wide variety of disciplines. Their legal content is principally Anglo-American, but a wide-ranging comparative approach is encouraged and authors are drawn from a variety of jurisdictions.

TOM D. CAMPBELL
Series Editor
The Faculty of Law
The Australian National University

1   Introduction

Democratic political systems are usually characterized by the fact that those who govern must win the approval of the people in competitive elections. Of course there are differences between systems but nearly all are based on the notion that the party that can control the parliaments has a right to govern (enjoying democratic authority to do so except when it tries to avoid future accountability, fails to respect limiting conventions or violates clearly delineated and traditionally accepted constitutional restraints).[1] Following Bruce Ackerman, I refer to this kind of democracy as 'monist'.[2]

What is interesting about recent theoretical debates in the United States is the prevailing understanding that the American system is different. Most legal commentators argue that the United States does not conform to the monist model of a democracy; more significant, they celebrate this fact, arguing that it should not. Instead, they recommend a conception of their system as a 'dualist' democracy.[3] As they see it, very significant restraints should remain on governments in a democracy even after the prevailing party has gained a mandate from the people in a national election. They take pride in the fact that the governing party must share powers with those who have no mandate from the people, and think it a good thing that recent administrations in the United States have not been able to secure all they may have wished to implement. They also claim that it is a good feature of the American system that the party in power (even when it controls both the executive and legislative branches) cannot always prevent others from securing policies it may disapprove.

What is contentious is not merely the desirability of restraints that prevent the governing party from cheating at the next election or from frustrating those who are organizing opposition. According to this vision, governments in the United States must accept that they share power because winning a national election should not and does not guarantee an unrestrained right to set the direction of pub-

1

lic policies. This circumstance is said to make American democracy an exception, as well as a model for the rest of the world to follow, for its practices are necessarily informed by constitutional doctrines that are quite different from (and, it is claimed, superior to) those that prevail in western and northern European systems and in most other democracies throughout the world.

One feature of the United States system that sets it apart is the role of the judiciary. Federal courts are responsible for upholding the Constitution and this requires judges to review any legislation proposed by the various parliaments. They must consider whether it conforms to the requirements of the Constitution – as interpreted by the judiciary. This role is not unusual, many democracies embrace judicial review;[4] what is different in the United States is the very wide discretion allocated to judges who are expected to make policy. The Supreme Court is said to be a co-equal branch of government, one institutional mechanism (among others[5]) by means of which countermajoritarian, dualist principles are actualized. Here, again, the American practice is said to be desirable, setting their democracy apart from other systems in a class of its own.[6] As Ronald Dworkin puts it, the United States political system is distinctive and to be preferred over those in Europe because it is a system in which:

> liberty and minorities have legal protection in the form of a written constitution that even parliament cannot change to suit its whim or policy ... and [in which] judges, who are not elected and who are therefore removed from the pressures of partisan politics, are responsible for interpreting and enforcing that Bill of Rights ...[7]

Thus, the American people are said to have wisely embraced a constitutional democracy, not a system that concentrates the authority to govern in the hands of a parliamentary majority or in an executive officer that has won a national mandate (or in a combination of both). In terms of this understanding, a constitutional system of the United States kind works well when judges embrace liberal principles as their guide and exercise a very broad discretion to set policies in conflict with those endorsed by the people through their elected representatives; and it works badly when judges defer on matters of principle to legislative or executive officials.

If we look for an exemplar of judicial leadership that illustrates why this kind of arrangement is important and desirable, those who defend dualism point to the period between 1955 and 1986 when the Supreme Court, under Chief Justices Earl Warren and Warren Burger, used judicial authority to expand the protection offered to individuals and groups by the Bill of Rights.[8] The Warren–Burger Court's first objective was to change social life in southern states challenging racial segregation and other practices that excluded African Americans from the political system. But it also tried to secure other changes that had a national impact. For example, it sought reforms to the criminal justice system so as to afford defendants greater protection; it redefined the separation of church and state doctrine to eliminate prayer from public schools; it recognized privacy as a right to free sexuality from the shackles of religious morality and to forbid state governments from preventing pregnant women from securing abortions; it redefined 'freedom of speech' to constitutionalize issues relating to libel and obscene speech; and it redefined 'the equal protection of the laws' to disallow some forms of discrimination against women.

Justice William Brennan is recommended by liberals who support these reform initiatives as the justice who most effectively enunciated the best understanding of the Constitution in the United States that is currently available but, of course, he was supported by others, such as Justices Hugo Black, Abe Fortas, William Douglas, Thurgood Marshall and Chief Justice Earl Warren; moreover, the activist role of the Supreme Court in this period is celebrated in the nation's law schools and supported by legal intellectuals.

This book will be about the growing disenchantment within the United States with this dualist paradigm. I will focus on the call to reconsider the importance of judicial deference and older ideals associated with the traditional understanding of 'the rule of law' (such as the notion that legislators and judges should strive for precision and that law is discovered, not merely made-up by a temporary coalition of judges who happen to share common values) that is gaining support among a small group of conservative intellectuals in the United States. These conservatives think that dualist constitutional theories are not helping their democracy to evolve in a constructive direction and they argue that Americans have more to learn about democracy from their European counterparts than vice versa. Indeed, they view the performance of United States institutions in the post-World War II years, when it has been guided by the prevailing dualist constitutional theory, as disclosing serious weaknesses in its assumptions.

Significantly, because of the influence Republican presidents have enjoyed over the appointment of federal judges, the resurgence of monist ideas in the United States is now influential within the federal judiciary itself (although this is counterbalanced to some extent by the prevailing dualist orthodoxy in the country's leading law schools).[9] Many United States judges reject the dualist approach, and they advocate a return to a vision of how their constitutional system should function that is focused on the need to allow those who win elections to govern.

I shall be concerned to explore these conservative concerns about their political system's performance and will show that there are good reasons for thinking that the United States works badly as a dualist system.

Intuitively we can see why this kind of reappraisal must be expected. Consider the way authority in the United States is divided between courts and parliaments, legislators and executive officials, state governments and the federal government. We must acknowledge that the following problems and tensions are likely to emerge:

1   conflict between the executive and legislative branches over shared powers and competing authority;
2   incoherence of the parliament and within the political parties (because Congress need not support the executive);
3   weak political parties (because power is dispersed and each candidate must virtually fend for his- or herself);
4   conflict between the states and the federal government;
5   legitimation difficulties because of the active countermajoritarian role of the judiciary.

In systems founded on a notion of checks and balances, unavoidable tensions of these kind often threaten the democracy. The restraints on governing parties may become so severe that the leadership elected officials are able to provide is ineffectual; this, in turn, leads to incoherence within the system as difference between the parties as well as discipline within them declines. The United States has experienced civil war, conflict between President and the Supreme Court, conflict between various states and the federal government, conflict between the executive and the legislature. Recently, 'gridlock' between the executive and legislative branches has made it difficult for politicians to face up to severe domestic problems (such as bankruptcy of major city governments, fiscal crisis of the federal government, trade imbalance and declining economic competitiveness, friction between racial groups, widespread poverty, the prevalence of guns in the community). In foreign policy we find that presidents, frustrated by a resurgence of Congress since the Watergate scandal in 1972, have pursued policies in secret or in contempt of Congress;[10] if the responsible officials get caught out, however, they may face vilification and even prosecution.

The United States is not unique. Almost every country that has embraced the Madisonian model has experienced difficulties and most have not managed to survive as functional democracies.[11]

I shall not be concerned with any broad comparative appraisal of the way the United States system works. My focus is with recent debates among constitutional theorists. In particular, I am concerned to evaluate the counter-revolution that has sought to reverse much of the Warren–Burger Court's work in securing civil and political rights. I shall argue that there is more to be said in favour of the view that American jurists have departed too far from norms accepted in other democracies and that a significant change of direction is now appropriate. Specifically, I approve the return to legal positivism that is manifest in the work of Justice Scalia and the caution about departing from conventional sources of law that is manifest in the work of other conservatives such as Justices Sandra O'Connor, Anthony Kennedy and David Souter. In this assessment I depart very much from the general run of opinions that prevail in United States law schools. But I shall persevere with my criticism of the jurisprudence that informed the Warren–Burger era because I believe there is a danger that American activist jurisprudence (based on dualist constitutional theories) is rapidly being exported. Perhaps we can avoid damage in other democracies if we first consider how badly these doctrines have served in the United States itself.

The Political Implications of Dualism: The Conservative Counter-Revolution

The dualist view of the role of the judiciary in the United States political system that I have been articulating was embraced by a majority of the justices on the Supreme Court during the period from about 1953 (with the appointment of Earl Warren as Chief Justice) until the retirement of Warren Burger as Chief Justice in 1986.[12]

This was a period of liberal dominance on the Court, but it would be wrong to think that liberalism prevailed in the United States during this time. Far from it – very conservative politicians were often elected to office. Although the Warren–Burger Court justices never intended to provoke a political backlash, their countermajoritarian orientation impacted on the political competition between the contending parties. This was inevitable given the very significant differences between the opinions held by ordinary Americans about civil liberties and those embraced by members of the legal elite (including Supreme Court justices).[13] President Richard Nixon understood the advantage that conservative politicians could gain by running against an unpopular Supreme Court and he initiated changes within the Republican Party so that it could seek to benefit from the national resentment against the Court's unpopular policies. For example, he understood the importance of 'law and order' as a political issue that favoured the conservative side of politics and foresaw that the public's concern with personal safety and the revulsion most people felt for criminals would lead to demands for increasing police powers, for relaxing controls over how evidence may be gathered, and for tougher sentencing – demands that went diametrically against the accepted wisdom on the Court. He must have been deeply grateful when the Court also became a perfect symbol of other unpopular policies. For example, the resented practice of school busing, initiated by the Supreme Court, was used to his political advantage; but other issues, such as liberal changes relating to the law of obscenity, were also significant. In the years following Watergate, Republican candidates were able to reassert their party's credibility at the national level by focusing on other court-imposed policies of concern to Nixon's 'silent majority', such as, school prayers, abortion, capital punishment and the use of racial quotas.

The overwhelming support for Nixon in 1968 and 1972, for President Reagan in 1980 and 1984, and the victory of George Bush (running as a Reagan candidate in 1988), demonstrate the success of the Nixon strategy;[14] and the counter-revolution against liberal elitism has prevailed because the Democratic Party has absorbed the lesson that it cannot succeed if it embraces countermajoritarian policies and because the Republicans have transformed the federal judiciary. (Bill Clinton has made every effort to distance himself from East-Coast Democrats in his public rhetoric and in the policies he endorses but he still makes efforts to please liberals when it comes to making appointments.) True to his electoral promises, Nixon made every effort to use the nomination process as a means for highlighting the political nature of the Court and to pack it with conservatives. He chose Lewis Powell, Warren Burger, Harry Blackmun and William Rehnquist – all extremely conservative on the issue of law and order and on many other issues. Reagan and Bush (building on the base secured by Nixon) ensured that conservatives would dominate the federal judiciary into the twenty-first century.[15] Reagan also changed the balance of power on the Supreme Court by elevating William Rehnquist to replace Burger as Chief Justice and, facing down opposition from some liberals in the Senate, he secured the confirmation of three other conservatives (Sandra Day O'Connor, Antonin Scalia and Anthony Kennedy). These appointments were later consolidated by Bush who secured the confirmation of David Souter and Clarence Thomas, both conservative judges.[16]

The result has been that the dualist understanding of the United States system has largely been undermined in practice. Many liberties that had previously been recognized are no longer protected. For example, the Court has: (a) restricted habeas corpus review, (b) allowed greater scope for police or other agencies to search or to administer drug tests, (c) allowed states to secure prosecutions by using evidence that it had previously excluded, (d) tolerated state regulation of abortions, (e) disallowed affirmative action when quotas are used, (f) refused to protect intimate relationships that are not conventional and (g) refused to protect those who possess child pornography or women who seek to dance naked in adult-only clubs.[17]

Given the support in the universities for the dualist notion of United States exceptionalism, these changes have been the subject of much controversy. Many liberal Americans find it troubling that the Supreme Court is no longer taking the primary responsibility for upholding rights. They worry that the states, Congress and the President will not meet the challenge and they fear that majority rule in the context of American society may well prove tyrannical. Many are also deeply suspicious of the way that the power of the President has been expanded since the New Deal, especially in conducting foreign policy.[18] They claim that the conservatives are insensitive to the unique nature of United States democracy and accuse them of reneging on their responsibility to subordinate the executive and to protect individuals against exploitation and discrimination.

Certainly, when we read the judgments of the various conservative justices, we cannot help feeling that there is a lack of generosity to the plight of those who are least advantaged or victims. What about Sergeant James B. Stanley whose life was ruined because the army secretly experimented on him (administering the drug lysergic acid diethylamide – LSD)?[19] He suffered severe behavioural problems, awakening during the night to beat his wife and children, breaking into sobs in front of his men, suffering short-term memory loss.[20] His life was ruined – he was discharged from the US Army and alienated from his family – but the Court found in favour of the Defence Department. What about mentally retarded and juvenile killers who had been sentenced to death? For example, Johnny Paul Penry who one clinical psychologist testified had 'the ability to learn and the learning or the knowledge of the average six-and-a-half-year-old kid'.[21] Surely the justices should have agreed that it is barbaric to execute retarded children? The Court found that issues relating to capital punishment are largely a matter for the states to resolve for themselves. What about Warren McCleskey who was sentenced to death even though he was able to demonstrate that he would have had a good chance of receiving a different sentence had he killed an African American rather than a white policeman? The Court ruled that sociological evidence that relied on statistical evidence to demonstrate racial discrimination was largely irrelevant in considering whether McCleskey had been afforded a fair trial, and held that he must prove that his own particular trial was unfair.[22] What about the 73-year-old Klamath Indian, Alfred Smith, who lost his eligibility for unemployment benefits because he was dismissed from his job for using the drug peyote as part of a religious ceremony (a practice dating back over ten thousand years)? Most people expected that the

Court would use the Establishment of Religion clause in the First Amendment to protect indigenous religious practices – but it ruled that the government was entitled to regulate the use of drugs so long as the laws it enacts apply generally.[23] What about Michael Hardwick, attacked by thugs and harassed by the police acting under a law that made sodomy a felony in Georgia? Surely what people do in their own homes should be their own business so long as they are not harming others? The Court ruled that the Constitution does not protect the liberty of anyone to practise sodomy.[24] Whatever their personal views about these individual cases and the competing values at issue, it is clear that the Rehnquist majority are unwilling to allow that they can read the United States Constitution in the manner that many liberals suggest to be legitimate.

Emotional responses to this change in the official interpretation of the meaning of the Constitution and especially of the Bill of Rights for Americans are understandable. It is easy to find cases (such as those cited in the last paragraph) in which the position adopted by the conservatives on the Court seems to conflict with the moral sensitivities of most decent people. But there is little point in denouncing the Court for moral failings in this way. The conservative justices are a product of the very forces that the Warren–Burger Court justices injected into the political arena. The backlash was predictable (given the attitudes of the American people).[25] The conservatives reject judicial elitism and regard themselves as guardians of a tradition of law that requires judges to be subordinate to those who are accountable to the people. Precisely because they are a product of a populist backlash, they claim Supreme Court justices are not appointed to impose their moral beliefs on the rest of the community.

The Conservative Agenda

Whether the United States will be a better society now that the Supreme Court is refusing to take primary responsibility for securing civil rights and liberties is difficult to say. It will depend partly on how diligently other branches of government respond to the change and partly on whether the costs incurred by retreating from the achievements of the Warren–Burger era are greater than the gains that will be achieved by requiring politically accountable leaders to shape policies.

By any reckoning it is a close call, for no one could possibly describe the United States over the past three decades as a model society. To understand the extent of the Court's responsibility for this record, however, it is necessary to make some judgments about the reasons for: the weakening of party affiliations, the dominance of the

Republican Party in presidential elections, the tax revolt, the increasing segregation and impoverishment of inner cities, the growing disparities in wealth, the increase in crime, the emergence of racial conflict as a national rather than regional problem and the failings of public schools.

Responsibility for these and the many other problems that the American people face today cannot be fairly directed at the individual liberal justices who in good faith sought to secure desirable changes by interpreting the Constitution as though it mandated a progressive agenda, allowing the Court to play the role of a guardian. These liberal justices were hoping to secure justice, not to undermine it. Nevertheless, the faith that the American people have recently placed in the capacity of the judiciary (in the 30-year period from 1955 to 1985) for achieving goals that the political system has had difficulty securing has surely had undesirable consequences. Some observers suspect that the Supreme Court's willingness to impose unpopular policies (even when as many as 80 per cent of the people indicate their opposition!) may have made it more difficult than it has been in other democracies to secure a national consensus to address pressing social problems (such as pervasive poverty, poor health services, and badly functioning schools).[26] Despite the manifest good intentions and high integrity of liberals such as Justice William Brennan and, say, Laurence Tribe (among many other academic supporters of judicial activism), it is plausible to view the legacy of the Warren–Burger era as something of a disaster.[27]

Whether one agrees with this perspective or not, it is necessary to take it into account if we are to understand and be fair to the conservative justices who are now on the Supreme Court. Anyone who thinks that judicial activism poses no dangers will simply reject their work as reactionary. They will hardly bother with their arguments because, from their point of view, there are no good reasons why the justices should not allow the Court to go on imposing desirable outcomes. Even if the conservative justices do not wish to impose their own policy judgments, it will be argued that they should at least employ the *stare decisis* rule (requiring deference to the Supreme Court's past decisions) to honour the legacy they have received from the Warren–Burger era. If no bad consequences have followed, what possible reason can there be for dismantling past actions of the Supreme Court that have produced the good results? Thus, the conservatives are condemned as irrational, ungenerous or bigoted (usually all three[28]) for trying to prevent liberal advances and for reneging on past commitments.

On the other hand, if we accept that conservatives may have good reasons for questioning the prevailing doctrine of United States exceptionalism that requires the judiciary to make crucial social policies, supposing that the Supreme Court's past activism has not been entirely beneficial, we can begin to appreciate their concerns. Their point of departure arises out of a judgment that courts cannot successfully substitute for parliaments in solving difficult social problems.[29] According to the conservatives, we are most unlikely to achieve a just society in the United States simply because the Supreme Court declares that this is what has to be. Conservatives in the United States have also noticed how, when the Court does make controversial decisions, politicians are sometimes left free to posture in unhelpful ways and that many of them may advocate policies they would not actually like to see implemented (for example, overruling *Roe* v. *Wade*, the controversial case upholding a woman's right to terminate her pregnancy in its early stages) to appeal for the votes of people who feel strongly about a single issue.[30] The conservatives may be right to suppose that these unscrupulous politicians (let us include Nixon, Reagan and Bush as chief offenders) may be more reluctant to do this if they know that the policies they propose will not be disallowed as unconstitutional. More to the point, the distribution of strong affects about a policy issue like abortion (that is, the groups in the electorate who may be prepared to shift their vote from one candidate to another because of it) will be different if the Court withdraws protection. (For example, when women were made aware that the right to choose an abortion was seriously under threat in 1989, they began to mobilize politically to prevent this, allowing Bill Clinton to secure an advantage over Bush in 1992.[31])

The political judgments that I attribute to conservative constitutional theorists seem sound. In the case of abortion, supposing that *Roe* v. *Wade* were to be overruled, state governments will be very reluctant to prosecute and punish doctors and women who violate laws prohibiting abortions. They will know that society has changed dramatically over the past twenty years and that opinion polls show that most people are much less influenced by religious beliefs than was the case even in the recent past. Politicians will know that moves, on their part, to forbid abortions by means of the criminal law will generate enormous protest. This pressure would probably ensure that most laws forbidding abortions are changed, ignored or found to be unenforceable.[32] Certainly the federal government would provide support for women who would need financial help to pay their physician and many ways (using public and private funding) would be found to facilitate any travel that may be required to ensure that every woman in the United States can get an abortion if she wishes it. More significant, the state and federal legislators who seek to please religious groups who oppose abortion may choose to put more of their energy into achieving practical goals. Instead of working to overrule *Roe* v. *Wade* (hoping that this will never happen), conservative politicians might actually reach a compromise with those who are pro-choice in order to help pregnant women secure financial and other forms of assistance. This may provide vitally needed resources for women who are reluctant to continue with their pregnancy because of financial problems or those who contemplate handing the baby over for adoption. Instead of the zero sum outcome that judicial resolution of the abortion problem seems to have generated in the United States both sides would gain through this kind of compromise.

What I am suggesting here is that we can see the embrace of various forms of 'conservative' jurisprudence as a form of pragmatism. The conservatives make the utilitarian judgment that the political system will function better if they recognize the constraints that are traditionally associated with the Benthamite understanding that judges are not free to impose their own values except in very special circumstances.

Thesis and Plan of Monograph

This book proceeds on the assumption that conservatives in the United States have a better understanding of the recent failings of their political system than their liberal critics. First, I look at the various strategies adopted by the Rehnquist group of justices to realize their own doctrine of judicial restraint; second, I explore the case that can be made against the liberal dualist conception of the Court's role.

As we shall see (in Chapters 3, 4 and 5, where I explore conservative views), the various conservative justices do have well-thought-out and defensible jurisprudential theories. This in itself, as I argue, is not enough to excuse what, in the light of the achievements of the Warren–Burger years, now seems a reactionary philosophy.[33] We can have little sympathy for these approaches if we assess them purely from an ethical perspective. I argue that the Rehnquist Court conservatives do have other good arguments but that these are not articulated in their opinions because they derive from political science, not law. I claim the conservative position only makes sense when we understand their constitutional theories in the context of their wider understanding of how the United States political system actually works. What I suggest is that two related questions need to be distinguished in analysing the work of the conservatives. The first concerns arguments that are internal to the law:

1 What guiding rules does each of the justices follow in reading the Constitution? How does he or she assess the importance, within constitutional law, of *stare decisis*? or of 'original intentions'? or of 'plain meaning'? How much respect does the justice show for

tradition? What other sources of law does he or she acknowledge? How does he or she respond when the requirements of the law are unclear? How does he or she respond when the Constitution presumes opinions that we no longer share (for example, that there is a natural right to property or that segregation by race is a defensible practice)?

In exploring this kind of question we can proceed by looking at various opinions, for the justices often take trouble to make their assumptions about how to determine the 'law' clear. Thus, in exploring this dimension of their work, we are able to proceed in a straightforward way. Here are some controversial opinions of this or that justice, how did he or she reach conclusions? We can look at a range of cases dealt with by a particular justice asking whether there is a coherent pattern in his or her work. Is the justice consistent? We can compare the approaches of the various conservatives. Are they approaching cases in the same way or are there discernible differences between them?

The second kind of questioning relates to the assumptions that the conservative justices seem to share about the nature of the United States political system:

2   How do the conservatives view the relationship between parliaments and courts in a democracy? What policy decisions, if any, do they believe are reserved for the judiciary? How do they think they should respond to public opinion surveys? To what extent do they think they should defer to the wishes of the Solicitor General? Why? When, if at all, do they think a constitutional court is entitled to act in a revolutionary manner, ignoring the Constitution?

These questions have a broader focus and are much more difficult to answer primarily because the justices do not feel obliged to make their opinions known. Here, unfortunately, we often have to speculate. All we can do is make clear what assumptions about the functioning of the system make most sense, given the caution the justices exhibit about judicial activism.

The questions I list under the first question will take up most of my time. Some of my chapters are devoted to exposition in which I explore the theories articulated by Justices Rehnquist, Scalia, O'Connor and Souter and the ideas of influential conservative scholars such as, Richard Epstein, Walter Berns, Charles Fried, Robert Bork and Stephen Macedo. In other chapters I look at conservative theories as these are applied; dealing with issues such as privacy (Chapters 5 and 6), affirmative action (Chapter 9) and capital punishment (see pp. 138–41).

Our speculations in answering the questions listed under the second question draw on a well-established tradition, associated with the opinions expressed in *The Federalist No. 78* by Alexander Hamilton who noted that:

> [the judiciary] will always be the least dangerous to the political rights of the Constitution; because it will be least in a capacity to annoy or injure them ... [it] has no influence over either the sword or the purse; no direction either of the strength or of the wealth of the society, and can take no active resolution whatever. It may truly be said to have neither force nor will but merely judgment; and must ultimately depend upon the aid of the executive arm even for the efficacy of its judgments.[34]

There is also a considerable body of scholarship that supports this view.[35]

In rejecting the view that a countermajoritarian institution can contribute very effectively, the conservatives also necessarily embrace what Gerald Rosenberg has recently described as the 'constrained court view'.[36] According to this view, the Supreme Court cannot effectively lead in achieving progressive social change because: (a) it lacks powers of implementation, (b) judges cannot enter into the political arena to defend its decisions, (c) it is vulnerable to various threats from the other branches and, ultimately, to transformation through the appointment power shared by the President and Senate, (d) it is badly equipped to make policy because it is not served by a professional bureaucracy and cannot adequately consult with various interest groups and (e) it must wait for suitable cases to arise before it can rule on an issue.

Contemporary conservatives in the United States give the 'constrained court view' an additional twist for they depart from the traditional understanding that the Supreme Court can cause little harm (as the 'least dangerous branch'); rather, they see judicial activism as positively dangerous.

The conservatives are clearly right in holding that it does not follow because the Court cannot do much good acting independently of other branches, that it cannot cause any harm. Contemporary conservatives maintain that an unbridled judiciary does indeed produce very serious and bad consequences and that this has become apparent in the United States during the years of well-meaning liberal activism. And there is good evidence to support the conservatives' claim. Not only does an analysis of the known cases of judicial policymaking show that judges are much less likely to make sound policy choices than legislators[37] but it also shows that their calculations about what is politically feasible have been less accurate than those of elected officials who are better placed to listen to representatives of various groups who may be effected by the proposed policies and to assess the mood of the community. Politics is ultimately about power, and if the judicial branch miscalculates in assessing its own influence, very serious consequences do follow.

This is why the conservatives are persuasive when they claim the Warren–Burger Court acted recklessly in stepping ahead of political leaders by endorsing policies that clearly did not have public support. It is one thing to frustrate local or even state governments when the Court is acting with the backing of the vast majority of other Americans, quite another to frustrate national leaders as the Warren–Burger Court sometimes did. This experience shows, according to the conservatives, that unpopular policies endorsed by the Supreme Court will not be implemented effectively and may not be sustainable in the longer term. They also claim that countermajoritarian policy making will bring the judiciary into the political process in ways that are extremely undesirable.

In assessing the conservative 'constraint-view-plus-political-caution' understanding of the desirable role for the judiciary in the United States, we must consider the claim that bad consequences have followed because the Supreme Court acted in a deliberately countermajoritarian manner. This is why I review a number of claims put forward by political scientists and other sociolegal scholars that seem to support conservative assumptions. For example, Robert Dahl tells us that liberal countermajoritarian theory is grounded on a false understanding of the political reality. In his view, it is not a possibility in a well-functioning democracy for a constitutional court to systematically defy more representative branches of government. In his view, the judges will inevitably reflect the policy choices embraced by the dominant elite because these officials will appoint them, and because there are other pressures on courts (for example, the prevailing attitudes in their home communities) that are likely to secure their subordination.

Dahl's claims challenge most dualist accounts because he shows why it is unrealistic to ask the Supreme Court to play a countermajoritarian role. Even John Hart Ely's advocacy of a representation-reinforcing role for the Supreme Court (recommending that it serve as some sort of umpire to ensure that democratic decision-making proceeds according to fair rules of procedure and that it protect groups that are vulnerable) is called into question by Dahl's evidence;[38] so also is Bruce Ackerman's view that the United States Constitution established a 'dualist' system in which 'higher lawmaking' needs to be distinguished from 'normal lawmaking'. Indeed, in the light of Dahl's evidence, 'dual track' and other countermajoritarian theories must be held fanciful.[39]

Although he wrote his original analysis in 1954, Dahl's conjectures are supported by recent experiences (for example, the transformation of the Warren Court by Nixon, Reagan and Bush) and other sociolegal scholars who having looked at the more recent evidence in a systematic way have defended his view. One writer is prepared to declare, boldly, that 'conventional wisdom among political scientists and sociologists who have studied these matters is that courts by themselves are not very powerful and, at best, are important at the margins or in conjunction with other government bodies'.[40]

As I have noted, the Warren Court was reconstituted by Presidents Nixon, Reagan and Bush who did not like what it was doing. But it took 30 years for Dahl's prediction to be vindicated. So we should consider the possible costs and benefits during transition periods. Did liberal countermajoritarianism secure good consequences by presenting the American people with an image of how their society could be – a society that takes rights seriously – or did it provoke a fierce undercurrent of ill-will, leaving a nasty legacy that will remain for a very long time?[41] Another question is whether it is better for a constitutional court to secure unpopular rights even when the justices know that their rulings will not be fully implemented by the responsible officials and are likely to be undermined by a political backlash. Isn't it better to go down supporting civil and political rights than to concede a narrow conception of the 'rule of law' to those who will use it to legitimate the exploitation of individuals and the violation of their liberties?

A considered answer to these questions requires an assessment of what can be lost when those who manipulate symbols insist on hoisting the flag of liberty, encouraging others to tear it down. Is a political culture likely to be damaged when politicians find it expedient to campaign against liberal ideals? No conclusive answer to this question can be provided but those who visit the United States today may decide for themselves whether the political culture in that society has come out of the decade of the 1980s in good shape.

What conservatives challenge, according to my account, is the notion that the United States Supreme Court should be viewed as distinctive. In a strange reversal of European political alignments, American conservatives worry about the fact that the Madisonian design that was embraced by the founders seems to allow power to be exercised by branches of government that have little incentive to respond to the will of the people. In contrast, American liberals seek to embrace a form of democratic elitism, although their guardians are supposed to embrace egalitarian values. This is why conservatives in the United States tend to agree that judicial theories that have guided judges in other democracies (where parliaments usually enjoy more capacity to intimidate the judiciary) should also be embraced within the United States. In their view, American intellectuals need to reconnect with European democratic ideals that draw on legal positivism, constrained pragmatism or on common law doctrines.

Those of us in other democracies who observe North American debates and study their institutions should respect the monist tradition now reasserting itself in the United States, and we need to take trouble to look carefully at the arguments put forward by scholars who are troubled by the countermajoritarian issue. We must seriously consider conservative criticisms of the Warren–Burger Court's record before we assume that our own systems will be improved by securing various forms of dualism as American liberals recommend. Perhaps we should be wary of following the advice of Ronald Dworkin and other dualists who advocate that most democracies will be improved if they embrace more court-centred approaches in securing rights. In any event, when we appreciate the nature of the changes that have been underway in the United States for the last 30 years, and the intellectual reappraisal of the Warren Court legacy that this has given rise to, we may wish to ask a few more questions before we assume that dualist views have triumphed. Why is it the case that the United States remains as one of the few democracies that has been seriously troubled by issues such as school prayer, abortion, affirmative action and capital punishment? Why is it the case that a country like Sweden, without a Bill of Rights, is able to boast a far better record in actually securing the well-being of its people? (Sweden offers a better deal to insular minorities such as the mentally ill, those in prison, and those before the courts than the United States, and Sweden has also exhibited a better control over the behaviour of its police and bureaucrats.[42]) Perhaps the explanation for these anomalies is that democratic processes matter; or to put the point in a slightly different way, community values are important and must be respected before progressive changes can be made.

In monist democracies reforms involving controversial matters, such as the abolition of capital punishment or the making of contraceptives available in schools, have been resolved after considerable negotiation and consultation with the communities effected, and only when politicians that are wary of any potential political backlash have decided that the public is ready for the change in question; they have sometimes been implemented surreptitiously by accountable elites who hope their involvement will not be noticed, but they are rarely instituted by fiat. In contrast, as I will show, the experience in the United States with a well-meaning judicial elite advancing programmes that enjoy little or no public support should serve as a warning. I will argue that democratic accountability is important because it serves as a mechanism for discovering when a society is ready for change. By allowing changes to occur only when politicians have secured significant public support, parliamentary processes serve as a safety device, in a similar way to a fuse in an electrical circuit. This is because accountable politicians can be relied on to retreat when they detect strong resistance in the community – this is how they survive to fight for the progressive changes they advocate at other more propitious times.[43] In contrast, a constitutional court is often disinclined to compromise over matters of principle.[44] Thus, community values are often completely disregarded when the liberal case that can be made out on one side of an issue is so compelling that judges feel obliged to ignore public opinion. But this arrangement is unsatisfactory because it inevitably leads to a situation where the progressive advance achieved on one front (for example, abortion or capital punishment) may necessitate a need to retreat on many others – as any honest reflection on the reasons for conservative successes in the United States over the past 30 years will show.

Liberal dualists may wish to respond to these monist concerns by making claims about the peculiar nature of the United States system. They might want to argue that the practice of using courts as substitute legislatures is essential in the United States because the complex Madisonian checks and balances make it virtually impossible for legislators to address certain kinds of problem. This line of argument accepts that judicial review (the overruling of duly elected parliaments) may prove counter-productive in other circumstances and societies (especially where a sovereign parliament can respond rapidly and decisively) but claims that the United States is distinctive in that this can never happen in this system.[45] On this account, each society must consider its own practices and we cannot decide in advance whether leadership by the judicial branch of government will produce good or bad consequences. What is essential in the United States may not be required in Australia or Sweden where Social Democratic social movements have managed to use the political process to good effect and would not as readily agree to be frustrated by a constitutional court.

On this view, in considering the United States, it could be argued that *Brown* v. *Board of Education* (requiring desegregation of the public schools in southern states) was absolutely necessary because reactionary southern Democrats were so firmly in control, not only in all the southern state legislatures but also within most of the important committees of Congress. Given that the politically accountable branches of government had failed to address such a major issue of principle as segregation (and they could not in the United States because of the entrenched and self-perpetuating power of the white southerners), the judiciary had to provide leadership. In terms of this account, then, the Supreme Court was the only United States institution that could conceivably have provided the initial (though ineffectual) confrontation with segregation and it was justified in doing so. To take a less controversial example, we could argue that it was/is necessary for the Supreme Court to establish guidelines in dealing with defamatory and obscene speech in the United States because the nation's media cannot be expected to operate effectively in circumstances where each of the 50 states is free to set different standards. Because the Constitution allocates responsibility to the states so that the United States Congress is impotent in this area, the Supreme Court was/is justified in taking the initiative in order to set a national standard.

I shall suggest that the conservatives are correct to view this appeal to unbridled pragmatism as well as claims about American distinctivism sceptically.

Even if I am wrong in holding that judicial activism is a practice that does more harm than good in the United States, other nations would be wise to think very carefully before they ask their judges to embrace a practice that can only be justified in the light of the very peculiar nature of America's constitutional democracy. It is an extremely dangerous practice for a constitutional court to frustrate a majority that is determined to secure well-defined policy goals. When countermajoritarian review has produced good results, this has usually been because the judiciary has acted only after making a careful assessment of the balance of political forces.[46] This is not to say that we should resist the international movement to do more to protect fundamental rights and liberties. But when any parliamentary democracy is persuaded to embrace a Charter of Rights (and most of them will by the turn of the century) we must hope that the judges who are asked to serve on its constitutional court are cautious about how they exercise their new responsibilities. They will find that they have much to learn from the experiences and opinions of the Rehnquist Court justices.

I shall briefly consider the question of what the experience in the United States with judicial review has to teach those of us in parliamentary democracies who are contemplating constitutional change at the end of my analysis, in my conclusion. Although I do not intend to present the United States system in comparative perspective, by focusing on theoretical debates and by considering the conservative side of the debate more sympathetically (and objectively) than most American commentators are inclined to, I hope to place the reader in a position to evaluate the case that can be made-out for expanding the policymaking role of judges. As will be seen from my commentary, I have reached the conclusion that it is necessary to resist the temptation to short-circuit parliaments in achieving progressive changes. In my view, the United States will become a better society now that its Supreme Court is committed to greater restraint. I argue that those of us in parliamentary systems have more to learn from examining the problems that are bothering American conservatives about judicial review than from accepting, on trust, the confidence of liberals that it has been a good practice.

A problem we face in recommending judicial caution about policymaking from the bench is that this sensible approach is not inspiring. Short-cuts in the name of justice have always attracted an articulate following. Judges like Ruth Bader Ginsburg or Sandra Day O'Connor who recommend cautious deference or a positivist, like Antonin Scalia, who recommends subordination of the judiciary to legislators, are unlikely to be thought of as legends. This kind of praise is usually reserved for those who use judicial power dramatically to secure good. Most young law students who read the opinions of liberal judges, such as Justices Brennan, will leave the library flushed with idealism and proud to be studying the law. Those who read Scalia will be outraged by his willingness to go along with injustice in the name of an abstract commitment to legal norms; those who read O'Connor, Ginsburg or Souter will be bored by their scrupulous concern to legitimate their opinions by citing appropriate legal sources. This is why I have embarked on the thankless task of reminding everyone that Justice Brennan's many victories have not endured. By closely examining the debate between liberals and conservatives, on its home terrain, those of us in other democracies will be able to make a more informed assessment of what is at stake. I shall argue that we would be foolish to allow Brennan's inspiring legacy to blind us to the political problems that have followed in its wake. There are no short cuts in securing justice. Neither symbolic gestures nor countermajoritarian judicial leadership will achieve it. If a society wishes to protect rights it will need to encourage politicians to go out and mobilize the necessary political support.

Notes

1   It is not necessary that the system be perfectly fair, or that it be characterized by competition between two disciplined and coherent parties. A two-party parliamentary democracy based on a first-past-the-post single member district electoral system is generally referred to as a 'Westminster' system. However, even the United Kingdom does not conform to this model today. Indeed, many well-functioning democracies embrace proportional representation and fall far short of the Westminster ideal, encompassing a variety of different mechanisms for ensuring accountability and stability, including judicial review and a federal division of powers. See Robert A. Dahl, *Democracy and Its Critics* (New Haven, Conn.: Yale University Press, 1989), 156–7.

2   See Bruce Ackerman, *We the People: Foundations* (Cambridge, Mass.: Harvard University Press, 1991). He contrasts 'monist' conceptions of democracy with those he calls 'dualist' and seeks to defend the view that the United States of America is best viewed as a dualist democracy, (pp. 3–32).

3   Ibid. Other influential writers who celebrate dualism include Ronald Dworkin, *Taking Rights Seriously* (Cambridge, Mass.: Harvard University Press, 1977), *A Matter of Principle* (Cambridge, Mass.: Harvard University Press, 1985), *Law's Empire* (London: Fontana Press, 1986); Laurence Tribe, *Constitutional Choices* (Cambridge, Mass.: Harvard University Press, 1985), (with Michael Dorf), *How to Read the Constitution* (Cambridge, Mass.: Harvard University Press, 1992); John Hart Ely, *Democracy and Distrust: a Theory of Judicial Review* (Cambridge, Mass.: Harvard University Press, 1980); Richard Epstein, *Takings: Private Property and the Power of Eminent Domain* (Cambridge, Mass.: Harvard University Press, 1985); Stephen Macedo, *The New Right and the Constitution* (Washington, DC: Cato, 1987, 2nd ed.); Walter Berns, *Taking the Constitution Seriously* (NY: Simon & Schuster, 1987); and to this list of distinguished legal scholars we must add the political philosopher John Rawls (see, *Political Liberalism*, NY: Columbia University Press, 1993). I discuss all of these authors in subsequent chapters.

4   Dahl, op. cit., 188; Of the 21 countries he lists as 'polyarchies', 13 have some form of judicial review. In most of these, however, the judiciary confines itself by convention, very rarely confronting legislators unless they are clearly in breach of a written constitution. In the systems that are not federations, half deny the judiciary authority to declare parliamentary acts unconstitutional.

5   The Constitution deliberately sets up one majority to check another by staggering the times set for elections and the period in office enjoyed by various officials. Americans are constantly in election mode but the result is that very little time is left to govern. More significant, it is often difficult to govern, even after a landslide election victory, because the government can be opposed by those who were elected at an earlier time. For example, a member of the House of Representatives must stand for office every two years, and must compete in a designated district for one seat; a Senator enjoys a term of six years but one-third of the Senate must compete at a state-wide level for two seats every two years; the President serves for four years but he or she must win a nationwide election. Other provisions also serve to make it difficult for a majority to implement its will. Thus, the President enjoys a veto to frustrate Congress (unless the legislators can marshal enough support to override); the Senate can frustrate the House of Representatives and vice versa; and some significant powers are shared, such as the power to secure treaties or to make high level appointments. All these arrangements (and others that could be listed) mean that even when a mandate is achieved at an election, the successful party's policies cannot easily be put into effect.

6   Political scientists have not been persuaded that a constitutional court can serve to restrain governments and are less enamoured with the United States system than most legal scholars seem to be. After comparing democracies throughout the world, Robert Dahl is amazed that lawyers in the United States can recommend 'dualism'. Yet they nearly all do. Dahl thinks that we must resort to the sociology of knowledge to explain this phenomenon. He even suggests that the parochialism of legal education and the fact that judicial review 'serves the corporate interests of the legal profession' are two possible reasons that can account for it. Dahl, op. cit., 358, n. 5.

7   Ronald Dworkin, *A Bill of Rights for Britain: Why British Liberty Needs Protecting* (London: Chatto & Windus, 1990), 13, stating his agreement with the opinions expressed in a lecture by French historian Francois Furet.

8   The Bill of Rights comprises the first ten amendments to the Constitution (1791). These specify limits to the powers allocated to Congress – it may not make

laws restricting the listed liberties. After 1868 with the ratification of the Fourteenth Amendment prohibiting the states from denying 'life, liberty or property', the situation changed. It was now clear that limits had been placed on what state governments may do and some argued that the best way of delineating what these limits were was to read the Bill of Rights as though it also applied to the state governments. During the period from the late 1920s to the late 1970s the Supreme Court slowly accepted that most of the Bill of Rights should be applied to restrain the activities of state governments. Thus, various liberties (although not all ten listed in the Bill of Rights) were selectively incorporated under the authority of the Fourteenth Amendment.

9   This dualist dominance is now in decline. One challenge comes from cynics who think that 'law' in the United States is simply what judges choose to make it. According to these writers, liberal jurisprudence offers nothing more than a 'noble lie' to manipulate the people so that democracy in the United States is now a farce (see Allan C. Hutchinson, 'Indiana Dworkin and Law's Empire', *The Yale Law Journal*, 96 (1987), 637–65). This is a plausible description of the practice in the Warren–Burger years when the Supreme Court did use liberal philosophy to support its imposition of judicial values, so it is not surprising that 'Critical Legal Studies' and 'Critical Race Theory' have been influential in the United States. These writers do not believe that liberals can deliver what they promise. A representative sample of the new cynicism is displayed in Allan C. Hutchinson (ed.), *Critical Legal Studies* (Totowa, NJ: Rowman & Littlefield, 1989).

10   James Sundquist, *The Decline and Resurgence of Congress* (Washington, DC: Brookings Institute, 1981).

11   F. W. Riggs, *Problems of Presidentialism* (1991), University of Hawaii, Institute of Government Studies (unpublished manuscript). Riggs provides a list of democracies in crisis. At the present time many political systems are struggling to emerge as democracies. In the light of Riggs's work, we may surely predict that those newly emerging democracies that are foolish enough to embrace dualist structures, modelled on the United States, are likely to face serious constitutional crises within a very short period.

12   The first sign of change was in 1925. A brief account of the incorporation doctrine, together with a list showing when various provisions of the Bill of Rights were incorporated, is provided in Jethro K. Lieberman, *The Evolving Constitution: How the Supreme Court Has Ruled on Issues from Abortion to Zoning* (NY: Random House, 1992). Incorporation became a political issue in the 1960s and 1970s.

13   In surveys conducted in 1976–77 and 1978–79 Herbert McClosky and Alida Brill show a huge gap in attitudes towards civil liberties between professionals (opinion leaders in education, the law, journalism and politics) and members of the general public (Nixon's 'silent majority'). See *Dimensions of Tolerance: What Americans Believe About Civil Liberties* (NY: Russell Sage Foundation, 1983).

14   Many other factors help account for these victories. The prevailing state of the economy is the most significant; but attitudes towards communism and the Vietnam War also come to mind. In 1980 Reagan also benefited from the Iran hostage crisis that made Jimmy Carter look so ineffectual.

15   Sheldon Goldman, 'Reagan's Judicial Legacy: Completing the Puzzle and Summing Up', *Judicature*, 72, (6), (1989), 318–30. Also, John Biskupic, 'Bush Treads Well-Worn Path in Building Federal Bench', *Congressional Quarterly*, 50 (1992), 111.

16   See David G. Savage, *Turning Right: The Makings of the Rehnquist Supreme Court* (NY: John Wiley & Sons, 1992).

17   See Erwin Chemerinsky, 'The Vanishing Constitution: The Supreme Court 1989 Term', *Harvard Law Review*, 103 (1989); also David Kairy, *With Liberty and Justice for Some: a Critique of the Conservative Supreme Court* (NY: The New Press, 1993).

18   A good example is Harold Hongju Koh, *The National Security Constitution: Sharing Power After the Iran–Contra Affair* (New Haven, Conn.: Yale University Press, 1990).

19   *U.S.* v. *Stanley* 483 U.S. 669 (1987).

20   Savage provides an account of the case, op. cit., 99–103.

21   Quoted by Savage, ibid., 243.

22   *McCleskey* v. *Kemp* 481 U.S. 279 (1987).

23   *Employment Division, Oregon Department of Human Resources* v. *Smith* 494 U.S. 872 (1990).

24   *Bowers* v. *Hardwick* 478 U.S. 186 (1986).

25   McClosky and Brill, op. cit.

26   Mary Ann Glendon, *Rights Talk: the Impoverishment of Political Discourse* (NY: The Free Press, 1991).

27   The lesson of the 1988 presidential election is that the American people are alienated from liberal ideals. This was absorbed by Bill Clinton and his advisers in the Democratic Leadership Conference. During the election in 1992 Clinton was able to persuade the suburban electorate that he was genuinely concerned about their interests and that he was not hostage to influential 'liberal' factions within the Democratic Party that represent the interests of minorities and the inner-city poor. Moreover, like Nixon and other successful Republican candidates, Clinton presented himself as a tough supporter of law and order policies. For example, in the midst of his primary contests, he returned to Arkansas to supervise the execution of a mentally handicapped African American convict. (He has continued to show this resolve. Recently, he supported a crime bill that will extend the death penalty and require states receiving federal money for new prison construction to adopt harsher sentencing rules.) But President Bush did not help his chances in 1992 by alienating many of the conservative supporters who had voted for him in 1988. He did this by, for example, agreeing to raise taxes, failing to veto the Civil Rights Act, failing to support his Education Secretary who had opposed programmes which offered scholarships on the basis of race, compromising over abortion.

28   David Kairy, op. cit.

29   A point that is well-supported by the evidence, as Donald Horowitz showed in 1977. See, *The Courts and Social Policy* (Washington, DC: The Brookings Institute, 1977). Another interesting analysis of the damage caused in five very different school districts through judicial interventions is provided by Raymond Wolters, *The Burden of Brown: Thirty Years of School Desegregation* (Knoxville, T.: University of Tennessee Press, 1984). Wolters's description of the consequences for the schools in the District of Columbia of Judge Skelly Wright's judgment in *Hobson* v. *Hansen* (265 F. Supp., 902, 1967) is a devastating caution against well-meaning judicial activism.

30   George Bush changed from a moderate pro-choice supporter (abortions should be allowed only when there is a good reason) to present as a pro-life supporter when he understood the advantage to him in 1988, but he tried to retreat back to his moderate position in 1992 after he saw the difficulties faced by Richard Thornburgh (who had served as Bush's Attorney General) when he failed to secure victory in a contest for the Senate in Pennsylvania in 1990 that he should have won easily.

31   The threat was credible after *Webster* v. *Reproductive Services* in 1989. See Lee Epstein and Joseph F. Kobylka, *The Supreme Court and Legal Change: Abortion and the Death Penalty* (Chapel Hill, NC: University of North Carolina Press, 1992), 292–8.

32   In *Abortion: the Clash of Absolutes* (NY: W.W. Norton, 1990), Laurence Tribe points out that pre-*Roe* laws and subsequently enacted abortion restrictions remain 'at least arguably on the books in thirty-three states' (p. 25). In his view some of these are likely to be reactivated if *Roe* were repealed and some enforcement efforts will succeed. This may be so, but the fact remains that prosecutions will be very unpopular – anyone who actually implements the pro-life agenda will soon learn

the political costs and most accountable politicians whose districts are not squarely in religious communities will start singing a different tune at the first opportune moment.

33   It is certainly not viewed as reactionary in other parts of the world. Indeed, the legal positivism which informs the work of Scalia, Rehnquist, White and Thomas has an honourable history as does the common law approach endorsed by O'Connor, Kennedy and Souter; both traditions are associated with the achievement of welfare states in Europe. When you can rely on parliamentary majorities to implement progressive policies, why allow judges to frustrate them? This sentiment is reflected in the thinking of some American jurists who were critical of the role of the Supreme Court in frustrating President Roosevelt's New Deal.

34   Clinton Rossiter (ed.), *The Federalist Papers* (NY: New American Library, 1961), 465.

35   As Bruce Ackerman notes, the conservatives can claim that their understanding of the 'countermajoritarian issue' has troubled many distinguished scholars and judges – Woodrow Wilson, James Thayer, Charles Beard, Oliver Wendell Holmes, Robert Jackson, Alexander Bickel, John Ely. See, Ackerman, op. cit., 7, citing: Wilson, *Congressional Government* (1885) and *Constitutional Government in the United States* (1907); Thayer, 'The Origin and Scope of the American Doctrine of Constitutional Law', *Harvard Law Review*, 7 (1893), (129); Beard, *An Economic Interpretation of the Constitution of the United States* (1913); *Lochner* v. *New York*, 198 U.S. 45, 74 (1905) (Holmes, J., dissenting); Jackson, *The Struggle for Judicial Supremacy* (1941), *Railway Express Co.* v. *New York*, 336 U.S. 106, 111 (Jackson J., concurring); Bickel, *The Least Dangerous Branch* (1962); Ely, *Democracy and Distrust: a Theory of Judicial Review* (1980).

36   See Gerald N. Rosenberg, *The Hollow Hope: Can Courts Bring About Social Change?* (Chicago: University of Chicago Press, 1991).

37   See Horowitz, op. cit.; and Wolters, op. cit.

38   Dahl denies this, op. cit., 191. He seems to think that Ely's moderate version of dualism is able to avoid the more serious problems of dualism. I do not see why even Ely's moderate dualist views should be exempted from his criticism. In any event, it is a close call. A constitutional court that acted cautiously in exercising representation reinforcing review, strictly along the lines advocated by John Hart Ely, would probably not be regarded as illegitimate. However, it is not always clear what 'fair representation' requires and a constitutional court may be tempted to make some controversial judgments (for example, the Australian High Court recently overruled Parliament on the issue of political advertising, giving us an Australian equivalent of *Buckley* v. *Valeo* (See, Tucker, D.F.B., 'Representation-reinforcing Review: Arguments about Political Advertising in Australia and the United States' in Tom Campbell and Wodtjec Sadurski (eds), *Freedom of Communication* (Aldershot: Dartmouth Publishing Company, 1994). This was controversial but it was accepted. It is, however, possible that future attempts by Parliament to deal with the problem of unfairness in political campaigns will also be frustrated and this could lead to a legitimation crisis if Parliament decided to assert itself. Another issue of potential significance in Australia is defamation law reform – if the Australian High Court was to follow its recent initiative with the equivalent of *New York Times* v. *Sullivan*.

39   When two houses of a parliament must share power, one usually becomes subordinate to the other (for example, the House of Lords in the United Kingdom defers to the Commons, and the Senate in Australia is very reluctant to confront the House of Representatives). As usual, the United States provides an exception to this generalization.

40   Malcolm M. Feeley, 'Hollow Hopes, Flypaper, and Metaphors', *Law and Social Inquiry*, 17, (4), (1992), 751.

41   One answer to this question is provided by Robert Hughes, *Culture of Complaint* (NY: Oxford University Press, 1993).

42   See Henry Milner, *Sweden: Social Democracy in Practice* (NY: Oxford University 1989).

43   President Clinton's record on abortion shows this. As Governor in a conservative state he understood that it would be foolhardy to recommend legislation that advanced a pro-choice position; nor did he oppose the enactment of a law that required parental consent before abortions could be performed on minors in Arkansas. If he had confronted his constituents on these issues, he would have found himself in a difficult position in 1992 when he was asking southerners to regard him as a moderate.

44   Glendon, op. cit., argues that American political culture has been distorted by 'rights talk'.

45   This is the position adopted by John Rawls, op. cit., who defends a dualist understanding of the role of the Supreme Court in the United States very similar to Ronald Dworkin's position (pp. 231–40). However, Rawls is more cautious about advocating dualism when the requisite 'historical circumstance and conditions of political culture' are lacking. Although he does not specify these circumstances in detail, he refers us to Robert Dahl, *Democracy and Its Critics* for guidance. (This is very like listing one's worst enemy as a character reference!)

46   In *Brown* v. *Board of Education* 347 U.S. 483, the Supreme Court anticipated support from the President and eventually from Congress. But its use of the phrase 'with all deliberate speed' in *Brown* II reflected a more pessimistic strategic judgement, in that no time limit for desegregation was set. The political judgment of the justices was not vindicated in the short term in this case because Eisenhower let them down, Kennedy was deliberately ineffectual, and the resistance in the South was more substantial than anticipated. The Court's ruling was ignored for ten years. Nevertheless, the justices understood that change in the South was inevitable.

2 Political Science and Sociology

Before I turn to consider various jurisprudential arguments, it is necessary to say a few words about my perception of the United States political system. As already noted, I challenge the prevailing view in the United States that the work that the framers accomplished in Philadelphia has provided a viable legacy for the twentieth century. My own view is more questioning of the dualist strategy of securing liberty through a separation and division of powers. I claim that this kind of system is not likely to secure good government in the circumstances faced by most modern communities. But these opinions are contested and are not widely shared in the United States among legal scholars. It is therefore necessary to spend some time reviewing the work of the political scientists whose research has influenced me most.

Most political scientists and sociolegal scholars adopt what is known as a realist orientation in trying to explain the behaviour of judges. This view is cynical about the claim that judges are bound by legal rules. According to it, we should understand courts and judges as products of politics; 'the law' is, usually, simply what judges choose to say it is. What they will choose to say in any given context is, of course, difficult to predict; but for sociolegal scholars, the values and political affiliations of a judge are as relevant in accomplishing this goal as knowledge of law. Thus, they argue that sociology and political science should supplement legal science for the judiciary is subject to some of the political pressures that influence other public officials.

Let me give some examples. Consider the circumstances of war. Those who value the First Amendment in the United States may expect that it will serve as a protection against censorship. But sociolegal scholars would expect very little protection for speakers in times of war. According to them, Supreme Court justices will be influenced by the same pressing concerns relating to national security that motivate other political leaders. And the historical record supports this view for, in fact, the Supreme Court has offered very little protection in cases impacting on national security. Even during the early stages of the Cold War, the Supreme Court did nothing to restrain the hysteria about communism that gripped American society, allowing Senator McCarthy to use congressional committees to wreck the careers of innocent citizens. (This disgraceful episode is hardly ever mentioned by those who hold the 'dynamic court' view but it should not be seen as an exception – the Bill of Rights will prove worthless precisely when it is needed most). The Fourteenth Amendment has also proved vulnerable in the circumstances of war. Again, this comes as no surprise to those who adopt a sociolegal approach for they would regard it as naive to suppose that Supreme Court justices will act in a principled manner when everyone else is calling for expedient measures (for example, in reviewing the military orders to intern Japanese Americans in California after the bombing of Pearl Harbour). Thus, they would suggest that the important *Korematsu* v. *U.S.* case should not be analysed without considering the context in which the decision was made.[1] According to those who advocate a sociolegal approach, then, we should not expect very much more from Supreme Court justices than we do from other politicians (especially when they enjoy a wide discretion to interpret legal rules 'in the best possible way').

There is another problem relating to judicial policymaking that troubles sociolegal analysts. This relates to the competence of judges to make a sound evaluation of the competing interests when dealing with difficult problems. Judges must usually operate under very severe time constraints, and without relevant bureaucratic support from people trained in accounting, economics, medicine, criminology and science; nor can they easily investigate or consult with relevant interest groups. Most significantly, judges are not well placed to anticipate how the public are likely to respond to their rulings for they are cut-off from ordinary life by their specialist training and circumstance – they only know what other lawyers think; and this problem is compounded by the fact that they are usually selected from a very narrow elite section of the community so that their personal experiences are of a more refined kind than those of the general public. (It is said that Justice Lewis Powell was curious when he noticed that his clerk was wearing blue jeans.[2]) It is also important to note that judges are constrained by convention and may not defend their policies in the public arena. Even when they have good reasons for making a choice, then, they must rely on others to support their judgment. These constraints, according to sociolegal writers, make it highly unlikely that a community will be better served when judges make policy than when accountable politicians are responsible.

Although sociolegal scholars allow that judges usually enjoy a greater degree of independence than legislators, in that they are appointed rather than elected to office and are guaranteed a generous remuneration during their lifetime tenure, they do not think this freedom from direct accountability makes much difference to the way they act. This is because indirect influences on courts are significant. This is why most sociolegal scholars are not surprised when the political forces that prevail in legislatures (or are able to influence the executive) are also able to shape judicial responses.

This conclusion is supported by the conservative legal scholar Alexander Bickel who points out, in one of the most influential books ever written about the Supreme Court in the United States, that the Court can do no more than to say something. 'The effect depends on others'.[3] To carry law into effect, goodwill, a great deal of money and much effort may well be needed. Most significant here is the possibility that a constitutional court's rulings will be ignored or opposed. State governments, Congress and President are all capable of organizing resistance to the Supreme Court in the United States. They do this by marshalling public opinion against the Court's rulings, by initiating attempts to amend the Constitution or by passing legislation that they believe will overrule what the Court has done.[4] As Bickel shows, this kind of resistance has been frequent. Thus Supreme Court justices are likely to be wary of inflaming opposition and are unlikely to dissipate their authority by ruling in ways they think will be ignored. Nor are they likely to engage in a conflict unless they are sure that they have sufficient support to win.

According to Bickel, judgments about the general acceptability of decisions are relevant in law – the justices on the Supreme Court must be guided by political calculations about what is feasible in any given circumstances. Indeed, he claims that if the Court is insensitive to the issue of legitimacy, it will eventually be forced to change. If the Court pushes its dominion too far, judicial review itself could be brought to an end.[5]

In this review chapter, I argue that the accumulative evidence about the role of the judiciary and the incapacity of courts to restrain parliaments offers convincing support to the constrained Court view. The Supreme Court in the United States should not be expected to bring about social reforms except under highly unusual circumstances. Once we recognize that judges play a vulnerable role within the process by means of which authoritative judgments about values are made, we must ask ourselves whether they can lead. Liberals urge the Supreme Court to assume leadership when most of the evidence shows that this is unlikely; moreover, they urge courts to make policy even though judges are likely to perform poorly in this role. In contrast, conservatives understand that courts are constrained arenas within which the nation's more important political battles should not be settled. As the conservatives see it, policies that are imposed by the judiciary will usually be challenged and are unlikely to be agreed to until the judiciary secures the support of one or other of the co-equal branches of government. When policies are made in more accountable arenas, on the other hand, these will usually be accepted as settled by those who disapprove the outcome. According to conservatives, then, the accumulative evidence about the position of courts in the political process shows why judges should strive to be followers, not leaders.

Sociological Assessments of the Role of the Court

Sociolegal scholars have been cautious in awarding high marks to the judiciary for its countermajoritarian policymaking.[6] Let me briefly consider some of the more influential contributions.

Robert Dahl's Assessment

Robert Dahl defends a reassuring assessment of the role of the Supreme Court. In a paper published in 1957 he argues that although the judiciary is necessarily and frequently engaged in policymaking, the role of the Supreme Court is effectively constrained by other political actors.[7] According to him, there are good reasons why Supreme Court justices tend to defer to the leadership of the other branches of government. One reason is the vulnerability of the Supreme Court because its members have no control over its own composition. Thus, the Court cannot frustrate a majority for any length of time because presidents will eventually be elected with a mandate to transform the ideological composition of the Court. The vulnerability of the Supreme Court as 'the least dangerous branch' is demonstrated in the record that shows, according to Dahl, that the justices have been reluctant to confront Congress and rarely invalidate laws in circumstances where it is clear that a majority of the existing members of Congress are resolved to secure a different outcome. In the few cases Dahl examines when the Court did act to challenge Congress (only 38 in the 167 years that Dahl has data for, and 12 of these occurred during the conflict over Roosevelt's New Deal so were quickly reversed) it has usually been unsuccessful in sustaining the judicial veto.[8]

Even when the Supreme Court finds a common resolve among the justices to confront the other branches, according to Dahl, it is usually unable to do more than delay important legislative changes; often, it quickly concedes once the justices are persuaded that a determined legislative majority is confronting them.

Dahl's 1957 account of the role of the judiciary in United States politics exaggerates the passivity of judges because he ignores the less dramatic ways that they can influence outcomes. For one thing, they can make policy when the legislators are unwilling to confront or unable to resolve a difficult policy issue; they can also intervene after legislators have exhausted themselves in conflict over the passage of a difficult piece of legislation (such as the Clean Air Act or the Civil Rights Act 1964). In these kinds of circumstances, judges often read a statute as they choose, knowing that it will be very difficult for the legislators to reverse their judgment. Indeed, in many instances legislators will know that judges are likely to hack their work to pieces and sometimes they deliberately agree to include vague phrases in a statute to encourage this. They usually do this in trying to reach consensus, choosing vague phrases precisely because no specific policy enjoys majority support. When legislators anticipate judicial resolution each side of a policy controversy can gamble that the presiding judges will see things its way. Sometimes the judiciary will side with one or other faction – often to secure outcomes that do not enjoy much support. (For example, there was very little consensus nationally in the United States about the use of racial quotas as a prophylactic against discrimination in employment, yet the Supreme Court read the Civil Rights Act 1964 in a manner that clearly contradicted the intentions of many of the legislators who voted for the Act, as well as the explanations offered by its sponsors, virtually making it mandatory for American companies to hire and fire in a manner that would enable them to secure the requisite number of the designated ethnic groups in their workforce.[9]) Of course, Congress is free to amend statutes that may have been butchered by the judiciary in ways most members disapprove (for example, Congress was free to amend the Civil Rights Act 1964 to prevent the widespread resort to racial-quota hiring and the race-norming of tests from continuing).[10] But this remedy is not always easy to accomplish when the outcome is likely to impact deleteriously on a mobilized section of the electorate or when most legislators are only too happy to avoid further controversy. (For example, a majority of the legislators who had considered the Civil Rights Act 1964 at great length in the United States Congress were exhausted by the contentious struggle over the issue of race discrimination and did not believe that they had much to gain by having the whole matter reconsidered.)

Another problem with Dahl's analysis is that, writing in 1957, he could not anticipate developments that occurred during the 1960s. It was too soon, at that time, to understand how the incorporation of sections of the Bill of Rights would empower the Supreme Court, allowing it to intrude into the affairs of the various states, imposing policies relating to police powers, voting rights, prisons, schools,

abortion, obscenity and many other matters. What occurred here was
the use of a federal agency, the Supreme Court, to impose on various
state governments on behalf of the nation as a whole. In this context,
the judiciary was not acting alone; indeed, it was able to succeed
precisely because there was no national opposition to its policies –
despite the very great resistance in particular states. If the judiciary
had chosen to step ahead of the general public, however, antagoniz-
ing groups on a national level and not merely within particular states,
a more formidable opposition could quickly have emerged. Indeed,
in cases where this happened (as in school busing), the policy changes
initiated by the Supreme Court proved unsustainable.

In a more recent work *Democracy and Its Critics*, Dahl again addresses the issue of countermajoritarian review in the United States,
that he describes as a system of quasi-guardianship. He summarizes
his conclusions by making the following observations that take account of some of the criticisms I have made:[11] First, when quasi-
guardians are made responsible for protecting fundamental rights
and interests, they will necessarily broaden the scope of their authority to 'take on the functions of making law and policy'. Second:

> No one has shown that countries like the Netherlands and New Zea-
> land, which lack judicial review, or Norway and Sweden, where it is
> exercised rarely and in highly restrained fashion, or Switzerland, where
> it can be applied only to cantonal legislation, are less democratic than
> the United States, nor, I think, could one reasonably do so.[12]

Third, judicial quasi-guardianship requires little self-control on the
part of citizens and politicians because they can rely on legal restraints being imposed; thus:

> Over time, the political culture may come to incorporate the expecta-
> tion that the judicial guardians can be counted on to fend off viola-
> tions of fundamental rights, just as greater self-restraint on the part of
> the demos and its representatives may become a stronger norm in the
> political culture of polyarchies without judicial guardianship.[13]

Fourth, most of the famous cases of the Warren Court involved state
or local laws that were of no great national significance, whereas
when the Supreme Court acted to frustrate Congress in the 1920s and
at other times, the cases were of genuinely fundamental importance,
'where an opposite policy would have meant basic shifts in the distribution of rights, liberties and opportunities in the United States'.
Fifth, the Supreme Court cannot offer much protection against Congress or President because 'the views of the majority of justices ... are
never out of line for very long with the views prevailing among the
lawmaking majorities of the country'. Sixth:

A heavy burden of proof should therefore be required before the democratic process is displaced by quasi guardianship. It should be necessary to demonstrate that the democratic process fails to give equal consideration to the interests of some who are subject to its laws; that 'the quasi guardians will do so; and that the injury inflicted on the right to equal consideration outweighs the injury done to the right of a people to govern itself.[14]

Donald Horowitz's Assessment

In another important sociolegal assessment Donald Horowitz takes a close look at judicial policymaking in practice. He agrees with Dahl that American judges are heavily engaged in policymaking exercising a wide discretion that goes well beyond a narrow focus on fundamental liberties, but does not share Dahl's complacency about this. For one thing, he notices how extensively the scope of judicial business broadened during the 1960s, so that courts in the United States became involved in making decisions about matters such as city planning, academic streaming in schools, abortion, that they would traditionally have been thought unfit to have opinions about.[15]

The issue that troubles most people about this development is the countermajoritarian problem: Are judges entitled to set out social policies when they are not accountable to the people? Is judicial policymaking a violation of democracy? Horowitz is more concerned to question competence. It is not that he thinks judges are less intelligent or fair minded than other policymakers, but they operate in the constrained circumstances of court hearings in which the information they receive is narrowly focused on the particular case before them. This is unfortunate, according to Horowitz, because policymakers must be concerned with the general problem in dealing with any issue, not whether one person should gain or another lose in a particular contest. Even if we agree that it is quite appropriate for judges to engage in policymaking, Horowitz urges us to consider whether they will do so competently. Are judges likely to make better choices than the legislators and administrators who have traditionally been responsible? Thus, his research is directed at discerning the impact that the manner by which a decision may have been reached is likely to have on the outcome.

To demonstrate that his reservations about the competence of judges are not merely speculative Horowitz presents four examples of judicial policymaking. By examining each case in great detail, looking over the shoulders of the judges at work with the benefit of hindsight, the disadvantages that judges face as policymakers come to be revealed. Horowitz claims that if we examine the case studies he presents carefully, we will see why judges are not likely to serve their

communities well if they take on far-reaching policymaking responsibilities.

Although Horowitz concedes that the adjudication process has
some advantages, he argues that its distinctive virtues render courts
unsuited to many tasks. As he points out, court procedures are designed to present issue in a particular controversy between two specific parties in a conflict, but this seems an unsuitable focus when one
is making policies that must apply generally. One problem that courts
face is that matters are brought before them by people with com-
plaints. The judges have little ability to avoid reaching a decision in
the case at hand before other cases of a similar kind have been
considered, yet there is 'no assurance that litigants constitute a random sample of the class of cases that might be affected by a decree'[16];
but, as Horowitz argues, this 'implies ad hoc decisions, one case at a
time' in dealing with overall policy choices.[17] He uses *Griggs* v. *Duke
Power Company* and *Lau* v. *Nichols* as examples of cases in which the
Supreme Court made policies for the nation after considering the
circumstances of unrepresentative complainants.[18] In the first, the
Supreme Court ruled on the use of an aptitude test in making employment decisions, a matter likely to affect the competitiveness of
United States companies and the manner in which they allocated
tasks to competing employees; but, in *Griggs*, the conflict before the
court involved a company with a general history of racial discrimination that had added the aptitude test requirement on the very date
that the law against employment discrimination became effective. In
the second case, *Lau*, the Supreme Court set national policy affecting
millions of Spanish-speaking children committing scarce educational
resources in a case brought by Chinese-speaking pupils who had
special difficulties coping in classes run in English. For Horowitz, the
most serious problem about judicial policymaking is that judges have
difficulty comprehending how their rulings will allocate scarce resources between competing ends. In his view, judges are unlikely to
keep in mind the troubling trade-offs that doing justice in one case
may entail for others (for example, if a court orders that government
funds be spent to ensure language instruction for students whose
home language is not English, it will not know where the necessary
money will have to be taken from).[19] Another problem about the
judicial process is that it is focused on presenting two sides, often
oversimplifying the policy dilemmas in an effort to direct the judge.
Thus, the competing advocates simplify the choice by marshalling
arguments in a coherent though biased manner. Nor are any of the
participants in this process necessarily equipped to make independent judgments for they are not specialists and enjoy few relevant
skills, if any, other than experience and training in litigation. In most
cases, the judge will also be a litigation lawyer by training; thus,

those who appear before him or her will need to explain complex specialist information as if to a layperson. The only experts who appear before the court will be witnesses who are paid and selected by the various parties and they will be led in presenting their evidence by the litigators, moreover the chosen experts are often highly partisan.

Horowitz compares the circumscribed and abstract manner in which a court must proceed with the circumstance of a specialist parliamentary committee advised by skilled and experienced administrators.[20] The court will make its decision untroubled by the presence of influential groups with whom it must negotiate. It can move to decision without bargaining. This is a problem, according to Horowitz, 'because it is precisely this ability to simplify the issues and to exclude interested participants that may put the judges in danger of fostering reductionist solutions'.[21] More serious is the difficulty that courts have in assessing costs and in framing appropriate remedies. Judges must focus on whether an individual complainant is entitled to a right – if so, they issue the relevant order. But an order requiring a party to do or refrain from doing something may not be the most appropriate remedy, given the costs to the community that this may involve. (On this point, Horowitz draws attention to the two criminal law cases he analyses, *Mapp* v. *Ohio* and *In re, Gault*.[22] From a legal point of view, these cases seem straightforward for the Supreme Court was hoping to assure the fair trial of defendants by insisting that strict procedures be followed. In *Mapp*, it forbade state courts to rely on evidence obtained in violation of the Fourth Amendment's guarantee of freedom from 'unreasonable searches and seizures'; in *Gault*, it required that juveniles who face confinement be represented by counsel, among other things, because they must be afforded the constitutionally protected privilege against self-incrimination. What the justices in both cases failed to take into account is that most criminal cases are resolved without trial. Thus they did not anticipate how police and other agents would actually respond to the new rules, and failed to adequately consider the impact these rules would have on the negotiations that are known as 'plea bargaining'.)

A related difficulty, according to Horowitz, is the incapacity of courts to monitor the implementation of their orders. If there is a lack of compliance or unforeseen difficulties make compliance costly and difficult, the court must wait for a party to return to the court seeking enforcement or dissolution of the injunction. But this is a clumsy process. Much more satisfactory in most circumstances are the options available to legislators and administrators who have an ability to adjust their regulative techniques in the light of experience. Although they can resort to the kinds of sanctions judges invoke, their power to control the flow of money allows them to discourage activity without forbidding it outright and to encourage behaviour they approve without making it compulsory. Thus, they:

> may use taxation, incentives and subsidies of various kinds, interventions in the marketplace, the establishment of new organisations or the takeover of old ones, or a number of other ways of seeking to attain their goals.[23]

They also have a capacity to review the impact of their chosen remedy as it is implemented to see how behaviour is actually influenced and to detect unforeseen difficulties. Thus, the remedy may be adjusted in the light of experience.

For all these reasons, Horowitz thinks that activist judges are likely to cause a good deal of harm, often imposing unhelpful outcomes that cost the community dearly.

Of course, all decisionmakers are likely to embrace bad policies and we cannot claim from these speculations that judges are likely to be less successful than legislators. For this to be shown, we must review courts in action, comparing their policy choices with those we have reasons for thinking would have been chosen by legislators. Horowitz, accepts this challenge and offers his four studies as a contribution to this ongoing evaluation. We need to ask whether the processes by means of which decisions are reached are likely to affect the kinds of outcomes we should expect. After looking at his chosen cases, Horowitz concludes that those who advocate extensive judicial involvement as policymakers should be aware of the institutional limitations of courts.

Horowitz's conclusion is troubling and persuasive. But his book did not have very much of an impact on the prevailing dualistic orientation supported by most legal intellectuals. Dualist assumptions about the leadership role of the judiciary have, however, again been challenged by another political scientist, Gerald Rosenberg, and this time there has been a significant response because he has taken the very important landmark cases of the Warren period as his focus and because he directly confronts the prevailing orthodoxy about the significance of the Warren Court in recent United States history. Let me now consider Rosenberg's work.

Rosenberg's Research

Rosenberg sets out to investigate when and under what circumstances the Supreme Court is likely to serve as an effective policymaking agency capable of securing significant social reform. As he points out, the judiciary is bound by precedent and other legal constraints, lacks independence, lacks the tools to readily develop appropriate policies, and cannot implement its rulings or enter into the political arena to mobilize support for them.[24] According to Rosenberg, these constraints make it virtually certain that the judiciary will not be successful when it pursues policies that do not enjoy support in the community or among the public officials who are crucial for their implementation.

Rosenberg's work is important because he does not stop at the point of decision – when he is satisfied that the justices have declared a preference for a particular policy outcome. He goes on to ask whether the decisions made are actually implemented and this is surely relevant when assessing the role of the judiciary in policymaking. As Rosenberg points out, it is one thing for the Supreme Court to bring down a ruling in a case that embodies a policy preference (for example, in *Brown*, that southern public schools should be desegregated) and quite another for its will to be carried out. For this to happen, many different agents may have to be persuaded to change their behaviour. Sometimes they will do this voluntarily if they recognize that there is political and popular support for the policy in question. Indeed, there are circumstances, as Rosenberg shows, where administrators may use a Supreme Court order to assist them in persuading others to go along with changes they may otherwise have resisted, and they can use the ruling as a shield by shifting blame for the unpopular policy onto the Court. But in these cases, agents who are crucially placed to assert leadership must support the Court. Sometimes administrators will not support the Court and may themselves need an incentive to change. For this to happen, however, the Court will usually have to rely on one of the other branches of government for support. Thus, we find that the Supreme Court in the United States can assert leadership when it correctly anticipates support from one of the other branches of government. For example, Congress and the President can impose costs on those who fail to comply (loss of federal funding is the usual penalty).[25]

Rosenberg's careful investigations, examining the consequences of landmark judicial rulings by the United States Supreme Court in a variety of settings, shows that the Court is highly constrained by other political actors and by the prevailing political culture; so much so, according to Rosenberg, that we can conclude that the Supreme Court in the United States is unlikely to secure significant social changes in circumstances where it is not supported by one of the other branches of government. As Rosenberg puts the point, 'Courts can matter, but only sometimes, and only under limited conditions'.[26] This is not to say that the Supreme Court will not try to bring about desirable social changes; nor can we conclude that it will not make a lot of bad policy judgments in trying to accomplish this. But we should be wary of concluding that it can act effectively on its own.

The Indirect Impact of Court Rulings

One important issue is whether Rosenberg's (and Dahl's) 'constrained court' view overlooks the indirect impact that landmark decisions may have. What I have in mind is whether courts can act as some sort of catalyst to facilitate the mobilization of political forces for change. Perhaps they can influence outcomes by shaping the political agenda so that issues that would otherwise escape attention are brought into public focus. Perhaps important cases serve as symbols so that the members of social movements are prevented from despair and even inspired to increase their efforts to work for change.

In a review of Rosenberg's *The Hollow Hope* Malcolm Feeley suggests that judicial decisions do produce indirect effects of this kind.[27] He wonders whether Rosenberg has overlooked the various and subtle ways that courts can raise expectations and, by offering a hope of victory, motivate reformers. Certainly the cases that Rosenberg focuses on in his study (*Brown* v. *Board of Education*, *Roe* v. *Wade*, *Mapp* v. *Ohio*, *Miranda* v. *Arizona* and *Baker* v. *Carr*) do serve as important symbols in United States cultural life.

Rosenberg answers this criticism claiming there is little evidence that courts have had any significant indirect effect.[28] In his view, it is wrong to suppose that any change that would not otherwise have occurred was accomplished solely because of judicial activism. Of course, this is not an easy claim to test empirically.[29] If we take changes in public opinion, in media coverage and in the behaviour of activists as evidence of such impact, however, Rosenberg's research shows that Feeley's claims are difficult to sustain. After an exhaustive effort to find evidence in appropriate places to support the Feeley view, he finds that it is mostly not there; and where it is, he dismisses it as of 'the subtlest nature'.[30]

This is not to say that controversial court decisions do not provoke people. But Rosenberg makes the interesting observation that they are more likely to influence outcomes when they provoke those who oppose than those who support the rulings. Indeed, he finds that countermajoritarian decisions are most likely to serve as a catalyst for those who seek to reverse the policies the courts are recommending. He summarises his findings in the following way:

> While I have found no evidence that court decisions mobilise support-
> ers of significant social reform, the data suggests that they may mobil-

ise opponents. With civil rights, there was a growth in the membership and activities of pro-segregationist groups such as the White
citizens Councils and the Ku Klux Klan in the years after *Brown*. With
abortion, the Right to Life Movement expanded rapidly after 1973.
While both types of groups existed before Court action, they appeared
re-invigorated after it.[31]

More important, symbolic victories may sometimes be taken for substantive ones. Many people like to believe that their society takes
rights seriously and they may feel reassured by decisions that seem
to fulfil this promise. If a constitutional court such as the United
States Supreme Court rules in a way that is supportive of rights (as
the Supreme Court did, for example, in the landmark cases *Escobedo*
v. *Illinois* and *Miranda* v. *Arizona* when it set out rules designed to
eliminate the possibility of police brutality[32]) many people may assume that all is well in the community – that rights are actually
protected – but they may well be wrong. (For example, anyone who
believes that *Escobedo* and *Miranda* put an end to arbitrariness and
police brutality in the United States is simply out of touch with
reality.) Yet many Americans do think their system is better in securing rights than other democracies because they trust the federal courts,
especially the Supreme Court (whereas, in fact, when we take into
account the conditions in which prisoners are kept, the prevalence of
capital punishment, and the frequent reports of brutal behaviour on
the part of the police, the record of the United States in confining the
coercion used by police and other officials is not very good when
matched against other democratic countries like Sweden, the Nether-
lands or even the United Kingdom).[33]

Judicial Liberalism, Public Opinion and Recent Elections

One way a constitutional court can have an impact is by generating a
backlash against its own policies. This is inevitable when the court
moves ahead of public opinion and it is the main reason why judicial
initiatives are largely self-defeating.

Consider the case of capital punishment in the United States. If we
look at opinions about the death penalty in 1936, only 33 per cent of
Americans are opposed and 62 per cent are in favour of capital
sentencing in serious cases.[34] This huge difference in the numbers
supporting and opposing the death penalty remained steady for about
20 years. However, in 1956 public opinion began to shift. We find
that although only 34 per cent are opposed to the death penalty in
1956, only 53 per cent now favour capital punishment (with the
number of people in the 'don't know' category growing dramatically

from 5 per cent in 1936 to 13 per cent in 1956); by 1966, as many as 47 per cent are opposed to the death penalty and only 42 per cent are in favour.[35]

Not surprisingly, in the light of these attitudes, attempts to secure reforms to eliminate capital sentencing as a practice in the United States were successful during the 1960s. Between 1964 and 1969 the death penalty was abolished in five states (Oregon, Iowa, Vermont, West Virginia, New York, New Mexico).[36] The reform process culminated in 1972 when, after considering a series of death penalty appeals, the Supreme Court announced in *Furman* v. *Georgia*: 'The Court holds that the imposition and carrying out of the death penalty in these cases constitute cruel and unusual punishment in violation of the Eighth and Fourteenth Amendments'.[37]

Unfortunately, the dramatic change accomplished by the Supreme Court ruling in *Furman* went ahead of the public in many states and the backlash was very significant. This was partly because two of the nation's most influential politicians were now able to use the issue for their own purposes. (Then) Governor Ronald Reagan in California whose death row population of 107 was the largest in the nation (and contained Charles Manson and Sirhan-Sirhan) proposed a public initiative – Proposition 17 – to restore the death penalty.[38] This was overwhelmingly supported by the people of California (a 2–1 margin) and other governors were encouraged to follow Reagan's lead.[39] President Richard Nixon also entered the debate, holding a press conference to declare his commitment to capital punishment for serious crimes just one day after the Supreme Court handed down *Furman*. He later submitted proposals to Congress asking the legislators to consider making death sentences possible for treason, kidnapping and hijacking. Less than one year later, Congress legislated a bipartisan reinstatement of capital punishment that was widely supported.[40] The success that Nixon and Reagan achieved by campaigning against the judiciary, together with the publicity generated by the legislative activity that followed their initiatives, also helped to reorientate public opinion (as Figure 2.1 illustrates, less than 50 per cent of the public favoured capital punishment in 1972, yet nearly 64 per cent did so by 1974; and the proportion supporting grew steadily reaching over 70 per cent by 1982).[41]

Just four years after *Furman* the Supreme Court reversed itself on capital punishment (in *Gregg* v. *Georgia*) illustrating once again how responsive the justices are to political pressures.[42] The case of capital punishment also demonstrates how populist politicians like Nixon and Reagan can gain from interventions by the judiciary. It shows how courts can cause harm when they place a controversial issue on the political agenda, forcing politicians to respond when public opinion is not favourably disposed to the reform in question. The most

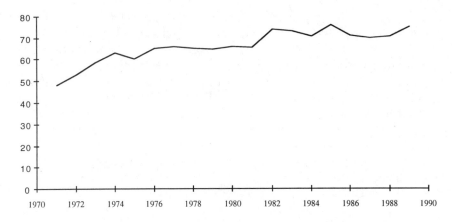

Source: Derived from Figure 4–2 in Lee Epstein & Joseph F. Kobylka, *The Supreme Court & Legal Change: Abortion and the Death Penalty* (Chapel Hill, NC: University of North Carolina Press, 1992), 89. They in turn cite H.W. Stanley and R.G. Niemi, *Vital Statistics on American Politics* (Washington, DC: CQ Press, 1992), 33.

Figure 2.1   Percentage of Population in Favour of the Death Penalty

important lesson for reformers that the Supreme Court's passage from *Furman* to *Gregg* illustrates is that they should not focus too much of their energy on securing victories in the courts. Whether the dramatic shift in public attitudes towards the present situation in which most people approve death sentences would have occurred in the United States if the Court had not dramatically intervened is difficult to say. We certainly cannot assume that the Supreme Court's intervention in *Furman* v. *Georgia* and the backlash this provoked had no effect.

But capital punishment is just one issue on which the public and the legal elite are seriously out-of-step in the United States. In two surveys conducted in 1976–77 and 1978–79, respectively, Herbert McClosky and Alida Brill show the enormous difference education makes in shaping peoples attitudes towards civil liberties.[43] According to them, precisely because the legal elite are better informed, they are far out-of-step with the general public on civil rights. This difference is most manifest with regard to issues relating to law and order (for example, only 40 per cent of the general public agree that forcing people to testify against themselves is never justified, yet 93 per cent of the legal elite think this would be wrong in all circumstances; only 55 per cent of the general public think that keeping people in prison for long periods before bringing them to trial should not be allowed, no matter what the crime, as compared to 79 per cent of the legal elite; only 11 per cent of the general public would acquit a defendant if the judge in the trial has made a mistake in legal procedure and 65 per cent think this would be carrying legal technicalities too far, yet 35 per cent of the legal elite would like to see a defendant acquitted in this circumstance and only 33 per cent think this would be carrying legal technicalities too far); but it is also significant in other areas such as in attitudes towards sexually related forms of expression, and towards the separation of church and state (80 per cent of the general public approve prayers in schools and only 10 per cent oppose prayers, yet only 48 per cent of opinion leaders approve prayers in schools and as many as 34 per cent are opposed).[44]

In all these areas, we must suspect that the capacity of liberals to use courts as a means for imposing elite values is limited. Experience tends to confirm this supposition. Many of the Court's policies have been undermined by administrative neglect or reversed by appointing more compliant judges. When they have not been, this is usually because public attitudes have come to change in the direction foreshadowed in the Court's rulings.

Even in cases where the Court's rulings are supported by a majority of the public, politicians threatening to reverse its policies may gain an advantage. If we take the case of abortion as an example, we see that the justices who decided *Roe* v. *Wade* in 1973 correctly assessed the direction in which public opinion would change.[45] More people in the United States today support the pro-choice position on abortion and only a very small proportion of the electorate (about 20 per cent) are keen to see *Roe* v. *Wade* reversed. This is one reason why Congress has never confronted the Court over abortion. Yet conservatives have managed to use the issue to their advantage. Consider how long abortion has served to agitate religious communities in the United States and speculate about how many votes may have been lost by liberal candidates bravely trying to support *Roe* v. *Wade*. The problem they faced is the difference in intensity with which the various contending affects are held by members of the electorate. Pro-life candidates may have annoyed many women but so long as the right to an abortion was assured, not many votes were at risk because the competing candidates were not assessed on this one issue by most of those who were pro-choice. In contrast, the 20 per cent of voters who were motivated by religious beliefs cared enough about abortion to change their voting behaviour – they were single issue voters and politicians who tried to accommodate them could gain an advantage.

The Judiciary, Liberalism and Recent Elections

The point I have been illustrating is that the backlash generated by an activist Supreme Court is likely to influence the political prospects of other political actors; indeed, that it is likely to provide an enormous advantage to those politicians who are unscrupulous enough to oppose the Court. We see this in recent presidential contests in the United States for the strategies adopted by the major political parties when conducting election campaigns have been shaped by an on-going debate about liberal values, partly provoked by the activities of the Supreme Court.

This phenomenon has been very significant in the South because the Supreme Court was involved as a key institution when the federal government brought segregation to an end. But the Warren–Burger Court's role as an unwitting *agent provocateur* for the Republicans, encouraging conservative communities to shift political allegiance away from the Democrats by presenting as a symbol of unpopular liberal principles, has not been confined to the issue of racial justice. The Supreme Court expanded the liberal agenda enormously by bringing down unpopular and controversial rulings relating to police powers, separation of Church and State, speech, and privacy. In a series of decisions, that stretch the legal imagination and ingenuity even of their defenders, it recognized a number of new rights that protected stigmatized groups that had little or no community support (for example, criminals, prisoners, atheists, pornographers, drug users);[46] even more controversially, it acted aggressively to withdraw protection from traditionally protected communities (such as poorly educated rural whites and the religious communities) by refusing to uphold claims to state autonomy (made in the name of the federal agreement originally embodied in the Constitution). The Supreme Court justices acted in the name of liberal values that had little community support and ignored the actual terms and conditions of the federal division of powers that were widely recognized and accepted.[47]

These interventions had the effect of placing progressive leaders in the Democratic Party in a very vulnerable position. Although they knew that they were unable to secure public support for the rights and liberties that the Court had decided to recognise, they felt obliged to defend the agenda the Court had foisted upon them. This was partly because of their own personal values. (How can someone who strongly believes that liberal ideals are worthy easily enter into a campaign to discredit the Court's imposition of those very values?)

Of course, the Supreme Court's role in projecting 'liberalism' as an issue that has polarised southern voters (and many others) against the Democratic Party is very much a supporting one. A much more serious problem for the Democrats is that a large number of the party's core constituents thoroughly approve of the liberal advances secured by the Warren–Burger Court. This is one reason why it has been so difficult for Democratic candidates to distance themselves from liberal ideals – they have had to fight in primary contests to secure nomination in circumstances where liberal values count for a good deal amongst core voters. This is a problem because the left faction within the Democratic Party has tended to shift too far from the centre of the political spectrum for the party to remain competitive. Until President Clinton's primary campaign in 1992, the Democrats were vulnerable to the charge 'that the people dependent on welfare, who are largely black and living in crime-ridden neighbourhoods, are at the heart of the Democratic power base in the big cities'.[48]

The national Democratic Party has endorsed school busing and affirmative action policies (knowing that vast numbers of voters are strongly against these programmes) precisely because left-of-centre supporters and intellectuals are often the most active within it. Moreover, it is the concerns of the 'left' within the party that have often been on display during party conventions. Jesse Jackson's primary campaign successes in 1984 and in 1988 are a testament to this. His speech at the 1988 Democratic Party Convention in Atlanta was moving and inspiring, yet it could not have helped Michael Dukakis's bid for the Presidency for the nation to see the extent to which Jackson's agenda was approved by the Democratic faithful.

Recent Democratic presidential candidates have failed to distance themselves sufficiently from Jesse Jackson (such as Walter Mondale and Michael Dukakis) and they have paid a significant price because of the widespread hostility that many Americans now exhibit towards his brand of liberal collectivism. In contrast, one reason why Bill Clinton was successful in 1992 is that he criticised Jackson for sponsoring an appearance of the rap singer Sister Souljah and managed to keep control of the party convention so that Jackson was not able to dominate. Moreover, he made clear that his welfare programmes were aimed at helping all Americans and he specifically addressed the concerns of suburban voters by offering help on college fees and health costs.

Bush helped him defuse the anxiety that white voters felt about racial politics by signing the Civil Rights Act 1992. As John Podhoretz explains in his recent discussion of the election, most of the Reagan loyalists among the Republican Party felt that it was essential to secure the association that many electors made between 'Democrat' and 'liberal'. In their view, the best vehicle for accomplishing this in 1992 was for Bush to go into the election after exercising a veto rejecting the Civil Rights Bill. But the President refused to do this. He thought that women and African Americans would give him credit for supporting civil rights, but they did not.[49] Clinton won the election because he was able to shift the agenda onto other concerns that also motivated the electorate.

Clinton's success shows that it is one thing to hold values in conflict with the mass public, quite another to embrace these values as part of a campaign to win elections. By resisting the temptation to campaign as a liberal he minimized the risk of losing the support of a very large proportion of southern white voters and most other middle-class Americans. Ironically, Clinton was helped in this strategy by Bush's extraordinary popularity – many potential candidates decided not to seek nomination. But he was also helped by the changing environment brought about by previous Republican successes. For example, because a conservative majority had emerged on the Supreme Court by 1989, it was no longer out-of-step on the left of the public; indeed, on many issues it had moved to the right of the spectrum, allowing Clinton to take the middle ground (for example, on abortion and discrimination against homosexuals).[50] Even on race relations, the Civil Rights Act of 1992 disallowed the more provocative forms of reverse discrimination and established a national consensus about more moderate programmes (claimed not to involve quotas and not to seriously disadvantage white males) to advance minorities and women. These advantages had not been enjoyed by previous Democratic candidates.

Was Republican ascendancy in presidential contests inevitable?

Not necessarily. The Civil Rights Movement received bi-partisan support (indeed, more Republicans than Democrats voted in favour of the 1964 Civil Rights Act in Congress) and, as we have seen, it was a Republican president, Eisenhower, who nominated the Republican Governor of California, Earl Warren, as Chief Justice. Also, the Republican Party had no substantial political base within the white South, so there were good reasons to expect that it would be the more aggressive of the contending parties in demanding changes in the southern way of life. They could have moved aggressively to try and capture the African-American voters who felt a great deal of ambivalence about the Democratic Party. Nor did there seem any good reason why the Democrats should have wanted to change. It had enjoyed a firm hold on a white southern base and there was no good reason, once the separatist movements had proved futile, why anyone should have expected any significant change in white southern voting behaviour in favour of the Republicans. By 1960, southern whites were isolated and simply had to accept that racial segregation could not continue.

Republican ascendancy in the South and in the nation as a whole in presidential contests was not inevitable between 1968 and 1992. White southern voters could have been enticed back to the Democratic Party once their initial anger and frustration had been dissipated. In any event, there is no obvious reason why there should have been any significant difference in the attitudes that the two contending parties displayed towards civil rights. If anything, one

would have expected the Democrats to have been the more conservative of the two, reflecting the long-standing influence of white
southerners.

Policy convergence did not happen because President Lyndon
Johnson had a different strategy in mind for his party when he
signed the Civil Rights Act 1964 and the Voting Rights Act. Although,
he had no intention of delivering 'the South to the Republican Party
for a long time to come',[51] he knew that this was a danger. His
strategy for future Democratic Party success depended on combining moderate white southern voters with the soon-to-be-mobilized
African-American section of the electorate. Certainly, his own decisive victory in 1964 involved winning all the African-American votes,
whilst securing a fair proportion of the white southern votes, showed
that this was possible.[52] In their analysis of southern politics, Earl
and Merle Black explain the new electoral competition in the South
that Johnson envisaged:

> In the old southern politics, before blacks voted in large numbers, the
> winner was automatically the candidate who received a majority of
> the votes cast by whites. This rule no longer held (after the passage of
> the Voting Rights Act). A candidate who received few votes from
> blacks now had to poll a landslide majority of the southern white vote
> (the specific percentage depending on the size and cohesion of the
> black vote) to obtain a bare majority of the region's total vote.

As Jimmy Carter showed in 1976 and Bill Clinton in 1992, Johnson's
strategy is viable. Carter won in most of the South by obtaining only
47 per cent of the white vote and Clinton won in Arkansas, Tennessee, Louisiana, Georgia and Kentucky even though he held the support of only 34 per cent of white southerners.[53]

The best strategy for a Democratic presidential candidate is to hold
the allegiance of enough white voters by offering policies on issues
other than race relations that they like and by not alienating them
unnecessarily. As Earl and Merle Black make clear, southerners are
interested in health, in education, in protecting the environment and
in securing employment. Thus, a Democrat advocating policies that
offer governmental help to troubled communities should be able to
defuse the disadvantage that the party carries because of its association with desegregation and civil rights.

I claim that one factor that has made it more difficult for Democratic candidates to succeed using Johnson's strategy is that the United
States Supreme Court moved ahead of public opinion on controversial issues leaving the Democrats with very little space to manoeuvre
into the middle ground. Thus, Democratic candidates entered presidential election contests with too many negatives. Their best elec-

toral strategy was to adopt policies that accommodated the African Americans while holding back liberal aspirations on other alienating issues such as abortion, school prayer and racial quotas. It was possible to find enough to please both moderate white southerners and African Americans in shifting towards a biracial coalition. But the party did not accomplish this. By embracing liberalism as a general orientation, and approving judicial policymaking in its name, the Democrats created a deeper split in the party than was necessary, causing far too many white southerners to become alienated for it to remain competitive in the region. The change allowed the Republican Party to use the South as a base and to provoke the Democrats further to the left than a majority of the electorate was prepared to tolerate.[54] Indeed, it is questionable whether Bill Clinton's recent victory in 1992 can be viewed as the end of this Republican advantage.[55]

There is some hope for the Democrats. This comes from the predominantly white suburban dwellers and those who live in the newer, growing predominantly white cities.[56] These communities will determine the outcome in future elections because they are now a substantial part of the United States population (the suburbs on their own had reached 44.9 per cent by 1986). Because these communities are overwhelmingly white, they are less concerned with matters relating to race relations than white communities in rural areas of the South and in the big cities; the suburban populations are also more liberal on women's rights and on matters relating to sexual morality. They are concerned about local autonomy, public safety, crime, drugs, job security, college fees, health insurance and with avoiding having to pay higher taxes that may be used to benefit others who are less privileged.[57] These voters are susceptible to Republican candidates – their 'silent majority' as Nixon referred to them – but, as President Clinton showed in 1992, they are open to the appeal of a Democratic Party that is willing to pander to their right-of-centre concerns.[58] Whether he can ensure that the Democratic Party's policy orientation remains centred on the suburbs when the party's own centre-of-gravity is largely in the left-of-centre factions living in the big cities is questionable. It is far more likely that the Republicans will find that the suburban voters gravitate back to them, so long as their party does not veer too far to the right in an effort to hold onto the declining number of voters who are influenced by religious concerns – provided that there is no substantial change in economic circumstances that Clinton can claim to have master-minded.

Conclusions

I have reviewed evidence from sociolegal research and psephology that provides good reason for questioning whether the leadership that the Supreme Court provided in making policy relating to civil rights has been beneficial in the United States.

As Horowitz's research shows, the justices often embrace counterproductive policies; and as, Rosenberg and Dahl have shown, it is unrealistic to expect the Court to secure countermajoritarian results. If the majority of Americans are resolved to violate rights, as during war and other national emergencies they sometimes are, the Supreme Court can offer little resistance and is unlikely to try. If it acts in a manner that is supported by a majority or by one of the more accountable branches of government, on the other hand, its leadership need not be countermajoritarian. More troubling are the political results of the Supreme Court's interventions. As we have seen, there was a Republican advantage in presidential contests during the Warren–Burger period of liberal hegemony on the Supreme Court. It is likely that the Supreme Court contributed to this outcome by constantly projecting controversial issues into the political arena. The Court presented Democrat contenders for the presidency with an unfortunate dilemma: they could defend the Court at the risk of losing a large number of supporters, losing the contest for office; they could oppose the Court and risk losing voters in primary contests, losing the contest for nomination. What usually happened is that candidates expressed commitment to liberal ideals in the primaries and then tried to retreat from this position in the presidential election. But the electorate punished them anyway.

Notes

1   *Korematsu*, 323 U.S. 214 (1944).
2   Reported by Laurence H. Tribe, *Abortion: the Clash of Absolutes* (NY: W.W. Norton, 1990), 13.
3   Alexander Bickel, *The Least Dangerous Branch* (New Haven, Conn.: Yale University Press, 2nd ed., 1986), 258.
4   Ibid., 244.
5   Ibid., 204.
6   Robert Dahl, 'Decision-making in a Democracy: the Supreme Court as a National Policy Maker', *Journal of Public Law*, 6 (1957), 279–95; Donald Horowitz, *The Courts and Social Policy* (Washington, DC: The Brookings Institute, 1977); Stuart Scheingold, *The Politics of Rights* (New Haven, Conn.: Yale University Press, 1974); Gerald N. Rosenberg, *The Hollow Hope: Can Courts Bring About Social Change?* (Chicago: University of Chicago Press, 1991).
7   Robert Dahl, loc. cit.

8   Dahl analyses cases in the 167 years between the adoption of the Constitution and his study.

9   When it ruled that employers could only rebut statistical evidence that suggested discrimination by showing that the outcome was necessary as a 'business necessity' (*Griggs* v. *Duke Power Co.*). This was such a tough test that most employers resorted to quotas to avoid litigation. See Hugh Graham, *The Civil Rights Era: Origins and Development of National Policy, 1960–72* (NY: Oxford University Press, 1990), 383–90.

10   Indeed, it did this in 1992 by including a provision that expressly forbids the 'race-norming' of test results.

11   Robert Dahl, *Democracy and Its Critics*, (New Haven, Conn.: Yale University Press, 1989), 189–91.

12   Ibid., 189–91.

13   Ibid., 189–91.

14   Ibid., 192.

15   Horowitz, op. cit., 4. Examples that Horowitz provides are the extension of judicial supervision 'to welfare administration, to education policy and employment policy, to road building and bridge building, to automotive safety standards, and to natural resource management'.

16   Ibid., 44.

17   Ibid., 22.

18   *Griggs*, 401 U.S. 424 (1971); *Lau*, 414 U.S. 563 (1973).

19   Horowitz gives the example of a district court order that had the effect of raising a state's annual expenditure on mental institutions from $14,000,000 to $58,000,000 over 2 years, op. cit., 6.

20   Ibid., 28–9.

21   Ibid., 23.

22   *Mapp* v. *Ohio*, 367 U.S. 643 (1961); *Gault, In re*, 387 U.S. 1 (1967).

23   Horowitz, op. cit., 35.

24   Rosenberg, op. cit., 9–22.

25   Ibid., 33.

26   Ibid., 106.

27   Malcolm M. Feeley, 'Hollow Hopes, Flypaper, and Metaphors', *Law and Social Inquiry*, 17, (1992) 752; Feeley cites Stuart Scheingold, *The Politics of Rights* (New Haven, Conn.: Yale University Press, 1974) as the source of this view.

28   In Rosenberg, 'Reply to Critics', *Law & Social Inquiry* , 17, (4), (1992), 761–78.

29   See Rosenberg's discussion of the problems, *The Hollow Hope*, pp. 107–11.

30   Ibid., 156 and 246; he reconsiders his evidence and reasserts his view after reading Feeley's comments, in 'Reply to Critics'.

31   Rosenburg, *The Hollow Hope*, 341–2.

32   *Escobedo* v. *Illinois*, 378, U.S. 478 (1964); *Miranda* v. *Arizona*, 384 U.S. 436 (1966). These cases give meaning to the Fifth Amendment promise that 'no person shall be compelled in any criminal case to be a witness against himself'. Even vague threats by the police when questioning a suspect or their failure to inform a suspect of his or her right to remain silent and to have an attorney present may disqualify a confession as acceptable evidence.

33   The United Kingdom is not a good democracy to compare to the United States in thinking about the protection of rights. This is because of the problems in Northern Ireland. I doubt whether any democracy would develop a liberal culture on issues relating to national security when the community is under systematic attack by an organization that has been as resourceful as the Irish Republican Army.

34   Lee Epstein and Joseph F. Kobylka, *The Supreme Court and Legal Change: Abortion and the Death Penalty* (Chapel Hill, NC: University of North Carolina Press,

1992), 47 (cited source: Harold W. Stanley and Richard G. Niemi, *Vital Statistics on American Politics* (Washington, DC: CQ Press, 1992).

35   Ibid., 47.

36   Ibid., 39.

37   *Furman* v. *Georgia*; discussed by Epstein and Kobylka, op. cit., 70–111.

38   Ibid., 83–90; The (then) Governor, Ronald Reagan, was responding to a ruling of the Supreme Court of California that anticipated *Furman* by one month (ibid., 77). The California Supreme Court wrote that the death penalty 'degrades and dehumanises all who participate in its processes' (id.). This *ad hominem* comment, though true, could not have helped secure any support for the ruling from those many people in the community who thought Governor Reagan was a thoroughly decent man – not unlike their own fathers who also, no doubt, believed that capital punishment was a reasonable response to vicious killers like Charles Manson.

39   Epstein and Kobylka list 37 states that took action to restore the death penalty shortly after *Furman* v. *Georgia*. (Most of these restored the death penalty by legislation without a referendum.) op. cit., 86–7.

40   Ibid., 84.

41   Ibid., derived from Figure 4-2 on p. 89. (Source: Harold W. Stanley and Richard G. Niemi, *Vital Statistics on American Politics* (Washington, D.C.: CQ Press, 1992).

42   *Gregg* v. *Georgia*, 428 U.S. 153, (1976).

43   McClosky and Brill, *Dimensions of Tolerance: What Americans Believe About Civil Liberties* (NY: Russell Sage Foundation, 1983).

44   Ibid., presenting findings on law and order (pp. 136–70), on sexually related forms of expression (pp. 207–8), on school prayers (p. 133).

45   McClosky and Brill's 1978–79 survey (ibid.) found that a majority of the general public in the United States believe that having an abortion is a matter for individual decision (p.217); only 23% of the mass public and 10 per cent of the legal elite think that 'like murder, it should be prohibited'. Epstein and Kobylka, op. cit. cite national Opinion Research Center General Survey data (1974–80) that show well over 80 per cent of respondents agreeing that abortions should be available in cases when (a) a woman's health is seriously endangered, (b) she is pregnant as a result of rape, or (c) there is a strong chance of serious defect in the baby. The respondents in these surveys are much less supportive when the grounds for abortion are that the income of the family is low, the pregnant woman is unmarried, or the pregnant woman simply declares that she does not want any more children. Less than 50 per cent favour abortion for these reasons (see Figure 6–4 on p. 233).

46   I do not wish to imply that these rulings were wrong as a matter of morality. It must be conceded that the United States would be a far better society if these stigmatized groups were properly protected. Although the courts can offer relief in particular cases when rights are violated they cannot offer more than symbolic victories to these groups as a whole for they have little capacity to implement their rulings. Thus, it is far more important to create an environment where politicians take their responsibility on civil rights seriously. This has not happened in the United States.

47   See Thomas Edsall and Mary Edsall, *Chain Reaction: the Impact of Race, Rights, and Taxes on American Politics* (NY: Norton, 1992), 45–6.

48   Thomas Byrne Edsall, 'Clinton, So Far' in *The New York Review of Books*, XL, (16), (7 Oct. 1993), 6.

49   It seems that President Bush was concerned about his standing with women and the African–American community after the Clarence Thomas–Anita Hill confrontation. Thus, he signed the Civil Rights Bill hoping to secure some goodwill. As it turned out, however, the civil rights community boycotted the signing ceremony. Nevertheless, the signing of the Bill by Bush eliminated quotas as an issue that he

could use against the Democrats in 1992. See John Podhoretz, *A Hell of a Ride: Backstage at the White House Follies 1989–1993* (NY: Simon & Schuster, 1993), 40.

50   Suppose that liberal justices still dominated the Supreme Court and that it had recognized a right of gay men to practise sodomy in private (that the Court in *Bowers* v. *Hardwick* had endorsed the policy advocated by the dissenting justices), or suppose that the Supreme Court had held fast to the notion that no restraints on abortion were permissible and that public funding must be provided. In this circumstance, the dynamic within the electorate would not have favoured Clinton as much as was the case in 1992.

51   Earl Black and Merle Black, *The Vital South: How Presidents are Elected* (Cambridge, Mass.: Harvard University Press, 1992) quoted on p. 6; Black and Black cite Joseph A. Califano, 'Tough Talk for Democrats', *New York Times Magazine*, 8 Jan. 1989, p. 28 as the source of this statement.

52   Black and Black estimate that he won only 45 per cent of the vote cast by white southerners (ibid., 202) but that in many states he was able to win by capturing all of the growing African–American vote and combining this with sizeable white support (as Johnson did in Florida, Virginia, Arkansas, North Carolina and Tennessee (see ibid., 207). In Texas he won a landslide with 63 per cent of the vote by 'polling all of the black vote, most of the Hispanic vote, and a clear majority of the white vote'.

53   *New York Times*, 5 Nov. 1992, p. B9 (Contains election results and analysis).

54   As Black and Black note in their analysis, 'No Democrat in American history has ever been elected president on the strength of northern electoral votes alone. Doing so would forfeit 147 electoral votes, 54 per cent of the total needed for victory' (op. cit., 360).

55   He did not do very well in the South, conceding Florida and Texas to Bush. Most indicators show that like the earlier southerner, Jimmy Carter, Clinton has quickly dissipated most of the goodwill that brought him into the White House. Whether he will be able to reverse this trend is too early to say. He is now seen as a liberal rather than a moderate so it looks as though he will need a lot of luck if he is to win a second term. He will have to persuade everyone that they are far better-off than they had been during the Reagan and Bush periods of office. See Thomas Byrne Edsall, 'Clinton So Far', op. cit., 6–9.

56   Ibid., 227.

57   Ibid., 228–55.

58   He won the contest for the suburban voters largely because Bush had lied about not raising their taxes and because he was prepared to tell the same lie – indeed that he would cut their taxes! – and managed to do so convincingly. He has since been caught out so the election in 1996 will be more difficult for him unless suburban voters feel much better off at that time and are prepared to forgive him. Suburban voters went for Clinton 41 per cent to Bush's 38 per cent in the North; 45 per cent to Bush's 39 per cent in the South; 41 per cent to Bush's 38 per cent in the Midwest and 43 per cent to Bush's 35 per cent in the West. *New York Times*, 5 Nov. 1992, p. 89.

3 Conservative Jurisprudence: The Natural Law Approach

In Chapter 2 I considered some of the reasons for questioning whether it is a good practice for the judiciary to try and assert dynamic leadership by moving ahead of public opinion without significant political support. I also demonstrated why Republican presidential candidates in the United States have benefited from the Supreme Court's activism during the 1960s and 1970s. It is against this background that we need to evaluate the jurisprudence of the Rehnquist conservatives.

As we shall see the Rehnquist conservatives offer competing accounts of how the Supreme Court can minimize the deleterious consequences of the dualist structure of the United States constitutional system. I list these as 'fainthearted originalism' and 'traditional conservatism' and will explore them shortly.

Before I turn to this task, however, it is necessary to consider conservative approaches that do not confront dualism. Not all conservatives would like to see the Supreme Court defer to Congress (one reason may be that it is controlled by Democrats) – and some would like to see it more active in supporting the Reagan agenda. These writers are somewhat frustrated by the deference shown towards Congress by the prevailing Rehnquist majority and would like to see the Court confront what they take to be the unbridled fiscal irresponsibility of New Deal Democrats. They think Congress is constantly tempted to use political power to bring about redistribution of wealth and argue that everyone would be better off if there was less scope for this practice. These conservatives wish to discourage what they refer to as 'rent seeking' and they usually embrace the libertarian economic theories of writers such as Friedrich Hayek and James Buchanan. Many believe that everyone would be better-off if governments were severely constrained in their ability to spend money. Indeed, some extreme libertarians would like to prevent gov-

51

ernments from taxing the rich disproportionately (advocating that revenues be raised only through a flat tax), and they fear the tendency of modern governments to offer services and benefits without first raising the necessary revenues to pay for them (advocating a constitutional amendment that would require balanced budgets). These conservatives view Roosevelt's New Deal as a disastrous turning-point in the history of the United States. They would like the Supreme Court to assist in restraining further government involvement in economic management and in winding back the welfare state. This is why they advocate that the Fifth Amendment's Eminent Domain Clause (which provides 'nor shall private property be taken for public use, without just compensation') be read in the light of common law assumptions about property, assumptions that informed the work of its framers. They would join the three rights of possession, use and disposition, as included under the concept of property reflected in the use of the term in the United States Constitution, making it very difficult for governments to allow rent seekers advantages.[1] According to this view, the United States Constitution presupposes a belief that the purpose of government is primarily to protect rights to liberty and property that existed prior to the formation of the state. The government is not free to take any citizen's property without just compensation.

I describe these approaches as 'natural-law foundationalism' and will devote the first part of this chapter to exploring the work of writers like Walter Berns, Richard Epstein and Stephen Macedo that exemplifies it.

Natural-law Foundationalism

Natural-law foundationalists share many assumptions about the propriety of countermajoritarian judicial review with their liberal opponents. They embrace dualism for they expect the Supreme Court to act to restrain officials even when they are acting with a mandate from the people. Thus, their position is vulnerable to many of the criticisms presented in Chapter 2. Indeed conservative dualists are even more unrealistic than liberals because the positions they ask the Supreme Court to adopt – returning to the kind of review the Court exercised before it was confronted by Roosevelt – enjoys so little support among the public that they are not taken very seriously. In contrast, there are significant interest groups who support the liberal civil rights agenda. This is one reason why all of the conservatives now on the Court reject natural-law foundationalism, agreeing that countermajoritarian judicial initiatives to secure the property right (listed in the Constitution in the Fifth and Fourteenth Amendments) would usually transcend their legitimate authority. They understand that an activist Supreme Court pursuing the goals of the political right would be even more deeply resented in the United States than the Warren–Burger Court pursuing an activism of the left has been.

Natural-law foundationalism also differs from liberal dualist theory in that the principle of justice it embraces, and claims to be embraced in the United States Constitution, is not egalitarian. Thus, natural-law foundationalists claim that liberal justices illegitimately impose a conception of justice that has no secure base in the Constitution's text or in American history. But they do not think that a constitutional theory can work without some commitment to justice. According to natural-law foundationalists, then, liberals pay too little attention to the Constitution as the source of law. They claim that libertarian principles of justice are implied in the Constitution's structural arrangements and in its actual text.

To understand their position we must begin by considering some of the problems that are associated with the view that we take the framers intentions seriously as a foundation in constitutional law, in thinking about how to read the United States Constitution. This is the position that is sometimes referred to as 'originalism' in the United States.

Difficulties with Originalism

At the theoretical level, as we have seen, hostility to the Warren Court's liberalism often manifests itself as a concern about judicial activism. Many Republicans argue that the Court should exercise its power sparingly and they accuse liberal justices of countermajoritarian arrogance. According to President Reagan's Attorney General Edwin Meese, for example, the activism of the Warren–Burger Court established a situation in which federal courts usurped powers that rightfully belong to citizens. In his view, the Court's liberals, by acting as though they are mandated to impose policies from the bench, have also claimed prerogatives specifically allocated to the Congress or President. Thus, he argues, if the Court is allowed 'to govern simply by what it views at the time as fair and decent', the democratic design of the United States system of government will be undermined; thus, he holds, the Supreme Court should restrict itself to enforcing the law by diligently upholding the intentions of the Constitution's framers.[2]

Meese's hostility to judicial activism is taken up in the rhetoric of Reagan, Bush and other prominent Republican Party leaders who offer a simple theory of constitutional interpretation. They claim Supreme Court justices should refuse to endorse modern conceptions of the meaning of the general phrases identifying rights in the

Constitution. (For example, because the Eighth Amendment's prohibition of 'cruel and unusual punishment' was originally understood as allowing for the death penalty, they claim it should not now be read as precluding this practice.) In terms of their view, then, it is beside the point whether nearly all contemporary justices think capital punishment is cruel, for judges (even on the highest tribunal) have no mandate to legislate this conception so long as this view was not shared by the framers. In their view, justices who impose modern conceptions of 'freedom of speech', 'cruel and unusual punishment', 'the equal protection of the laws' bring the Constitution into disrepute.

There are serious problems with this version of originalism that need to be considered.[3] These are the common criticisms:

1   The text of the Constitution is not conclusive in establishing the intentions of the framers. Indeed, their intentions are often impossible or very difficult to establish even when historical analysis of English precedents, together with materials such as the records of the 1787 Convention and the ratification debates, have been considered. As a result, historical analysis is often inconclusive, allowing for a great deal of controversy and for the manipulation of historical evidence so that it supports whatever result is favoured.

2   The fact that the Constitution's promises are vague does not help. For example, it is not easy to see how general phrases like 'the equal protection of the laws', 'Commander in Chief of the Army and Navy', ' [the right] to declare war', 'abridging the freedom of speech, or of the press' and 'the right of the people to keep and bear Arms' are to be interpreted. Nor is there any assurance that the framers did not hold conflicting understandings of the meaning of these phrases.

3   Those who framed the constitutional arrangements may have had poor judgment about the feasibility of what they were accomplishing. For example, they thought a subordinate executive desirable without realizing the functional need for coherent leadership, dispatch and secrecy in foreign policy; they allocated significant powers to the states without anticipating the need for unified laws that has manifested itself in the modern period; they endorsed Lockean rights without anticipating the complexity the concept of property must have in modern economies.

4   Ratification of the Constitution is surely important, yet the opinions of those who approved the arrangements are difficult if not impossible to determine.

5   Circumstances have changed in ways that could not have been foreseen by the framers that makes interpreting the Constitu-

tion's text very contentious. For example, it clearly, makes good sense to hold that the 'Commander in Chief' role, assigned to the President, now includes command over the air force, but it is much more difficult to say whether the First Amendment's protection of speech applies to the broadcast media and to cable and whether it embraces commercial speech. Similarly, the Constitution's Fourth Amendment prohibition against government intrusion is easy to understand when searches involved physical entry into private premises, but the framers cannot be said to have expressed any views about wire-tapping, electronic eaves-dropping or surreptitious mail reading, nor can we discern their views about the propriety of searching motor vehicles. Even when the framers intentions are clear, they may no longer be appropriate, for example, 'advice and consent of the Senate' meant meeting with the 26 members but such consultation is difficult now that the members number 100. Similarly, the framers clearly wished to exclude obscene speech from the protection offered by the First Amendment but should 'obscenity' mean the same thing to us today as it did in the eighteenth century or should the Court change the standard to take account of modern sensibilities? Even the size of the United States today calls the original understanding into question; what may have been appropriate in 1787 may not also be so when the population is over 248 million and the number of states has increased to 50. And why should 'commerce' be held to mean the same today as it did when the means of transport was the ox cart? Questions of this kind inevitably make constitutional analysis enormously controversial.

6   Over the 200 years since the ratification many controversial interpretations and conventions have changed the political system in fundamental ways. For one thing, the system is much more democratic and this has affected the relationship between the competing institutional sources of power. Most significantly, the Presidency now enjoys unique democratic authority as the only office (apart from that of the Vice-President) requiring a nation-wide election. These changes did not result from a better-informed understanding of the framers intentions but because members of the Supreme Court (and others who had political influence) realized that departures from that understanding were necessary or desirable.

If we are to return to 'original understanding' as a guide, then, we must be told how this historical evolution is to be evaluated. Should the United States system revert into the kind of federal division agreed to in the eighteenth century, when the loyalty of citizens to their state governments was at least as strong as their commitment to the union, when democratic sentiments were not so widespread and when commerce was primitive? Alternatively, why must the contemporary Supreme Court refrain from imposing modern conceptions of what is a 'cruel and unusual punishment', 'freedom of speech' or 'the equal protection of the laws' if there is no need for it to defer to eighteenth century conceptions of federalism or the separation of powers?

Finally,

7   When the intentions of the framers are closely analysed, we find that there is no expectation on their part that subsequent generations would be bound by their intentions. They seem to have assumed either that the courts should be bound by the common understanding of plain words or that courts should interpret the provisions of the document according to the traditions of English common law. Paradoxically, then, a jurisprudence of 'original intentions' cannot claim that the framers forbade us to depart from what they intended.[4]

Walter Berns and Stephen Macedo: Natural-law Foundationalism

One reason someone may wish to embrace originalism may be to honour 'what was agreed to' in the constitutional contract. This is why the framers' intention could be seen to be significant in establishing the requirements of the law – the intentions are the law because the Constitution is regarded as a binding contract that defines all rights and obligations. In terms of this conception, the justices have a responsibility to honour what the framers intended because this is what the people ratified.

Unfortunately it's not easy to honour the framers' intentions because the phrases they included in the Constitution (agreed to at various times, for example, 1787, 1791 and 1868) must be understood as reflecting the liberal political philosophy that was shared by the negotiators at the time. This common philosophy is said to fill in the gaps of the Constitution's text and to provide guidance when its words are ambiguous or have to be adapted to modern circumstances. It is to be discovered through historical research and certain documents and statements have special authority, for example, the Constitution's Preamble, the Declaration of Independence, and the Federalist Papers. In terms of this account, constitutional lawyers and judges should aspire to think like the framers and their work should be informed by what we know of the unpublished debates at the Constitutional Convention held in Philadelphia. In terms of this view, we also understand the framers intentions by ourselves embracing and learning to appreciate the influence of significant authors, such as John Locke and Thomas Paine, and the work of jurists such as William Blackstone. It is the liberal principles that we can distil from a reading of these works that should help us to appreciate what the Constitution means. This liberal philosophy should inform the way we apply the Constitution to the problems of our own day.

This is not to say that anyone believes that natural law doctrines can simply be read into the Constitution so that the contemporary Court may implement a Lockean agenda. But it is argued that the Bill of Rights and the Privileges or Immunities Clause of the Fourteenth Amendment cannot be fully comprehended without understanding that they were motivated, in part at least, by the natural-law doctrines that many of the framers shared. According to natural-law foundationalists, this background is essential in understanding what it is that the framers proposed and what was entrenched in the law as protected liberties. Thus, they argue that there is absolutely no warrant for supposing that the framers authorized modern justices to roam broadly imposing any political philosophy they approve, as Ronald Dworkin and other egalitarian liberal scholars seem to suppose;[5] rather, the listed liberties and rights must be taken to embody a specific commitment to a distinctive natural-law conception (which, for example, requires us to read the Eminent Domain Clause of the Fifth Amendment as placing severe limits on governmental agencies who wish to regulate business).

Stephen Macedo develops this kind of approach to defend Justice William Brennan's view that the Constitution is a living document in that its meaning evolves because of 'the adaptability of its great principles to cope with current problems and current needs'.[6] Unlike Brennan, however, Macedo thinks that the liberal principles endorsed by the framers have an enduring significance so that the twentieth century is linked to the eighteenth century by the liberalism that must inform any coherent understanding of the Constitution's significance. Macedo is not troubled by this because he thinks that classical liberal ideas remain defensible today. In his view, contemporary Americans are well-served by the foundations that the framers secured and would be wise to continue to allow liberal ideals to sustain their common life, adapting the Constitution to serve their own concerns.

He illustrates this approach in considering Justice Douglas's reasoning in his opinion for the Court in the important privacy case *Griswold* v. *Connecticut*.[7] According to Macedo, Douglas should be praised for seeing that there are implicit penumbral rights that can be deduced because of the liberal philosophical assumptions that make most sense of the liberties listed in the Bill of Rights. But he criticizes Douglas for not noticing strong similarities between his approach and the jurisprudence that informed the work of the Court in *Lochner* v. *New York* when economic liberties were recognized as constitutionally protected.[8] In his view, Douglas is not free to choose only those elements from the eighteenth-century legacy that he finds congenial for he must work from the Constitution's text. If he commits himself to upholding liberty – and he is right to have done this in *Griswold*, according to Macedo – he cannot jettison the economic rights that the framers, following John Locke and William Blackstone, took to be fundamental. Thus, he concludes:

> Why not read economic liberty, after all, as a penumbra or emanation of various constitutional specifics? The contracts and taking clauses, and the protection of property in the due process clauses of the Fifth and Fourteenth amendments, would all appear capable of casting shadows broad enough to limit government economic policy. From these and other specific protections one might discern a general constitutional concern with economic liberty which could then be taken to inform the due process clause, and we wind up with a 'Griswoldian' defence of *Lochner*. Moreover the protection of economic liberty was certainly on the minds of the framers and it has a prominent place in our history. So why is privacy fundamental whereas economic liberty is not?[9]

This is unabashed dualism and the question put is addressed to liberals like Ronald Dworkin who share Macedo's view that rights are implied and can be deduced using the correct liberal philosophy. The difference between Dworkin and Macedo is that the former thinks that we can choose what we take to be the most adequate liberalism to inform our deliberations; whereas the latter thinks we are bound to honour the Lockean commitments the framers used as their point of reference.

Although Walter Berns shares Macedo's view that we cannot understand the United States Constitution without appreciating the liberal philosophy that influenced its framers, he recommends a very different approach. He thinks that most attacks against originalism are ill-considered; and he challenges the related claim that the meaning of the Constitution necessarily evolves.[10] According to Berns, the work of the founding generation was possible because they all shared the view – as self-evident truth – that certain rights were natural. Thus, the purpose that informs their work is not opaque. He also claims that once we realize that the Constitution is informed by a shared natural-law philosophy, we can identify the meaning of its various phrases. In his view Americans would be better-off if they read the Constitution more carefully and if everyone considered his or herself bound by its terms. He claims, then, that originalism can be defended and urges Americans to be less tolerant of judges who seek to rewrite the text. In his view they should be required to uphold the Constitution as it was originally written.

The most influential statement of this kind of approach has been provided by Richard Epstein in his provocative book *Takings: Private Property and the Power of Eminent Domain*. Like Berns, Epstein uses history and natural law theory to make sense of the Constitution's text. Let me consider his approach briefly.

Epstein's Approach: Natural-law Formalism

Like Berns, Epstein is worried about the practice of judicial review in the United States. As he points out, the Constitution sets out an elaborate political system that, in large measure, relies on a separation of powers, empowering the Supreme Court to strike down legislation that is incompatible with its terms. Although he approves of this system, Epstein worries about the very broad discretion that justices like William Brennan and William Douglas seem to claim. As he explains, 'the mission of constitutional government must soon founder if judges can decide cases as freely with the Constitution in place as without it'.[11] But he admits that the ambiguities in the Constitution's text make it difficult to see how wilful justices are to be restrained.

Epstein illustrates his argument by considering the language of the Eminent Domain Clause ('nor shall private property be taken for public use, without just compensation'). As he shows, even the relatively ordinary language of this clause uses terms that are not defined within the Constitution itself. What is to count as 'just' compensation? What government actions must be regarded as a taking of a person's property? The central difficulty with American constitutionalism, according to Epstein, is that the power of language to bind requires a clarity and precision that the actual Constitution fails to exemplify.

Epstein's concern about ambiguity in constitutional law is shared by legal positivists. But he is unpersuaded by the Benthamite claim that natural law theories need to be jettisoned as unacceptably vague. He does not agree that judges should decline the invitation to exercise review when constitutional provisions appear to afford them an unbridled discretion. According to Epstein, this kind of self-denial by Supreme Court justices would undermine the American ideal of a constitutional democracy that is informed by the framers Lockean ambition of securing the prior rights of individuals. The problem they faced, as he sees it, was to specify the rights and liberties they meant to protect from possible federal government violation with enough specificity to bind judges.[12]

Epstein thinks that the framers accomplished this goal in a satisfactory manner when they made use of terms from the common law, such as 'life', 'liberty' or 'property', which had a relatively clear meaning in the eighteenth century; but he argues that their work has been undermined because a subsequent generation has considered itself free to substitute different meanings, especially when reading the Bill of Rights. This departure from constitutionalism represents a fatal error, according to Epstein. Thus, like Berns, he challenges the view that the Constitution is an invitation to perpetual revision – a living Constitution – arguing that it is difficult to understand why the framers bothered to set out terms for government in the first place if subsequent generations did not have to accept them as binding. In his judgment, any constitution whose key terms can be said to mean whatever future judges would like them to mean would allow a travesty of the rule of law.[13] This is why he recommends an approach to the United States Constitution, in reading the Eminent Domain Clause of the Fifth Amendment and as a general guide to interpretation, that seeks to fix meanings (of, for example, 'private property', 'taken', 'just compensation' in the Eminent Domain Clause) by determining how terms are used 'in the normal social and cultural discourse' characteristic of the late eighteenth century. In recommending this use of historical sources, however, Epstein is careful to point out that he does not require the justices to take into account the 'actual historical intention of any of the parties who drafted or signed' the Constitution.[14] The language used in a constitution should not be bound by the specific motives that inspired its inclusion in various clauses, but necessarily has a general application whether or not this was foreseen at the time. Thus, Epstein tells us that historical sources should be used with care in constitutional law. They 'are exceedingly helpful in allowing us to understand the standard meanings of ordinary language as embodied in constitutional text', but they should not be used to limit the reach of important clauses by 'isolating the collective purposes and hidden agendas that secured its passage'.[15]

Besides history, the justices may rely on reasoning from analogy, 'from core cases to their close substitutes'. Thus, Epstein allows that it would be foolish not to allow 'that the taking of property necessarily includes the destruction of property as well'.[16] He also allows that drastic circumstances may require us to acknowledge exceptions when governments violate a right with good reason (for example, freedom of speech must be suspended if the life of a government agent is likely to be placed in jeopardy by the dissemination of certain facts); but he warns that the exceptions allowed for must be severely limited for otherwise the right in question will become redundant.[17]

This approach is a qualified form of originalism because we are not entitled to substitute a twentieth-century conception of, say, 'property' for the meaning of the term that prevailed among the framers. Epstein requires a strict construction of the meaning at the point of ratification. He is also concerned to disallow changes that have been accepted through past judicial initiatives (in particular, the reading of the Eminent Domain Clause accepted by New Deal justices). Indeed, he recommends that we review this modern development – the legitimation of the regulative, welfare state, and the case law history that has followed over the past 60 years – as an error that must necessarily be remedied. The New Deal has no constitutional standing, according to Epstein, because the notion of a 'living constitution' whose meaning is adapted by judges to varied historical circumstances offers no clear guidance that can confine judicial policymaking. Thus, he advises Supreme Court justices to work as though the 'eighteenth-century Constitution' was adopted yesterday. In his view, the justices have a responsibility to honour the understandings of the framers, disregarding the fact that the Supreme Court has itself departed from them.

Epstein adds some qualification. For example, because some offending taxes and regulations have been operating for decades and people have come to rely on the continuation of this order, he concedes that modern justices should work cautiously in securing remedies for some constitutional violations.[18] But he insists that the Court should not give away the possibility of securing remedial solutions, even though this task may seem somewhat drastic and, at times, unfair. Where 'the reliance interest is powerful and pervasive', however, the justices should be sensitive 'in selecting and sequencing remedies'.[19]

Epstein's work has been subjected to sustained criticism and he is vulnerable to many of the problems associated with originalism that I listed in the preceding section.[20] My major difficulty with his proposals relates to the abstract nature of his project. Although he makes use of history, he does so in a very unlawyerly manner.[21] For most practical purposes, the eighteenth-century Constitution that Epstein is using as his guide is not relevant to the concerns of practitioners involved in twentieth-century constitutional analysis – even conceding that Epstein has correctly described the ordinary meaning of eighteenth-century terms. The problem of relevance goes to the nature of 'law' for Epstein is recommending what H.L.A. Hart calls a 'rule of recognition', yet this is something that lawyers should discover by looking at the practices of their community.[22] They have no authority to make-up any rule they like. Epstein's book, like Berns's *Taking the Constitution Seriously*, provides arguments for suggesting rules that he thinks would serve better than the rules that are actually followed by advocates and judges today. This is very different from suggesting minor revisions in current practice that will facilitate changes that most people approve. We must ask, then, how Epstein's use of history is different from simply making up the rules. It is true that

Epstein sees the need for an objective source for law, but he thinks that he is free to recommend his own favoured source. He likes the eighteenth-century Constitution and dislikes the processes by means of which the twentieth-century Constitution has been amended through judicial interpretation. But who appointed Epstein to invent what is to count as constitutional law in the United States? Why should he be free to ignore *stare decisis* as an important source of constitutional change? The problem we face here is that 'law' is a result of political forces even when there is a written document to refer to as 'the Constitution'; so it matters that the American people, under the leadership of a President who had mobilized the support of Congress and intimidated the Supreme Court, decided that the federal government had to be allowed to raise revenue and to regulate the national economy in ways that Epstein disapproves of as unjust. It is true, as Epstein points out, that this development required a very strained reading of both the Commerce Clause and the Eminent Domain Clause, but there were pressing reasons for this transformation; and the change has been sustained for 60 years.

This history also complicates Epstein's utilitarian analysis. He thinks that people in the United States would be better-off if everyone accepted that the Eminent Domain Clause should be read in the way he recommends, that is, as it was understood in the eighteenth century. This may be true – although most people doubt it. But Epstein's analysis is complicated by the fact that he admits that his recommendations represent a radical departure from conventional wisdom about what counts as 'law' among lawyers. Indeed, the judicial role it would entail is also unacceptable to most people in the United States who want modern governments to provide economic management, social insurance and to regulate commerce to secure public goods. This means that a Supreme Court that decided to act on his advice would be throwing the nation into the kind of turmoil they faced when President Roosevelt threatened to pack the Court. When we take into account the countermajoritarian nature of this recommendation and the departure from conventionally recognized legal practice it entails, we see that Epstein's utilitarian calculations are misleading – most Americans would not be better off if their nation was launched into a constitutional crisis. The problem manifest here is that abstract models are often a poor guide in social science. What Epstein fails to see is that they offer much less help to constitutional lawyers.

A final word about Epstein's natural-law foundationalism is worth adding. Let us suppose that we agree that the framers were all committed to a political philosophy that assumed that the purpose of the state is to protect a natural right that individuals enjoy to own property; assume that they embraced the principle of justice defended by Robert Nozick:

> From each according to what he chooses to do, to each according to
> what he makes for himself (perhaps with the contracted aid of others)
> and what others choose to do for him and choose to give him of what
> they've been given previously (under this maxim) and haven't yet
> expended or transferred.[23]

What follows from this? Are we not free to declare that the framers'
conception of justice is indefensible? What if we prefer the approach
defended by the philosopher John Rawls or are convinced that utilitarian theorists have more to offer. If the framers' assumptions are no
longer convincing to us, why should we feel bound by the Bill of
Rights? A reasonable response when we find that a phrase in the
Constitution that relies on outdated or highly contentious assumptions is simply to hold that it no longer applies. Another is to substitute our own better understanding.

Some of the liberal writers whose work I review in later chapters
claim that judges are free to substitute their own conception of the
various open-ended concepts listed or assumed in the Bill of Rights.
For example, Ronald Dworkin argues that a Rawlsian approach should
be adopted so that we read the Bill of Rights as though it was intended to ensure that the interests of every citizen are treated by
governments with equal concern and respect. This interpretation allows Dworkin to make more sense of recent history than Epstein
who prefers Nozick's principle of justice. But this merely reflects the
fact that the Warren Court was partly a product of Roosevelt's New
Deal. It cannot be argued that a Dworkinian Constitution bears even
a family resemblance to the Constitution actually endorsed by the
framers in 1791 or that there is any consensus in America that the
nation's major policy choices should be determined by nine guardians. We may well ask of those who approve this kind of judicial
leadership: If the New Dealers are allowed to appoint justices to
facilitate a dramatic change why are the Reagan forces debarred
from doing the same? Dworkin's point of departure in Rawls's philosophy although far more congenial to those of us who support
social democratic ideals is no less arbitrary than Epstein's view that
we should read the Bill of Rights as though it was intended to ensure
that property is not taken without just compensation.

Those who are persuaded that the United States would be a better
society if governments were required to justify the taking of any
property in the manner Epstein recommends, have argued that the
most satisfactory way of achieving this outcome is by using the
authority of the Constitution to control the federal government's
power to raise taxes and to regulate economic life. They need a
countermajoritarian constitutional court because they suspect that
governments that are accountable to a majority of the people will

often tempt the electorate by offering to redistribute resources in the name of social justice. Some libertarians advocate following the procedures listed under Article V for formally amending the Constitution. But why not amend it informally through judicial interpretation in the manner recommended by Epstein? Once the propriety of judicial amendment is conceded, it is not at all clear that Dworkin and other liberals can provide good *legal* reasons why their particular conception of the Bill of Rights should be privileged. Yet they do want to disqualify those on the right of the political spectrum from doing what they think those on the left are entitled to do when reading the Constitution – substituting their own favoured conception of various rights.

I consider various responses to this challenge in subsequent chapters. Here I merely note that most conservatives reject dualist theories of this kind. Thus, they hold that neither the right nor the left are entitled to amend the Constitution by judicial fiat. These conservative theorists are reluctant to conclude from the fact that the framers' political theory is inadequate that they are now free to impose their own favoured views. Most argue that when the assumptions that make sense of the framers' work are no longer compelling or when history shows that the Supreme Court has ignored the framers' intentions for a long period of time, judges should be very reluctant to embrace broad interpretations of the Bill of Rights, substituting their own preferences. That there is good sense in this caution is illustrated by problems constitutional scholars have with the Second Amendment that establishes a right to bear arms. Presumably no American court will want to hold that Congress may not legislate to deal with the serious problem that the proliferation of firearms now poses. A good reading of the words of the Second Amendment right of the people to keep and bear arms is that it is otiose because the listed right assumes circumstances that do not apply in the twentieth century, namely that 'a well regulated Militia is necessary to the security of a free state'.[24] We cannot conclude from this that judges are now free to start imposing their own favoured policies about how Americans may go about defending themselves.

Natural-law originalism is not widely shared in the United States for not many people are prepared to accept the drastic implication that would follow if it were adopted by Supreme Court justices as their guide. As Senator Biden rather dramatically points out, its adoption could lead to the invalidation of 'virtually every single modern legislative scheme to regulate the economy, the environment and the workplace'.[25]

Some libertarians, such as Epstein and Macedo, approve this result, believing that Americans would all be better-off when the government is limited severely. But most people are less inclined to pursue abstract philosophies without concern for the immediate consequences and they prefer courts and politicians to act more pragmatically. Nevertheless, if as a matter of legal doctrine we embrace originalism, saying that the intentions of the framers are to be taken as determining the significance of the rights that are listed as protected in the Constitution, the natural-law interpretation is plausible.[26] Indeed, a natural-rights reading of the Constitution seems to have been embraced at times by Justice Clarence Thomas in some of his papers, in various speeches he has delivered and in remarks he has made answering questions at the time of his nomination.[27] But he has shown that he is unwilling to embrace natural-law foundationalism as a member of the Supreme Court. As his answers to Senator Biden's probing questioning during the nomination hearings make clear, he understands very well how many far-reaching changes to existing practices would have to be implemented if this interpretation of the Constitution were to be embraced by a majority on the Court.[28] His gruelling examination must have persuaded him that contemporary Americans simply do not share the beliefs embraced by the framers. This is probably why he has sought ways of reaching decisions that are easier to defend politically. A justice of the Supreme Court must not only find good legal arguments but he or she must also understand what is feasible.

In any event, we find that Thomas prefers to join Justice Scalia in many cases. As the information presented in the annual summaries provided by the *Harvard Law Review* shows, he has been far more likely than any of the other conservatives to reach agreement with Scalia. The figure below summarizes as a percentage the information provided.[29]

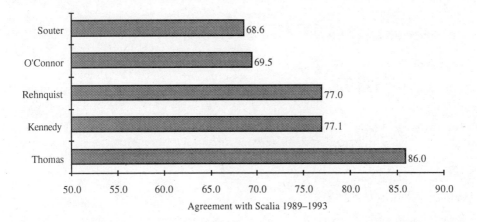

Agreement with Scalia 1989–1993

We see from this evidence that Thomas is now inclined towards legal positivism and has accepted that it is not appropriate for him to impose his personal values as a deeply committed Christian. Strong additional evidence for this is provided by the fact that Thomas joins the two opinions by legal positivists (written by Rehnquist and Scalia respectively) in the important abortion case *Planned Parenthood of South East Pennsylvania* v. *Casey* that I discuss in Chapter 6. Had he wished to make a religious statement about the right to life, this would have been the place to contribute. Thus, it is safe to conclude that he has elected to abandon the natural-law approach.

Notes

1   Richard Epstein, 'Reply to Critics', *University of Miami Law Review*, vol. 41, no. 1 (1986), 258.

2   Edwin Meese, III, Address to the American Bar Association, 9 July 1985, published in *History Today* (15 Nov. 1985).

3   See, Stephen Macedo, *The New Right and the Constitution* (Washington, DC: Cato, 1987, 2nd ed.), 5–31.

4   Ibid., 14ff.

5   Ronald Dworkin, *Taking Rights Seriously* (Cambridge, Mass.: Harvard University Press), 136 ff.; Laurence Tribe, *Constitutional Choices* (Cambridge, Mass.: Harvard University Press, 1985), ch. 1, and *Abortion: the Clash of Absolutes* (NY: N.W. Norton), 88–99.

6   William J. Brennan, Jr., 'The Constitution of the United States: Contemporary Ratification' (Address at Georgetown University, 12 Oct. 1986, p. 7, quoted and cited by Walter Berns, *Taking the Constitution Seriously*, NY: Simon & Schuster, 1987), 235).

7   381 U.S. 479 (1965).

8   198 U.S. 45 (1905).

9   Stephen Macedo, 'The Right to Privacy: a Constitutional and Moral Defence', *Political Theory Newsletter* (Canberra, ACT: Australia: RSSS, Australian National University, CPN Publications), vol. 2, no. 2 (1990), 192–3.

10   Berns, op. cit., 233–41.

11   Richard Epstein, *Takings: Private Property and the Power of Eminent Domain* (Cambridge, Mass.: Harvard University Press, 1985), 20.

12   Epstein's reliance on natural rights is, at one level, purely semantic. He explains that he does not mean to question the positivist view that unjust laws are 'law' but merely to insist that what makes a law 'just' or 'unjust' cannot depend on the question of its legality. This is an uncontroversial thesis for a self-proclaimed natural rights supporter to embrace. Moreover, Epstein's affinity for legal positivism is strengthened further when he asserts that the proper way to evaluate legal rules is through an assessment of their social consequences. As he explains, there are very good utilitarian reasons for recognizing that individuals enjoy 'rights to acquire and own property, and to have the exclusive liberty to control one's person and labour' – rights that are usually identified as natural rights. See Epstein, 'Reply to Critics', op. cit., 257.

13   Epstein, *Takings*, 24.

14   Ibid., 27–9.

15   Ibid., 29.

16 Epstein, 'Reply to Critics', 266; *Takings*, 37–9.
17 'Reply to Critics', 267.
18 *Takings*, 324.
19 Ibid., 326.
20 See the collection of papers from the 'Symposium on Richard Epstein's *Takings: Private Property and the Power of Eminent Domain*' in *University of Miami Law Review*, vol. 41, no. 1 (Nov. 1986).
21 This point is forcefully made in a slightly different context by Bruce Ackerman, in his contribution to the Symposium on Epstein's work; *ibid.*, 56–7.
22 H.L.A. Hart, *The Concept of Law* (Oxford: Oxford University Press, 1961), 92–107.
23 Robert Nozick, *Anarchy, State, and Utopia* (Oxford: Blackwell, 1974), 160.
24 The phrase in quotation marks is taken from the Second Amendment, United States Constitution.
25 *Report of the Senate Judiciary Committee on the Nomination of Clarence Thomas to be an Associate Justice of the U.S. Supreme Court*, 1 Oct. 1991 (Congressional Session 102-1, CIS No. 91-S524-2) at p. 52.
26 The approach is defended by Walter Berns, op. cit., Richard Epstein, *Takings*, and by Stephen Macedo, *The New Right and the Constitution*.
27 Clarence Thomas, 'The Higher Law Background of the Privileges and Immunities Clause of the Fourteenth Amendment', *Harvard Journal of Law and Public Policy*, vol. 12 (1989); and 'Notes on Original Intent', submitted to the Judiciary Committee at the time of the Hearings on his Nomination. See the response of Senator Biden, pp. 11–19 in *Report of the Senate Judiciary Committee on the Nomination of Clarence Thomas to be an Associate Justice of the U.S. Supreme Court*, 1 Oct. 1991 (Congressional Session 102-1, CIS No. 91-S524-2).
28 The most critical problem is that a natural-law reading of the Constitution would seem to support the controversial ruling in *Lochner* v. *New York*, 198 U.S. 45 (1905).
29 The information summarized is provided at the end of each of the Supreme Court's terms in *Harvard Law Review*; see vols. 103, 104, 105, 106, 107 (1989–93).

4 Conservative Jurisprudence and the Rehnquist Justices: The Harlan Legacy v. Fainthearted Originalism

Let us now begin a consideration of conservative approaches that do not assume that the twentieth century is somehow bound by the precise terms of agreements entered into in the eighteenth and nineteenth centuries.

One group of conservatives, including Justices Souter, O'Connor and, perhaps, Kennedy explicitly draw on the legacy of the most influential dissenting justice during the Warren years, John Marshall Harlan. The jurisprudence of Harlan has been significant (for example, he also influenced Justice Lewis Powell) and his position has been ably defended and systematically elaborated by his one-time clerk Charles Fried. Indeed, Fried's own influence on the Court has also been substantial for he served as Solicitor General for President Reagan. As the person responsible for marshalling the arguments to support Reagan's policies, Fried constructed a strong case for rejecting the collectivist egalitarianism that now informs so much of the 'civil rights' agenda in the United States and is a champion of limited government. Fried offers a powerful statement of a conservative legal philosophy and is very good at presenting the intellectual aspects of what we now refer to as the 'Reagan Revolution'. His work is also interesting because of the clarity with which he articulates competing conservative theoretical positions.

Harlan's approach is important because he respects history without being bound by the past in the way that 'natural-law' originalists are. Thus, he does not think that judges are free to make the law what they would like it to be. Nor does he think that modern judges interpreting a document framed in the eighteenth century are bound by the common law. In his view, a constitution must necessarily evolve and judges who are authorized to interpret constitutional clauses have an obligation to look back over legal materials to determine what the law is. They may not ignore the work of earlier courts and must attempt to discover an evolutionary thread; yet they should not substitute philosophy for law simply to achieve coherence. Cases matter and a judge must focus on the particular circumstances of different cases in seeking grounds for developing law through the discovery of analogies. A backward-looking approach that is focused in this way will ensure that legal change is slow – unless legislators choose to act. Judges will be bound by the particular circumstances of the case before them, justifying their rulings by securing links between past cases and the present. According to Harlan, the common law may have been largely abandoned but the methods of common–law judges cannot be.

Harlan never articulated his approach in a systematic way. Thus, I have chosen to focus on Charles Fried's statement of the orientation. In later chapters I will also explore his views on abortion and affirmative action. I claim that Fried's view of the proper role of the judiciary (a) is more defensible than approaches, like the various forms of originalism, that bind judges to the past; (b) allows judges a wide discretion to impose their philosophical preferences; and I argue (c) that it has some advantages over alternative conservative approaches and (d) is often able to secure the support of a majority of the justices now on the Supreme Court because most are happy with the direction it recommends.[1]

Another approach favoured by conservatives embraces legal positivism. This is the other position that I will explore in this chapter.

Positivists hold that it is important to insist on preserving a distinction between legal, philosophical and moral reasoning. Thus, judges should not treat the imprecise phrases in the Bill of Rights as an open-ended invitation to impose some favoured philosophy – even the philosophical ideals and understandings of the framers – and must cite non-subjective sources in establishing the law's requirements.[2] This approach embraces a qualified originalism and is favoured by Chief Justice Rehnquist (when he chooses to embrace a judicial theory) and by Justice Antonin Scalia. It is a form of originalism because it requires us to understand the various controversial terms and phrases of the Constitution in the light of the meanings prevalent towards the end of the eighteenth century. In terms of this orientation, we should not be concerned with the intentions of the framers but should try to determine how controversial phrases were understood at the time of the drafting of the Constitution.

As we have seen, crude originalism is very difficult to defend. This is because it embraces a static conception of the Constitution as forged in the eighteenth century yet the meaning of the text, for the Court, has inevitably evolved over the years with changing circumstances. The Court no longer operates in a society in which the loyalty to state governments is deeper than the loyalty to the union, in which commerce is primitive and the Presidency mostly a ceremonial office. Today, the United States is the leading power of the world and the President is a national and world leader. Thus, the Supreme Court would be foolish to embrace a doctrine that required it to impose only those conceptions of controversial constitutional phrases that were embraced by the framers. But the Court would be equally foolish to assume that it is free to impose any conception of 'freedom of speech', 'the equal protection of the laws', 'liberty', 'property' and other vague but important terms that are found in the Constitution.

I show how Rehnquist, Scalia and Thomas seek to face these problems. I claim that Scalia's articulation of legal positivism, like Charles Fried's development of Harlan's position, offers a viable way forward in the United States.

Fried's Recommendations

Fried defends a complex conception of the rule of law, relying on the tradition of professionalism within the judiciary. In terms of this account, we come to know the law through a process of reasoned debate in which practitioners are disciplined by a respect for precedent and are trained to recognize analogies between the circumstances of one case and another.[3] The judicial task is not always easy, however, for it requires a close examination of a number of competing sources (for example, constitutional phrases, statutes, principles, customs and accepted practices). Judicial reasoning, in terms of this conception, must reflect a respect for the past and even Supreme Court justices should accept the past decisions of the Court as authoritative. This recognition establishes a presumption that past rulings will be honoured; it does not require that *stare decisis* should always prevail. In some cases, even when a justice believes that a past opinion was badly argued, she may accept it as a binding precedent so long as it is not in clear conflict with some other significant case.[4] A further significant aspect of this orientation is that legal knowledge (for example, our conception of the various liberties and rights listed in the United States Constitution) is seen to be evolving and can never be dissociated from history. Thus, we require the justices of the Supreme Court to situate their rulings against a complex background of shared public understandings about the salience of various principles and precedents. The aim is to force the Court to develop a coherent but disciplined way forward or backward, working on a case by case basis.

Justices Sandra Day O'Connor, Anthony Kennedy and David Souter seem to be sympathetic to Fried's approach for, like him, they place a good deal of weight on *stare decisis*. But they do not follow Fried or Harlan faithfully and significant differences emerge that I explore in Chapter 6.

Why does Fried reject originalism? In answering this question, let me concentrate on what he takes to be a central weakness. There are other problems with originalism that he also notes, but I will not concern myself with these as I have already listed most of them.

As we have seen, those who seek objective meaning for constitutional phrases and those who embrace seventeenth-century, natural-law conceptions of the listed rights hold a static conception of the Bill of Rights – it means for them today precisely what it meant to the framers. But as Fried points out, because of this static view of the Constitution, they necessarily have difficulty coming to terms with or accommodating the many landmark precedents that seem to have no warrant in the original constitutional design, such as the doctrine of federal government supremacy (a reading of the Commerce Clause so as to facilitate revolutionary changes in the relationship between the states and the federal government), the incorporation doctrine (a reading of the Fourteenth Amendment to include the procedural safeguards listed in the Bill of Rights, to ensure that they also apply to the activities of the state governments), the anti-segregation doctrine (a reading of the Fourteenth Amendment so as to overturn 150 years of southern history), the political equality doctrine (a reading of the Fourteenth Amendment to allow the Court to adjudicate questions concerning the drawing of district boundaries for purposes of political representation), the political speech doctrine (a reading of the First Amendment to protect defamatory attacks directed at public officials or public figures), the privacy doctrine (a reading into the Constitution of novel rights, such as the right to view pornographic material, to use artificial methods of birth control and, for women, to choose whether to terminate a pregnancy in its early stages).

What troubles Fried, is that if we take originalism seriously we are required to embrace a revolutionary change of direction overruling most of these developments.[5] For example, the New Deal decisions that facilitated regulation of the economy by the federal government in 1937 violates the Contracts, Takings and Due Process Clauses.[6] But this conclusion is unacceptable to Fried because very few Americans would wish to support a wholesale retreat from the doctrine of federal government supremacy.[7]

Of course, not all defenders of originalism advocate a complete retreat from the results of past judicial activism. Most prefer to honour some doctrines while disavowing others. For example, Robert Bork acknowledges that the federal government must not be frustrated in the way that it was in the *Lochner* v. *New York* case,[8] and he accepts the *Brown* v. *Board of Education* ruling that establishes the anti-segregation principle, although he rejects the companion case, *Bolling* v. *Sharp*, that applies the requirements of *Brown* to the federal government.[9] On the other hand, he dislikes the protection of privacy offered in *Griswold* v. *Connecticut* and has doubts about the incorporation doctrine. Stephen Macedo approves the recognition of an implied privacy right and accepts the reasoning of Blackmun in *Roe* v. *Wade* and he also supports *Lochner* (with qualifications), challenging the validity of the doctrine of federal supremacy over the economy.[10] But the criteria various writers use for selecting good from bad constitutional developments are not usually sensitive to the concerns that had actually influenced the Supreme Court in securing the developments in question; more significantly, they often offer no satisfactory explanation for accommodating the radical departures from precedent that they advocate as correct (for example, Bork can give no coherent reason for accepting *Brown*, apart from the fact that he dislikes the practice of segregating schools on the basis of race and approves the fact that most Americans embrace an anti-discrimination principle as part of their political morality[11]).

Fried seeks a conservative position that is not revolutionary in its implication because it is not confined in the way originalism is to eighteenth-century understandings. In terms of Fried's analysis of 'law', our conception of the Constitution's requirements must inevitably evolve and should reflect changing circumstances. In his view, judges enjoy authority to manage the evolution of the law as they respond to issues from case to case, although they have no mandate to 'roam where unguided speculation might take them' and must be 'disciplined by a respect for tradition, professionalism, and careful and candid reasoning'.[12] Fried's concern is to save the Reagan Revolution from the excesses of abstract theorizing by offering a common law reading of the work of the Supreme Court. He is not against judicial policymaking as long as it is done in what he claims is the proper manner:[13] moving from one case to the next at hand, consistently and cautiously; exercising discretion only when a resolution is absolutely necessary or judicial intervention appropriate. Like the originalists, he is against the unbridled resort to abstract ideas so characteristic of American jurists who argue as though Supreme Court justices are authorized to impose their favoured political theory and may ignore the expressed wishes of other branches of government.[14] Fried's goal is to reverse this practice of excessive judicial activism by encouraging the Supreme Court to rule in a manner that slowly narrows the salience of the more controversial, open-ended, precedents of the recent past.

Fried cautions against the strategy of securing an overruling of most of the precedents set in the Warren and Burger eras, when liberal jurisprudential ideas seems to have influenced the Court to embrace an unbridled activism. Rather than a frontal charge (seeking to secure the Reagan administration's ambitious programme that included the overruling of decisions such as *Griswold* v. *Connecticut, Roe* v. *Wade, Regents of the University of California* v. *Bakke, United Steelworkers of America* v. *Weber, Baker* v. *Carr, New York Times* v. *Sullivan*), he offers a less formalistic and rigid departure from this unsustainable legacy. His preference is for the initiation of a quiet change of direction that allows most of the landmark cases to remain but in a much more confined way. For example, although he advocates overruling in *Roe* v. *Wade* he supports the recognition of a privacy right; his problems with *Roe* stem from the fact that (a) it cannot be accepted as a legitimate development from *Griswold* v. *Connecticut* and (b) the moral dilemmas surrounding the practice of abortion cannot be resolved without going beyond 'law'. In dealing with the Fourteenth Amendment, he argues that *Brown* v. *Board of Education, United Steelworkers of America* v. *Weber* and *Regents of the University of California* v. *Bakke* are all sustainable decisions but that the collectivist interpretation of these precedents, reading them as though they require federal courts to sustain claims to group rights is unacceptable.

By assisting the Court to move backward in short but firm steps, Fried tells us, the defensible aspects of 'the Reagan agenda' was implemented in a satisfactory and good tempered manner: the justices were asked to identify what is sensible and sustainable in the past and to endorse measured changes that reflected the values of the American people. In contrast, originalism did not prove successful as a working orientation for the Court because it entailed far-reaching consequences that seemed difficult to contain in a plausible manner.

Originalism and Bork–Rehnquist Approach

Many of the most serious criticisms of originalism were articulated at the time of President Reagan's unsuccessful nomination of Judge Robert Bork for the position of Associate Justice of the Supreme Court. He was identified as a leading exponent of the doctrine and many of his critics thought that this was sufficient reason to question his candidacy. Indeed, this partly accounts for why the hearings in the Senate Judiciary Committee went beyond a scrutiny of his legal competence and integrity. Although it is misleading to claim that the negative judgment of the Senate constitutes a rejection of originalism, it is clear that many senators did have reservations about the doctrine, at least in the form it was articulated by Bork at the hearings. Not surprisingly, Judge Bork has now published a systematic attempt to answer his critics, addressing some of the problems I have listed.[15] It will be useful to briefly consider his revised statement.

Judge Bork addresses two central problems: historical indeterminacy and the issue of evolutionary change. Thus, he tries to reassure those who believe that it is impossible to establish what the Constitution's framers would have thought or did think about a number of controversial questions, and those who question why constitutional analysis should be bound by eighteenth-century conceptions.

Bork confronts the charge of historical indeterminacy by claiming that controversies can usually be avoided if we seek to establish the understandings people could have been expected to have had about constitutional provisions at the time of their ratification. In his view non-subjective forms of evidence such as 'debates at the conventions, public discussion, newspaper articles, dictionaries in use at the time' should be of greater relevance to the jurist than speculations about what motivated the framers. Of course, if the intentions of the framers are clearly articulated or easy to deduce and if they are also coherent, they must be decisive; but as this is not usually the case, Bork argues that contemporaneous understandings are enough to secure the meaning of the controversial, constitutional phrases in question.

On the issue of evolutionary change, Bork's response is simple – jurists should rely on other branches of government to take the initiative or the Constitution should be amended. If changing circumstances make it impossible to determine the framers intentions with any certainty, Bork advocates judicial restraint; in his view, relevant policy choices about how to proceed should be made by authorities who are accountable to the people. Thus, the jurist should act as though there is no applicable law, '[t]here being nothing to work with, the judge should refrain from working'.[16] This is a crucial claim because it shifts the burden of responsibility for change away from the courts, turning a favourite argument of critics against themselves. As Bork notes, the fact that it is sometimes impossible to determine the meaning of the Constitution's key phrases is not a warrant for judicial activism; to the contrary, it compels the judges to stand aside for they have no other source of authority.

On this conception, the role of a judge is confined for he or she must cite sources and should not merely articulate value preferences when exercising authority. As Bork presents the position, originalism is simply a sophisticated form of legal positivism – it insists on the distinction between legal and moral reasoning. In the case of constitutional adjudication, the judicial sources are the words of the document amplified by what can be known of the framers' common understandings and the meanings that would have been attributed to these words by people at the time of ratification. Thus, even if a Supreme Court justice believes that capital punishment is a 'cruel and unusual punishment', he or she will have no authorization for imposing this value because the death penalty was not thought of as 'cruel and unusual' by those who ratified the Eighth Amendment of the Constitution in 1791. Even if capital punishment is a practice that violates fundamental moral sensibilities today, Bork refuses to concede that the Court is entitled to cite the Eighth Amendment as a warrant for imposing this point of view. His positivism holds that the Supreme Court is not responsible for articulating or imposing the will of the people but may act only to enforce the law. It is legislators in the various state parliaments who are normally responsible for articulating public morality in the United States, and they are in the best position to ascertain and implement appropriate policies. Supreme Court justices have no prerogative to secure the morality of the people except when this manifests itself in law.

On this understanding, then, there is a conflict between judicial policymaking and democratic accountability and judges should not presume to displace legislators when this can be avoided. Of course, Bork concedes that the Supreme Court enjoys a special authority specifically provided for in the Constitution to uphold the listed liberties and, thus, that it may sometimes have to overrule those who are elected to make policies. However, he argues that if the justices are to act within the framework of law, they must limit their discretion, especially when reading the more open-ended phrases of the Constitution; and if a policy problem could not have been contemplated at the time of ratification, they must proceed with the greatest caution for judges should defer to those who are in a better position to discern and articulate the values of the people.

Bork's views echo the opinion of Chief Justice Rehnquist who, in a lecture he delivered at the University of Texas Law School (1976), is concerned to distinguish two competing senses of the phrase 'the living Constitution'. The first, which he approves of, regards the courts as having a responsibility to apply the general language of the Constitution to cases that the framers might not have foreseen. Thus, the Constitution's First Amendment protection of freedom of speech may be applied in the context of modern electronic media and the President's Commander-in-Chief power can be extended to include command over the air force, even though these developments could not have been foreseen or contemplated by the framers. In instances of this kind, however, the justices will feel bound by the values that can be derived from the language and intentions of the framers. Thus, if the framers excluded obscene speech from their conception of the speech that the First Amendment embraces, allowing state legislators to protect citizens from exposure to what they regard as offensive materials, the Court must be bound by this even if a majority of the justices on the Court today share a more libertarian conception of 'freedom of speech'. The second sense of a 'living Constitution' Rehnquist identifies (and disapproves of) is more permissive for it allows courts to substitute their own conception of the Constitution's protected liberties, 'making the Constitution relevant and useful in solving the problems of modern society'. Thus, the justices dealing with an obscenity case, as contemplated above, need not defer to state legislators because they could justify exercising judicial review by accommodating their libertarian standard under the general phrase 'freedom of speech' protected in the First Amendment. In this way, Rehnquist insists, policy conflicts that should be resolved within the political process are illegitimately settled by the Supreme Court.

Like Judge Bork, then, Rehnquist argues that this kind of usurpation is countermajoritarian and dangerous; in his view, it also misconceives the nature of the Constitution that places responsibility for change in the popularly elected branches of government.[17]

Criticisms of the Bork–Rehnquist Approach

The most serious problem with the Bork–Rehnquist approach is that the Court has never acted in the deferential manner they recommend. Thus, they need to explain how they intend to deal with the many landmark precedents that seem to have no warrant in the original constitutional design. Of course, neither Bork nor Rehnquist advocates a wholesale rejection of the Court's past precedents. They accept that they must defer to some of the landmark decisions that are the result of activism on the part of Supreme Court justices, even when they believe that these decisions exhibit unwarranted policymaking. But each prefers to honour some doctrines (such as federal supremacy, incorporation, anti-segregation) while disavowing others (such as privacy). But the criteria used by each of them for selecting good from bad developments are difficult to fathom and have not been clearly articulated. One suspects that their caution about openly espousing the full revolutionary implications of their doctrine is guided by nothing more than the political climate of the times and their own values.

Although he is very sympathetic to qualified originalism because it offers the hope that legal reasoning may proceed with reference to objective standards, Justice Scalia acknowledges that some of the serious problems I have listed are fatal.

In the first place, he does not think that Bork has effectively disposed of the problem of indeterminacy, for lawyers are not normally qualified to do and do not have the time for historical research. Yet there seems no other way a judge can find the correct meaning of controversial constitutional phrases. As Scalia points out, the one example we have of a genuine attempt to fulfil originalism's methodological requirements took more than a year-and-a-half to accomplish and was published three years after the Court first heard the case.[18] (Nor can we be sure that the results of such research would be conclusive; and even when they are, anyone who wished to evaluate the ruling would have to review the supporting research, assessing the primary sources in the light of all the contrary opinions about their significance.) Clearly, then, historical research is uncharacteristic of legal reasoning and is unlikely to prove dispositive (as is illustrated by the fact that Scalia notes, that Taft's opinion was overruled in 14 pages, just eight and a half years later).[19]

Despite this problem, Justice Scalia is sympathetic to the position adopted by Bork and Rehnquist. Indeed, he cynically deplores the fact that contemporary lawyers are less hypocritical than lawyers in the past who at least paid lip service to originalism, even though they did not conduct their debates in the light of historical analysis. In Scalia's view, the search for original intentions, even if this cannot be accomplished very adequately, has a far better claim to integrity as an orientation than its major competitor, which virtually abandons the notion that fidelity to the text of the Constitution is an overriding principle of adjudication. In his view judges must reason from some specific sources if they are to establish their authority and he claims that their opinions will be arbitrary if they abandon this ideal. This is why he is so critical of the modern tendency, prevalent among liberal judges and constitutional theorists, to substitute political philosophy or pseudo-sociology (identifying the fundamental values of the community) for historical commentary when considering the meaning of the Constitution's more controversial phrases. Scalia believes that the lawyer's craft is different from that of the politician, philosopher, historian or sociologist; and argues that the integrity of 'law' depends on distinguishing legal reasoning from ethical, economic and political concerns. In his view, those who embrace originalism as their legal philosophy are to be commended for attempting to establish the autonomy of law.

Scalia's views about the inappropriate resort by judges to political philosophy echo Bork in his Francis Boyer Lectures on Public Policy

(1985). There are two serious difficulties that conservative theorists raise about philosophical approaches to law: the problem of their fit with the more traditional sources of law and the related issue of indeterminacy.

The most important of these concerns is the seeming incompatibility of current, liberal, philosophical trends with some phrases in the Constitution. This is a problem of the fit between a legal theory and the sources of law. For example, many liberal lawyers today think that it is appropriate for judges to ignore the fact that capital punishment was recognized as a legitimate practice in the eighteenth-century (as noted at various points in the Constitution), and they also wish to ignore the specific use of 'property' in the Liberty Clauses in the Fifth and Fourteenth Amendments. Of course, there are good reasons for regarding capital punishment as a 'cruel and unusual' form of punishment that should be prohibited, regardless of what the Constitution says about it; and there are also good reasons for questioning Locke's defence of property rights. But if liberals wish to pursue a practice of ignoring what they dislike in the Constitution, their claims to legal authority start to look very questionable indeed. This problem is, of course, compounded when protections that are not specifically listed are read into the Constitution, using the authority of the Ninth Amendment's caution that 'the enumeration in the Constitution of certain rights, shall not be construed to deny or disparage others retained by the people' as a justification.

Liberal writers are not insensitive to this criticism and have made some efforts to explain their approach. For example, Ronald Dworkin uses a distinction between 'concepts' and 'conceptions' to justify adopting what many regard as his rather cavalier treatment of the Constitution's actual requirements. In his view, we are entitled to read the listed rights in the Constitution as a special kind of instruction, requiring us to develop and apply our own conception of rights when controversial cases arise. In terms of his account, then, judges are not bound by the specific understandings about rights or liberalism shared by the framers but are empowered to decide between competing conceptions of political morality. He writes:

> So it is wrong to attack the Warren Court, for example, on the ground that it failed to treat the Constitution as a binding text. On the contrary, if we wish to treat fidelity to that text as an overriding requirement of constitutional interpretation, then it is the conservative critics of the Warren Court who are at fault, because their philosophy ignores the direction to face issues of moral principle that the logic of the text demands.[20]

But what if a judge wishes to abandon individualism in order to embrace a conception of group rights, as some liberal justices do in affirmative action cases? What if she embraces socialism as an overriding goal, simply recognizing those entitlements that will facilitate the realization of this objective? Surely there are some limits to the rival conceptions that may be appropriately embraced.

Dworkin has very strong views about what kinds of argument are acceptable in delineating the sphere of 'law'. Thus, in a recent article, he takes issue with Charles Fried arguing that he fails to provide a principled defence of the conservative judicial revolution in his memoir of the Reagan years.[21] Dworkin disallows Fried's approach because, he claims, it fails to respect the integrity of law, which, he tells us, requires that judicial interventions proceed on the basis of principles applied consistently.

Unfortunately, besides failing to provide any historical evidence that the framers share his particular conception of what can count as an acceptable constitutional argument, Dworkin fails to show why it is inappropriate to put forward – as a constitutional principle – the view that judges should defer to the branches of government who are accountable to the people. Nor does Dworkin's distinction between matters of principle and questions of policy seem to help, here, for it surely is the case that questions about the appropriate role of courts in a democracy do raise issues of principle.[22] The central issue is what form of democracy has or should be embraced in the United States of America. Dworkin's view that the framers intended to institutionalize a form of democracy in which the protection of individual rights is a precondition begs many questions about how they intended to ensure this. His claim that they required judges to face many questions of political morality and that this was the main mechanism they used to secure political rights is contentious. In particular, it may be argued, as Rehnquist and Bork do, that the division of powers between the federal and state levels of government was seen by the framers as a far more significant guarantee. In any event, it is not clear why the framers' intentions should be determining. Scalia can simply declare that the American people have become more democratic and are, rightly, suspicious of judicial policymaking.

Dworkin also seems to overlook the fact that the framers had no intention of empowering future generations in the way he claims. It is one thing to suppose that they did not require their own specific conception of particular liberties to be binding on future generations and quite another to suppose, as Dworkin does, that they mandated future justices to impose quite different political moralities. This assumption is implausible because it is clear that many of the framers held very strong views about the specific natural rights that they

took to be fundamental. Most shared Thomas Jefferson's individualism, embracing the kind of Lockean sentiments we find in the Declaration of Independence. Their primary concern was to maximize
individual freedom by ensuring that governments would be constrained through appropriate checks and balances. Although they
never contemplated modern collectivist views, it is clear that they
would not have supported the view that governments may act
coercively to establish positive liberties. They most certainly would
be surprised to hear Dworkin argue that the value that makes best
sense of the constitutional arrangements is not liberty but fairness
(or, as Dworkin puts it, that individuals be treated with equal concern and respect). As for the view that the Constitution should be
read so that it affords fairness to groups rather than to individuals,
this is totally alien to the thoroughly individualist vision the framers
shared.

I shall consider these issues in greater detail in Chapter 8 when I
review Dworkin's views. Here I merely note that Scalia is on strong
ground when he questions contemporary liberal approaches for playing fast and loose with the Constitution's text. A further aspect of the
liberal approach that bothers him is its indeterminacy. The two issues
are related because if the fit between a theory and the sources of law
are as loose as we have found liberal theory to be, it would seem to
be the case that anything goes. What Dworkin has to show, then, if
he is to convince a sceptic such as Scalia about the propriety of his
approach, is that his version of liberalism exhibits a greater fidelity to
the spirit of the text than, say, the thoroughgoing individualism of
Stephen Macedo and Walter Berns. But this cannot be done convincingly. Alternatively, he must show that his political theory is superior
and that this justifies an abandonment of the traditional sources of
law. But although Dworkin is on stronger ground when he claims
that fairness is a better foundation for a liberal political theory than
liberty, there is no way in which the superiority of his egalitarian
vision can be demonstrated conclusively.

Scalia's response to the philosophical debates is somewhat surprising for one would expect him to join Stephen Macedo and others in
advocating a revival of classical liberal ideals, using the Supreme
Court to establish the kind of constitutional reform which some conservatives have advocated.[23] As we have seen, libertarian political
theorists have an advantage in the political debate because their
philosophy accurately reflects the values of many of the eighteenth-
century lawyers who helped to draft the Constitution. But Scalia
resists the temptation to suppose that it is now the turn of a different,
intellectual elite to impose its values, refusing to join the philosophical battle from the conservative side.[24] Instead, he prefers to treat the
Constitution as a flawed document because of its many vague phrases

and embrace of natural law theory. In his view, its requirements should be narrowly interpreted so that modern courts are not compromised by these problems. Thus, he embraces the Protestant idea that law resides in the common understanding of plain words, rather than in philosophical ideals, which in his view, should be expunged from the law. Thus, he would ignore the Ninth Amendment completely, on the grounds that such a vague statement of intent cannot bind a court.[25] In his view, judges should defer to other branches of government unless established legal doctrines or a clear constitutional requirement can be cited to support their rulings.

Justice Scalia is also concerned because originalism is incompatible with the notion that courts should be bound by precedent. Yet no serious exponent of the law would really wish to abandon *stare decisis* 'so that *Marbury* v. *Madison* would stand even if Professor Raoul Berger should demonstrate unassailably that it got the meaning of the Constitution wrong'.[26] The problem here arises from the 200 year history in which many of the Constitution's provisions have been systematically ignored by the Supreme Court and other branches of government.

Related to this, Scalia expresses a further reservation about originalism because he claims most of us would not be prepared to apply the doctrine consistently. For example, most people deplore Judge Bork's claim that *Bolling* v. *Sharp* (ruling that the Fourteenth Amendment's Equal Protection Clause applies to the actions of the Federal Government) is an unjustified rewriting of the Constitution. As Scalia notes, they find it unthinkable that the states should be forbidden to segregate and the Federal Government allowed to. While Bork is clearly right in claiming that a consistent 'originalist' must allow this anomaly, Scalia is clearly correct in concluding 'so much the worse for originalism'. Other controversial cases that are difficult to justify as an originalist readily come to mind (such as *Brown* v. *Board of Education*, *New York Times* v. *Sullivan*, *Baker* v. *Carr*, and *Griswold* v. *Connecticut*). Yet in all of these, and others that could be considered, an alternative result seems unthinkable and outrageous. But this is the kind of consequence, which Scalia correctly sees, follows from the demand that the Court protect only those rights that are readily identifiable in the Constitution's text and only if they are supported by what we know of the values embraced by Americans in the eighteenth century.

Scalia's Fainthearted Originalism

These are serious problems that certainly call into question even Judge Bork's recent version of originalism. There have been many

landmark holdings by the Supreme Court, reshaping legal developments in very significant ways that appear to be either unanticipated
by, or incompatible with, the values of the framers. Even Chief Justice John Marshall's two landmark decisions *Marbury* v. *Madison* and
McCulloch v. *Maryland* are not easy to justify if the sole test of legitimacy is the conformity of a judgment with the intentions of the
framers. Changes accepted by the Supreme Court or initiated by it,
affecting the institutional arrangement put in place by the framers,
have occurred to meet the demands of a modern society. Without
these changes (in the balance of power between the Congress and the
President, between the state governments and the Federal Government, and between the Supreme Court and the other branches of
government) the system in the United States is unlikely to have
endured for 200 years.

Scalia thinks we should recognize the contradictions between the
framers' intentions and what has evolved; and argues that history,
tradition and the past decisions of the Supreme Court ought to be
taken into account by judges when they reach their decisions. Thus,
he advocates a form of originalism that he frankly calls 'fainthearted'.[27]
By this he means that it is flexible enough to understand that no
constitutional theory is perfect and that judges will often face cases
in which reality dictates a certain amount of inconsistency. Scalia is
prepared to live with this so long as the rules by which the Supreme
Court supposes that it is bound are clear. If changes are desired,
these can then be made in the appropriate manner. What he wishes
to avoid is a situation where the Court imposes its judgments in a
manner that does not allow for review by the other branches. Of
course, this cannot be avoided in every instance for the Court is
responsible for interpreting vague constitutional phrases. However,
Scalia proposes caution and seems to endorse the following rules of
thumb:

1   when the Constitution is clear, this should be adhered to unless a
    precedent allowing a different approach has been well-established
    (the appropriate manner for change in this context is a constitu-
    tional amendment);
2   when the Constitution is ambiguous, the Court should endeav-
    our to leave most of the initiative for policymaking with other
    branches of government;
3   when the Court does impose its own reading of a controversial
    phrase, it should formulate a clear rule that it is prepared to
    enforce consistently.

In place of the originalist's commitment to remain true to one
source (that is, the Constitution as understood in the eighteenth cen-

tury), Scalia allows more flexibility and creativity. Judges may consider precedent and they may also review the historical record to identify traditionally accepted liberties. What he insists, though, is that ingenuity be used to limit the discretion judges claim for themselves. This does not mean that the Court must take responsibility for dismantling the legacy of its own past judicial activism. Other branches of government should take the greater responsibility for this, supposing change is desirable, and co-equal branches will be forced to take more responsibility in providing leadership if the Court is clear about its own presumptions. The Court's responsibility is to show its unwillingness to be manoeuvred into making unpopular choices that politicians prefer to avoid (for example, allowing or denying abortions, regulating morality, requiring affirmative action). The Court can do this by, for example, construing vague and ambiguous phrases narrowly or by refusing to uphold them.

What we find Scalia recommending, then, is a form of positivism which is self-consciously based on a normative commitment: that legal authorities ought to seek ways to refrain from policymaking. He accepts the Bork–Rehnquist view that the judiciary has no democratic authority and that it is, therefore, inappropriate for judges to make policy; but he does not accept that an adequate jurisprudence can be founded on the originalist doctrines they advocate. The judicial ideal he advocates is similar to theirs (that of the objective umpire) and, like them, he holds that judges must seek objective sources but he is less convinced that his ideal of law can be fully realized. Indeed, he allows that some exceptional cases will arise in which a court will be justified in establishing policy (or in confirming policy judgments made by activist judges in the past). In these cases, however, Scalia requires that the standards that the modern Supreme Court acknowledges be clearly identified.

Despite differences of emphasis, for example O'Connor and Kennedy place greater weight on the importance of *stare decisis*, Scalia's views seem to have some support among the present justices (see Figure p. 65). Rehnquist, Kennedy and Thomas often join his opinions. Thus, even if 'fainthearted-originalism' is unlikely to be the favoured approach on the Court as we move into the twenty-first century, it will be influential.

Conclusion

I have argued that 'fainthearted originalism' offers a coherent way forward for the contemporary Court.[28] In terms of this approach we require the justices to embrace a form of positivism that is self-consciously based on a normative commitment: that legal authorities ought to seek ways to refrain from policymaking. The fact that the Constitution is vague should not be taken as a blank cheque offering unfettered discretion to the justices; rather, a lack of precision signals that they should defer to other branches of government who have greater authority to act on behalf of the people.[29] What the Court has a responsibility to do, when it chooses to assert legal authority, is to articulate clear rules and to cite sources. These latter can be: an established reading of a provision in the Constitution, the rules established in previous cases under *stare decisis* or, in some circumstances, the traditions of the American people (not what the justices wish them to be). What Rehnquist, Scalia and Thomas insist, though, is that ingenuity be used to limit the discretion the justices claim for themselves. This does not mean that the Court must necessarily dismantle the legacy of its own past judicial activism for the justices are bound by rules that enjoy an accepted and established place in the system. But the Court must show its unwillingness to be manoeuvred into making unpopular choices that politicians prefer to avoid.

Scalia is most responsible for recognizing the need to be 'fainthearted' in applying legal positivism to the inhospitable terrain of United States constitutional law. Thus, he allows that the development of the law must necessarily be somewhat inconsistent and that the justices will need to be governed by what is feasible and practical. Nevertheless, Scalia suggests that many of the more important changes countenanced in the past are justifiable because they are supported by what he regards as good legal arguments. Thus, he tells us that the justices who supported the controversial decision in *Lochner* v. *New York* were correctly overruled because they erroneously argue that 'liberty' in the Due Process Clause of the Fifth Amendment encompasses a right to make contracts, yet, as Justice Holmes pointed out in his dissent, there is no objective basis for reaching this conclusion. Its plausibility depends on the economic theories that the justices embraced, rather than on legal arguments. Similarly, the arguments of the Court in *Plessy* v. *Ferguson* ignore what Scalia believes is the best reading of the Equal Protection Clause in the Fourteenth Amendment.[30] In his view, the best justification of *Brown* v. *Board of Education* (overruling *Plessy*) is to be found in John Harlan's dissenting judgment – the Constitution's mandate prohibits segregation.[31] Although he concedes that it may not be possible to show that this reading of the Fourteenth Amendment was intended by the framers, it makes good sense to adopt it as a rule because it offers the Court an objective basis for justifying the initiative it took and a means for guiding the Court's rulings in future cases. (I discuss the application of Scalia's orientation to the problem of affirmative action in Chapter 9.)

Notes

1   Chief Justice Rehnquist and Justice Scalia often vote with Justice O'Connor (see the evidence provided in the table on p. 90; and Erwin Chemerinsky, 'The Vanishing Constitution: The Supreme Court 1989 Term', *Harvard Law Review*, vol. 103, no. 1 (1989). Scalia sometimes expresses his frustration with what he takes to be O'Connor's excessive caution; see his opinion in *William Webster* v. *Reproduction Health Services* 109 S. Ct. 3040 (1989).

2   See Edwin Meese III, 'Interpreting the Constitution' in Jack N. Rakove (ed.), *Interpreting the Constitution* (Boston, Mass.: Northeastern University Press, 1990), 13–23; Robert H. Bork, *The Tempting of America: the Political Seduction of the Law* (NY: The Free Press, 1990); William Rehnquist, 'The Notion of a Living Constitution', *Texas Law Review*, vol. 54, no. 4 (1976), 693–706 and 'Government by Cliche', *Missouri Law Review*, vol. 45, no. 3, (1980), 379–93; Antonin Scalia, 'Originalism' *Cincinnati Law Review*, vol. 57, (1989), 849ff.

3   In its most recent manifestation in the United States, this orientation derives its bearing from the commentaries of the legal scholar Alexander Bickel and from the work of Associate Justice, John Harlan. Charles Fried served as a clerk for Harlan and attaches a quotation from his dissenting judgment in *Poe* v. . *Ullman* 367 U.S. 497, 542 (1961) as a manifesto for his chapter 'Privacy' in *Order & Law: Arguing the Reagan Revolution* (NY: Simon & Schuster, 1991).

4   In a recent article ('*Metro Broadcasting Inc.* v. *FCC* [110 S. Ct. 2997]: Two Concepts of Equality', *Harvard Law Review*, vol. 104, (1990), 107–27. Fried draws attention to the conflict between the recent affirmative action cases *Croson* and *Metro Broadcasting*; Justices Stevens and O'Connor would uphold *Weber* even though they both regard it as poorly argued. O'Connor (with Justices Kennedy and Souter) takes the same attitude to *Roe* v. *Wade*; see their opinion in *Planned Parenthood of S. E. Pennsylvania* v. *Casey*.

5   This argument made by Fried is articulated by many other critics of originalism. See especially Henry Paul Monaghan, 'Stare Decisis and Constitutional Adjudication' in Jack N. Rakove (ed.), op. cit., 263–313.

6   See Fried's discussion of the New Deal, *Order & Law*, 68–70.

7   Even Macedo qualifies his effort to rehabilitate the reading of the Constitution that preceded the New Deal – exorcising the ghost of *Lochner* v. *New York* – by adding: 'The court should, while not leaping back to *Lochner*, at least add a measure of substantive "bite" to the rationality standard it applies in the economic sphere' 'The Right to Privacy: a Constitutional and Moral Defence', *Political Theory Newsletter* (Canberra, ACT, Australia: RSSS, Australian National University, CPN Publications), vol. 2, no. 2 (1990), 192–3.

8   He tells us that the federal supremacy doctrine amounts to a constitutional amendment, *The Tempting of America*, 56–7.

9   Ibid., 83–4.

10   Stephen Macedo, op cit., 192–3.

11   Bork's account of *Brown* is in *Tempting of America*. Cf. Raoul Berger, *Government by Judiciary: the Transformation of the Fourteenth Amendment* (Cambridge, Mass.: Harvard University Press, 1977), 100–10, 117–33; Alexander Bickel, 'The Original Understanding and the Segregation Decision', *Harvard Law Review*, vol. 69 (1955), 1ff.; also Ronald Dworkin, *Law's Empire*, (London: Fontana Press, 1986), 359–63.

12   Fried, *Order & Law*, 70–1, quoting from Justice Harlan's dissenting judgment in *Poe* v. *Ullman*, 367 U.S. 497, 542 (1961).

13   See his account of 'continuity and change', ibid., 68–70, where he discusses the New Deal and *Brown* v. *Board of Education*.

14   For example, Laurence Tribe, 'The Futile Search for Legitimacy' in *Constitutional Choices* (Cambridge, Mass.: Harvard University Press, 1985), 3–9 and, gener-

ally, Part 1, 3–29; Ronald Dworkin makes an attempt to narrow the kind of philosophical argument that can be resorted to within legal arguments by distinguishing between arguments that cite principles and those that recommend policies in, *Taking Rights Seriously* (Cambridge, Mass.: Harvard University Press, 1977), 22–8 and 90–100 but he also allows such a wide discretion to judges that the distinction does not serve as much of a restraint in practice (see, generally, *Law's Empire*).

15   Bork, *Tempting of America*, 161–85.

16   Ibid., 166; See also John Hart Ely, *Democracy and Distrust: a Theory of Judicial Review* (Cambridge, Mass.: Harvard University Press, 1992), 41, 'If a principled approach to judicial enforcement of the Constitution's open-ended provision cannot be developed, one that is not hopelessly inconsistent with our nation's commitment to representative democracy, responsible commentators must consider seriously the possibility that courts should simply stay away from them'.

17   Rehnquist, 'Living Constitution', 609.

18   Chief Justice Taft's 70-page opinion in *Myers* v. *United States*, 272 US 235 is cited by Scalia as the case in question.

19   Scalia, 'Originalism', 851.

20   Dworkin, *Law's Empire*, 136.

21   Ronald Dworkin, 'The Reagan Revolution and the Supreme Court', *New York Review of Books*, xxxviii, no. 13 (1991).

22   Dworkin, *Law's Empire*, 22–8.

23   James Buchanan and Geoffrey Brennan, *The Reason of Rules: Constitutional Political Economy* (Cambridge/NY: Cambridge University Press, 1987).

24   I do not deny that Scalia, like most judges, may not be guilty of imposing his own values. See Jeffrey Rosen, 'The Leader of the Opposition', *The New Republic*, (18 Jan. 1993), who accuses him of imposing subjective values in cases involving affirmative action, property rights, executive power and school prayer. I have reservations about whether Scalia is guilty as charged because, as I show, he has a more complex approach than most other originalists. But even if Scalia is guilty of judicial policymaking, at least he tries not to rely on his own prejudices and sense of morality. More significantly, unlike liberals who embrace activism, he accepts that he ought not to allow his passions to dictate his responses. He would acknowledge that Rosen's charges are very serious and would make efforts to correct himself so that he does not abuse his judicial authority in the ways alleged.

25   Scalia, 'Originalism', 853.

26   Ibid., 861.

27   Ibid., 849.

28   I have discussed Scalia's 'fainthearted originalism' at greater length in 'Conservatives on the Supreme Court', *Constitutional Political Economy*, vol. 3, no. 2, (1992), 197–221. My discussion in this chapter draws on that account.

29   As Robert Bork puts it, '[t]here being nothing to work with, the judge should refrain from working', *The Tempting of America*, 166.

30   1992 U.S. Lexis 4751 ff.

31   For Scalia's views on *Brown* v. *Board of Education*, see his dissenting opinion in *Casey* (1992 U.S. Lexis 4751).

5 Privacy and Abortion

As we have seen, the conservative justices who now constitute a secure majority on the Supreme Court disagree about the nature of judicial reasoning for some are legal positivists while others are traditional conservatives who follow the second Justice Harlan. They also offer different accounts of the proper scope of the Supreme Court's authority and competing strategies for the future. Indeed, we find that there is an emerging alignment on the Court under Rehnquist. In one camp we find William Rehnquist, Antonin Scalia and, on some issues, Byron White (now retired), Anthony Kennedy and Clarence Thomas; in another Sandra Day O'Connor and David Souter with Kennedy joining them on some issues. But these divisions do not occur all that frequently and are largely confined to cases raising claims to First Amendment protection, including those that rely on the Establishment Clause, and cases dealing with some aspects of privacy. If we take the number of 5–4 decisions in each term as a measure of the Court's cohesion we find that the conservatives have established dominance since the appointment of David Souter in October 1990. Consider the following pattern in the decline of the number of close decisions.[1]

Year	Number of 5–4 decisions
1985–86	45
1986–87	12
1985–88	33
1988–89	39
1989–90	21
1990–91	17
1991–92	14
1992–93	18

In all, the impact of the O'Connor–Kennedy–Souter agreement has resulted in only eight decisions in which the three traditional conservatives form the core group in the majority when Scalia is excluded, out of a total of 53 of the close 5–4 decisions in the period after Souter joined the Court (that is, the 1990–91 term through to the end of the 1992–93 term). The O'Connor–Kennedy–Souter group will, of course, occasionally find support from members of the Court who are not conservatives, but these are included in the eight that I have counted. Thus, the defection-rate away from conservatism is not very high.

This chapter and Chapter 6 will be concerned to explore the intellectual basis for this splintering of what, on most issues, remains a secure consensus among the conservatives on the Court. As can be seen from the figure presented below, O'Connor and Kennedy are more likely to vote with Rehnquist than Scalia is. It is also clear that the conservatives agree on many issues of very great significance. The considerable support that Rehnquist has enjoyed from the other conservatives shows that it is more usual for them to reach a consensus over how to resolve difficult cases, than to allow theoretical differences to split the conservative majority. Indeed, the willingness of all of the conservative justices to vote with the Chief Justice shows that the Rehnquist Court is cohesive (using data provided in the annual summaries provided by the *Harvard Law Review*).

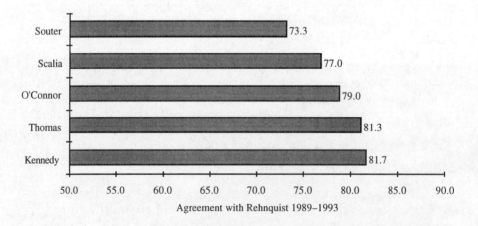

Agreement with Rehnquist 1989–1993

We see from this that theoretical disagreements among conservatives does not place Rehnquist's ability to secure majority support in jeopardy. Justices O'Connor and Kennedy are just as likely as Scalia to vote with Rehnquist and are equally convinced that activism by judges during the Warren–Burger era resulted in undesirable consequences. Nevertheless, in a few cases the justices are divided about what to do. In particular, the conservatives have difficulty agreeing about which of the controversial rulings of the Warren–Burger era to overrule. Some of the justices believe that *stare decisis* requires them to uphold most controversial precedents even when they rest on flawed assumptions about the nature of constitutional adjudication; others are eager to overrule precedents that they view as having no basis in recognized sources of law. The issue has been troubling the justices for some time and has come to a head in *Planned Parenthood of Pennsylvania* v. *Casey* in which the Court decided (in a five to four decision) to uphold the important abortion case *Roe* v. *Wade*.[2] *Casey* offers a good focus for my analysis of the competing points of view because each side goes to some trouble to explain and justify its understanding of the *stare decisis* rule.

I shall consider *Casey* in Chapter 6. It is here that I explore the consequences of the theoretical disagreements that have already been identified and will continue to explore in this chapter. I shall also compare the approaches of other conservatives who have examined the debates about privacy, such as Stephen Macedo and Charles Fried. These debates among the conservatives are important because no right to privacy is listed in the Constitution as protected; yet some such right seems to be implied. As the *Casey* case illustrates, the competing judicial philosophies among the conservative justices will sometimes give rise to unexpected results, when the usual consensus between them breaks down so that moderates on the Court (justices like Harry Blackmun and John Stevens) can influence the outcome. I claim that this will not happen as often as many liberals might hope, however, because the agreement between the conservatives is extensive. Even those conservative justices who place great weight on *stare decisis* are concerned to dismantle the legacy of the Warren period and, in most cases, a consensus will be found in support of this agenda. Nevertheless, the dispute between the conservatives, which has impacted on cases involving abortion, religion and some aspects of free speech, is significant and interesting.

I argue that Rehnquist and Scalia's analysis dissenting in *Casey* (recommending *Roe* v. *Wade* be overruled) is the more coherent, and offers clearer guidance to those who must apply the law about what the justices are trying to accomplish. Their legal doctrines are also easier for the justices themselves to apply than any of the competing orientations and will give rise to greater certainty and consistency. But the brand of conservatism they represent is deeply resented in the United States. Americans have lived with an interventionist Court for nearly half a century and have come to accept this as normal. Indeed, many people in the United States turn to the Court, rather than to Congress or the Executive, for guidance and leadership and are deeply troubled by the changes the conservatives hope to accomplish. A large number of critics are lawyers, especially those with influence in law schools and the media who seem to have embraced a perception of themselves and their discipline that is flattered by the central role that the Supreme Court has recently played in their system of government. The most vocal are, however, those who speak for groups who feel that their interests are under attack.

It is partly in response to the sustained criticism of the Rehnquist Court that Souter, Kennedy and O'Connor recommend greater caution. Their decision in *Casey* not to overrule *Roe* v. *Wade* is partly politically motivated. By showing a willingness to compromise with the activist past they hope it will prove easier to sustain a change in direction. Nevertheless, as I show, the concessions they have made in this case, if followed systematically, are likely to leave the jurisprudence of the Court in some disarray, and the justices will be accused of making arbitrary judgments.

Before I consider *Casey*, however, it is necessary to explain why privacy cases have proved so controversial. This will be the task of the present chapter.

Controversy over Privacy

In the Unites States, privacy has usually been protected incidentally, as an aspect of the First Amendment's guarantee of free speech, by the Third Amendment's recognition of the sanctity of the home, by the Fourth Amendment that prohibits unreasonable searches and seizures, and by the Fifth Amendment in its Self-Incrimination Clause.[3] In the landmark case *Griswold* v. *Connecticut* the Supreme Court went beyond this, recognizing privacy as a fundamental liberty, protected under the Liberty Clause in the Fourteenth Amendment (which forbids any state to deprive any person 'of life, liberty, or property, without due process of law'). This means that state governments that violate privacy must show that they have a compelling reason for doing this; their motives and interests will be subjected to an exacting scrutiny by the Court even though privacy is not independently listed in the Bill of Rights.

By recognizing privacy as a constitutionally protected liberty interest in *Griswold*, the Court signalled its willingness to address a range of issues relating to the decisions people make about reproduction;[4] finally, in the controversial *Roe* v. *Wade* ruling it recognized that a woman's right to terminate her pregnancy before the foetus is viable is an aspect of privacy and must be regarded as a protected liberty.[5] Since that time it has sustained *Roe* on numerous occasions although in recent years it has allowed state governments to impose quite severe restrictions.[6] In *Casey*, it confirmed that *Roe* and the other abortion decisions represent a coherent development of the legal principles consolidating the privacy right recognized in *Griswold*. It argued that the rule articulated in *Roe* has not been found unworkable and no subsequent legal developments have weakened its doctrinal footings.

Privacy Doctrine

What are the doctrines articulated in *Griswold* and why have conservatives found them so troubling?

The Court was asked to invalidate a portion of a Connecticut statute that made it illegal for married couples to use contraceptives. Thus, the case involved a claim to marital privacy. The reasoning of the Court is of considerable interest because the majority had no hesitation about exercising judicial oversight to protect the unenumerated privacy right. Justice Douglas expressed the opinion of the Court, arguing that it is legitimate to recognize privacy as a 'penumbral' right because respect for personal autonomy and bodily integrity are recognized as important values, as is shown by the fact that they are substantially protected, even presupposed, in many of the listed rights. If marital privacy is not specifically listed, Douglas argues, this can be presumed to result from an oversight by the framers (who cannot be expected to have foreseen every contingency). It follows that the Court is justified in acting to correct this. In his concurring opinion, Justice Goldberg went further. In his view, the Court is entitled to recognize privacy under the authority of the Ninth Amendment which states: 'The enumeration in the Constitution, of certain rights, shall not be construed to deny or disparage others retained by the people'.

Ninth Amendment jurisprudence and the recognition of unenumerated rights goes to the heart of the dispute between conservatives and liberals. Conservatives are not happy to allow the Court to decide the liberty interests presupposed by the term 'liberty' and those that are unprotected. In particular, they are unwilling to resolve the problem by articulating abstract political theories in terms of which rights are deduced. In their view, it is impossible to reconcile the competing claims of liberty and equality in an objective manner and the Court should not attempt to do so. As for the claim that the Ninth Amendment provides a justification for indulging in this kind of jurisprudence, the conservatives are sceptical. Although the provision can be read as an open-ended invitation to treat 'liberty' as embracing whatever the justices deem to be a fundamental interest, as Goldberg recommends, the conservatives are not tempted to do this. In their view the Ninth Amendment is unacceptably vague and should be read narrowly, if not ignored. It is not, therefore, surpris-

ing to find that the positivists (within the originalism school of interpretation, that is, Rehnquist, Scalia and Thomas as well as more
traditional conservatives, such as O'Connor, Kennedy and Souter),
who now make-up part of the new conservative majority on the
Supreme Court, have been unwilling to follow the lines of reasoning
articulated by liberals. This is not to say they all wish to overturn
Griswold;[7] but they do intend to contain the ruling so that its invitation to embrace competing philosophical conceptions about the
nature of liberty, citing the Ninth Amendment to justify imposing
any recommendations thought desirable, is firmly declined. Indeed,
nothing seems to provoke conservative constitutional scholars more
than the decisions of the Court in which a general right of freedom of
choice in matters not directly affecting other people was recognized.
This powerful abstract principle, which is defended in the classical
liberal tract by John Stuart Mill, is also said to encompass a woman's
choice to terminate her pregnancy;[8] but although it is clearly assumed by many of the arguments embraced by liberals and is a
logical implication of their reasoning in dealing with privacy problems, it seems to have no clear status as a constitutional principle.
Not surprisingly, it irritates the conservatives that liberals embrace
methods of interpretation that allow them to give abstract principles
of this kind so much weight in their deliberations.

The Court's willingness to recognize a privacy right brought it
under sustained public scrutiny because religious groups confronted
feminists about their willingness to tolerate abortions and there was
no common ground.[9] Indeed, this is precisely the kind of deep-
seated and unresolvable controversy between advocates of competing absolute values that conservatives think will eventually harm the
status of the Court, if it is foolish enough to take one side or the
other. In their view, it would have been better had the competing
choices between a woman's right to choose and the right to life been
dealt with as a political conflict and not as a civil rights matter.
According to them, the liberal justices who supported Blackman's
judgment in *Roe* v. *Wade* disempowered the millions of Christians,
and others, who believe that the practice of abortion violates the
sanctity of life.

Once the Supreme Court has ruled, there is no further avenue for
redress without changing the Constitution or the composition of the
Court. Thus, the religious groups frustrated by *Roe* turned to the
political process and persuaded many voters to switch from the Democrats to Republicans in presidential elections.[10] Because Republican
candidates such as Reagan and Bush promised to appoint more conservatives to the federal benches, especially the Supreme Court, and
unabashedly supported 'family values', they were able to win-over a
significant number of voters who had previously supported the Demo-

crats. There were other reasons why the Democrat candidates have been unable to succeed in presidential elections, of course; but it cannot be denied that the political response to judicial activism may have left the United States a much more divided society than it would have become had the politicians made more of the policy choices (see my discussion in Chapter 2).[11]

Not surprisingly, conservative jurists see *Roe* as an appalling decision. Why should the people of the United States accept that the nine Supreme Court justices have any special authority to resolve a moral issue of this kind? Although the Republicans have benefited from the activism of the Court in political terms and the justices who have been recently appointed to the Court personally owe their elevation to this political backlash, conservatives believe that the political involvement of the Court is undesirable and that the nomination process has become much too politicized. Nevertheless, they understand the frustration and anger of the Christian fundamentalists, Catholics and others who oppose *Roe* v. *Wade*. Although they are by no means a majority in the country, and it is likely that more pragmatic responses to the practice of abortion would be adopted by most politicians if they had to take responsibility for enacting laws that actually impact on people's lives, the pro-life groups feel cheated by the Court. What makes their targeting of the Court and judiciary seem justified is that the reasons given by the Court in support of the *Roe* ruling do not cite any listed right in the Constitution, nor is the liberty to end a pregnancy recognized in English common law.[12] Indeed, as evidence placed before the Court makes clear, the practice of abortion has never previously enjoyed a privileged position within the traditions of the American people. Suppose the Court had ruled that the foetus enjoys a right to life, citing the Liberty Clause of the Fourteenth Amendment as a justification for overruling liberal, prochoice statutes enacted by various state governments. In this event, feminists and liberals would have been justifiably angry and unwilling to accept the outcome for it is clear that the Liberty Clause was not intended to achieve this objective. According to the conservatives, Christian fundamentalists, Catholics and other pro-life advocates have as much justification to object to *Roe* because there are no good reasons why the justices (as opposed to members elected by the people to the legislative branches) should have taken responsibility for resolving the national controversy about abortion. In terms of their view, the members of the Court enjoy no authority to resolve any moral disputes unless they are able to cite agreed sources of law (that is, the Constitution, legal precedents, uncontroversial conventions and the identifiable traditions of the American people).

Conservative Views on Privacy: The Positivist Approach

How should the Court have reasoned in *Griswold*?

Justice White provides an answer which has been endorsed by the positivists. In his view, privacy can be protected if the liberty in question falls under one of the listed constitutional rights (the Ninth Amendment does not count). Alternatively, the Court can scrutinize the motives of those who have legislated to restrict privacy to see whether the regulations they have proposed are rationally related to a legitimate purpose. For example, in the Griswold case, White finds no acceptable reason why the state of Connecticut should wish to regulate the relationships between married couples; and he holds that the reasons that the state itself provides (that the restrictions advance good health and safety) are not a convincing justification for the restraints because it is not clear how forbidding the use of contraceptives is supposed to advance the listed goals. Thus, White votes with the liberal majority to uphold *Griswold* and also joins them in the other early privacy case involving a claim to gain access to contraceptives, *Eisenstadt* v. *Baird*.[13] But his concurring opinions in both cases make very clear that he disagrees completely with Justice Douglas's reasoning in *Griswold*.

The full implications of Justice White's disagreement with liberals has become manifest in more recent privacy cases. Indeed, he is the principal author in the controversial 1986 sodomy case, *Bowers* v. *Hardwick*,[14] in which the Court ruled that there is no broad-ranging privacy liberty that protects consensual, private, unharmful relations between adults. Here, White clarifies the unwillingness of the conservative justices to make use of the Ninth Amendment. He tells us that the Court must avoid exercising any unnecessary discretion to make policy by reading the general phrases protecting rights in the Constitution narrowly. The purpose of such a restrictive reading of the Constitution's text is to ensure that most of the controversial policy issues are resolved by legislators and not by judges. In the particular case, for example, White asks us to consider whether the liberty claimed by homosexuals to engage in acts of sodomy can possibly be regarded as a practice the framers intended to protect. For White, this interest was not afforded protection in the past and could not claim to be rooted in the traditions and conscience of the American people. Certainly it is possible to argue, as Blackmun does in a dissenting opinion, that sexual intimacy is part of a general right to liberty that ought to be protected in a civilized society, but White is not prepared to read this claimed right into the Constitution. As he puts it:

> There should be ... great resistance to expanding the substantive reach
> of [the Due Process Clauses], particularly if it requires redefining the

category of rights deemed fundamental. Otherwise the judiciary necessarily takes to itself further authority to govern the country without express constitutional authority.[15]

This view requires the justices to scrutinize every disputed prohibition to see if it involves a constitutionally protected right. Only those liberties that are actually listed in the Constitution or that can be shown to reflect traditional values may be treated as protected.[16] In the particular case, of course, Hardwick could show that sexual intimacy is a basic value shared by most Americans. But White (and he is joined by Scalia, Rehnquist, O'Connor and Kennedy) will not accept this appeal to an abstract value. What he requires is a showing that the specific practice in question, that is, an act of homosexual sodomy, is listed as protected or is valued. Thus, in terms of this interpretation, Hardwick was required to show that the American people have placed significant value on protecting homosexuals if he is to secure the protection of the Court.

We can see, then, that the positivist way of dealing with the issue of what is to be accepted as a fundamental right foreshadows many future judgments in which the Court is likely to step back sharply from its earlier liberalism. *Hardwick* signals the resolve of the more conservative members of the Rehnquist Court not to achieve desirable, policy changes by means of constitutional adjudication.

Fried on Privacy

Fried is most unhappy with this development and opposes White's reasoning in *Hardwick*, which he describes as 'stunningly harsh and dismissive'.[17] What he requires is a careful analysis of Justice Douglas's reasoning in his opinion for the Court in *Griswold* (which, he explains, relies on arguments developed by Justice Harlan in his dissenting opinion in an earlier case *Poe* v. *Ullman*).[18] In his view, Douglas is correct to follow Harlan's method, interpreting the broad language of the Due Process Clause of the Fourteenth Amendment in a manner that takes the Bill of Rights, as a whole, as a guide. As Fried puts it, Harlan's reasoning takes the constitutional guarantees 'as points on a graph, which the judge joins by a line to describe a coherent and rationally compelling function'.[19] Fried claims that Harlan's deduction that privacy protection extends to include marital intimacy – securing the bedrooms of American couples from the intrusion of the criminal law – is a correct exercise of reasoning from analogy: if the sanctity of the home is given some recognition in the Bill of Rights and the autonomy of individuals is also recognized in some circumstances, marital intimacy must also be protected.

Following Harlan's strategy, Fried finds it easy to move from a principle that protects marital intimacy, as established in *Griswold*, to one that offers protection to those engaged in consensual but unconventional sexual relations in private. As he points out, Hardwick's activities were an act of private association and communication and, as such, caused no harm except to those who are offended by the mere knowledge that homosexual relations take place.

Interestingly, Fried does not include any recognition of an abstract right to reproductive freedom in this acknowledgment of a privacy right. He claims that all couples have a constitutional right to protection from intrusion when they are intimate in their homes but he does not argue that governments may not forbid the distribution of contraceptives or that they must disseminate advice about contraception. Thus, in his commentary on *Eisenstadt* v. *Baird*, he praises Justice Brennan for declining to identify a fundamental right to obtain contraceptives and criticizes him for suggesting, as he does in a subsequent case, that *Eisenstadt* demonstrates a 'constitutional protection of individual autonomy in matters of childbearing'.[20]

Dworkin and Macedo on Privacy

What further legal implications can we deduce from *Griswold*?

As we have seen Stephen Macedo argues that we can make an analogous argument about economic liberty: if we identify the Contracts and Takings Clause and the Due Process Clauses as points on a graph we must surely see that there is a general constitutional concern with economic liberty so that 'we wind up with a "Griswoldian" defence of *Lochner*'.[21] Ronald Dworkin argues that once we start delineating the profile of a right to privacy in the manner recommended by Justice Douglas in *Griswold*, we must come to acknowledge a general right to freedom of choice in matters not directly affecting other people; and he concludes that when this principle is applied to the case of abortion, we must surely see that it protects the right of a woman to choose whether or not to terminate an unwanted pregnancy in most circumstances.[22]

Fried resists both these lines of argument. Before we can decide whether the Court should expand or contract any particular right, he tells us, we must first assess the salience of the competing public interests. If these are significant so that the state can make out a compelling reason for restricting the liberty in question, and if the balance that needs to be struck is unclear or the competing considerations cannot be rationally explored using the techniques characteristic of legal reasoning (for example, if it is necessary to collect a substantial number of facts or to proceed by cautious experimentation or if the ethical issues involve more than a concern for justice),

judges should usually defer to legislators. It is a matter of professional pride. Judges should think like lawyers, resisting any temptation to find cases analogous when they present different, pressing,
issues of public policy.

In confronting Macedo's argument, Fried points out that the New
Deal changes that the Supreme Court initiated in 1937, by removing
the constitutional impediment to the federal government's role in
regulating the national economy (previously sustained for 40 years),
are based on a sound instinct for judicial deference. Thus, he tells us
that the Court should not be criticized because its reversals seem to
have been abrupt and drastic.[23] In his view, the economic circumstances of the late 1930s ensured that the Court could not continue to
ignore the fact that the economy had become interrelated and
national; thus, it had to conclude that 'old concepts the Court had
invoked to confine national regulation just could not bear the weight
that was put on them'.[24] This is because the public interest in regulation had become compelling. To insist on imposing a legal
straightjacket would have been arrogant – elevating abstract legal
reasoning above common sense. Thus, Fried approves the Court's
decision not to regard a seventeenth-century conception of economic
liberty as relevant to the circumstances of the twentieth. In his view,
the New Deal changes are an example of the Court's historical sensitivity and he claims the justices were wise to infer that enormous
changes in the economic life of the nation required them to defer to
the leadership of co-equal branches of government. The Court correctly perceived the need to abandon legal instruments that had
served their time and were merely an impediment to considered
policymaking.

With regard to abortion, in considering Dworkin's argument, Fried
argues that it is improper to treat abortion as an aspect of privacy or
to regard contraception and abortion as analogous – the former practice involves the ending of an innocent human life whereas the latter
merely prevents a life from coming into being. This is a significant
difference, according to Fried, which makes it illegitimate to include
a woman's liberty to terminate her pregnancy as an aspect of the
autonomy usually extended under privacy principles. For one thing,
those who disapprove of abortion because they think the practice
morally wrong cannot be expected to regard their concerns as trivial
– as though the taking of innocent life is the kind of practice we
should tolerate even when we disapprove of it. If large numbers of
people in a particular state believe abortion is an unjustifiable taking
of human life, the legislators cannot be expected to remain insensitive to their *compelling* concerns;[25] nor is it irrational for a secular
state to adopt the view that it has a *compelling* interest in sustaining
human life.[26] Fried illustrates his point by making a subtle distinc-

tion between circumstances in which the state chooses to place value on sustaining human life and the circumstances that could arise were the state to decide to control population growth by insisting that abortions are performed. In the former case, the Constitution is silent with regard to the competing values for the practice of abortion can be regulated without intruding into people's homes but, in the second, there are protections listed in the Constitution that prohibit the state from seizing the bodies of women to secure its goal (unless it has a compelling interest and no other reasonable alternative means is available). So, Fried argues, the issue of justice to the woman concerned and the vitality of constitutional rights would be paramount in the latter case, as it is not in the former. Even if we concede that controlling population could become a *compelling* interest in some circumstances, we must allow that there are many ways that this goal could be achieved without forcing women to undergo abortions.

Fried's case against Justice Blackmun's reasoning in *Roe* v. *Wade* rests on his claim that it is impossible for lawyers to determine the point at which the state's interest in sustaining human life should be regarded as *compelling*. In his *Roe* judgment, Justice Blackmun tells us that it is reasonable to suppose that this comes about after six months but, as Fried notes, this claim seems arbitrary. Why is it irrational (or constitutionally impermissible) for a government to suppose that potential life is of significance at the time of conception? Nor is it clear why it is constitutionally impermissible for a government to decide that a woman's choice to terminate her pregnancy should always be deferred to, yet Blackmun supposes that the state's interest in protecting the foetus becomes strong enough to force her to carry it to term once the foetus is viable outside of the womb. So long as there is nothing in the Constitution that tells us that the preservation of human life cannot be regarded as a *compelling* state interest, the *Roe* v. *Wade* ruling must be regarded as a clear case of judicial policymaking.[27] Indeed, Fried tells us that Blackmun 'gives legal reasoning a bad name' by disregarding profound disagreements over the importance of life; his fixing of an arbitrary rule to resolve the competing interests would have been perfectly acceptable had he been a legislator but it is quite impermissible for a judge to impose a rule of this kind unless this is required as a matter of law.

Professor Dworkin is unhappy with Fried's reasoning.[28] In his view, Fried's analysis of *Griswold* and *Hardwick* commits him to recognize a general right of freedom of choice in matters not directly affecting other people. This abstract principle is so powerful, according to Dworkin, that it encompasses a woman's choice to terminate her pregnancy so that Fried's reasoning, in analysing *Roe*, is in conflict with his reasoning in *Griswold* and *Hardwick*. If Fried is to meet this charge of inconsistency, Dworkin argues, he must demonstrate that abortion involves the serious harming of another person; otherwise his application of the general liberty principle is arbitrary. But, as Dworkin points out, the only harm that abortion involves is to the woman concerned or to the foetus she is carrying. Thus, Fried must show why we should recognize the foetus as a person whose rights compete with those of the mother for the purposes of constitutional analysis. Dworkin argues that this burden cannot be met in a satisfactory manner because (a) Fried accepts that the Constitution does not recognize the foetus as a person, and (b) the notion that state governments may choose to recognize new persons is indefensible.

Dworkin misstates Fried's argument. The privacy right Fried deduces from Harlan's dissenting judgment in *Roe*, which he applies in analysing *Griswold* and *Hardwick*, is very different and much narrower than the conception of privacy that Dworkin attributes to him. It rests on the acknowledgment that the Constitution establishes a presumption that people should be secure to do as they please in their homes; it certainly does not entail the baggage of a general liberty principle, as Dworkin claims. For example, we cannot deduce from Fried's narrow conception of privacy anything about an alleged constitutional right to gain access to contraception, sexual aids, pornography or prostitutes.

Dworkin notices that Fried holds the view that the *Griswold* case 'only concerned whether the police should have the power to break into bedrooms to search for contraceptives'; but he dismisses this narrow reading of the case by noting that the Supreme Court, 'in cases after *Griswold*, which Fried does not suggest were wrong, decided, for example, that the states could not forbid the sale of contraceptives in drug stores, a prohibition that could certainly have been enforced without midnight raids on marital bedrooms'.[29] Presumably, Dworkin has in mind *Eisenstadt* v. *Baird* (1972), a case in which the Court struck down a statute forbidding the distribution of contraceptives to unmarried persons. But, as we have seen, Fried argues that the constitutional value at issue in this case is equality, not privacy, and that it was dealt with under Equal Protection Clause of the Fourteenth Amendment.[30] It is clear from Fried's discussion that he certainly does not recognize any constitutional right to have access to contraception. As far as Fried is concerned, under the privacy protections that can be found in the Constitution (as opposed to one that can be deduced from some abstract principles of political philosophy), governments are free to regulate the availability of contraceptives so long as they treat people equally and the sanctity of the home is properly respected.[31] As for abortion, this is a public matter; and, according to Fried, the Constitution is neutral about abortion, as it is about contraception and prostitution.[32] If legislators conclude that public policy requires the imposition of some restraints on purveyors of contraception or on abortionists and prostitutes, whether for paternalistic or other reasons, they are free to license health clinics, brothels and pharmacists or to establish other more severe restraints of one kind or another;[33] on the other hand, they are also free to use their power to uphold a woman's right to obtain contraceptives and good advice or to help her to terminate her pregnancy if she chooses.

Concluding Remarks

In this chapter I have considered the various approaches adopted by conservatives in dealing with privacy. We have seen that there are theoretical disagreements; and that in some circumstances the conservative justices on the Supreme Court are inclined to vote in different ways. It is now time to consider the most important case in which these differences have manifested themselves, *Planned Parenthood of South East Pennsylvania* v. *Casey*.

Notes

1 The information is taken from the *Harvard Law Review* statistical summaries, presented at the end of each Supreme Court term.

2 1992 U.S. Lexis 4751; *Roe* v. *Wade* 410 U.S. 113 (1973); earlier cases in which the divisions are manifest include: *City of Akron* v. *Akron Centre of Reproductive Health, Inc.*, 462 U.S. 416 (1973); *Webster* v. *Reproductive Health Services*, 109 S. Ct., 3040 (1989).

3 This list follows Justice Douglas's opinion in *Griswold* v. *Connecticut* 381 U.S. 479 (1965).

4 *Eisenstadt* v. *Baird* 405 U.S. 438 (1972); *Carey* v. *Population Services International* 431 U.S. 678 (1977).

5 *Roe* v. *Wade* 410 U.S. 113 (1973).

6 See Laurence H. Tribe, *Abortion: the Clash of Absolutes* (NY: W.W. Norton, 1990), 16–21.

7 Most of them are prepared to accept *Griswold* but not for the same reasons. See the views articulated by Justice White in his concurring opinion 381 U.S. 507 (1965).

8 Ronald Dworkin, 'The Reagan Revolution and the Supreme Court', *New York Review of Books*, XXXVIII, 13, (1991), 23ff.

9 Indeed, *Roe* v. *Wade* was one reason why those who opposed the Equal Rights Amendment were able to mobilize opposition so effectively – religious groups resented the intrusions of the Court in the name of liberal values and mobilized supporters against the ERA so as not to empower the judiciary to make policy relating to women.

10 See Tribe, *Abortion*, 143–50.

11 See Kevin Phillips, *The Politics of Rich and Poor* (Random House, 1990); Thomas Edsall, *Chain Reaction* (NY: W.W. Norton, 1992), Peter Brown, *Minority Party* (Washington, DC: Regnery Gateway, 1991).

12   See Scalia's dissenting opinions in *Planned Parenthood of South East Pennsylvania* v. *Casey*.

13   405 U.S. 438 (1972).

14   106 S. Ct. 2841 (1986).

15   Ibid., 2846.

16   See Scalia's opinion for the Court in *Michael H.* v. *Gerald D.* 109 S. Ct. 2333 (1989).

17   Charles Fried, *Order & Law: Arguing the Reagan Revolution* (NY: Simon & Schuster, 1991), 83.

18   *Poe* v. *Ullman*, 367 U.S. 497 (1961).

19   Fried, *Order & Law*, 74.

20   Ibid., 77, quoting Brennan's judgment in *Carey* v. *Population Services, Intern.*, 431 U.S. 678, 687 (1977).

21   Stephen Macedo, 'The Right to Privacy: a Constitutional and Moral Defence', *Political Theory Newsletter* (Canberra, ACT: Australia), 193.

22   Dworkin, 'Reagan Revolution', op. cit., 24ff.

23   The cases Fried cites are *West Coast Hotel* v. *Parrish* and *NLRB* v. *Jones & Laughlin Corp.* See *Order & Law*, 68ff.

24   Id.

25   I highlight 'compelling' in this context because this is the term used to describe the burden that the state must meet when it acts in a manner that violates people's constitutional rights. It must show (a) a compelling interest, and (b) that its remedies are narrowly tailored to securing its stated purpose; and (c) no reasonable alternative means for securing its compelling interest is available.

26   As Fried points out, the controversial *Roe* v. *Wade* judgment itself acknowledges that it becomes reasonable and appropriate for the state to decide that 'another interest, that of ... potential human life, becomes significantly involved' at some point during a pregnancy. Fried, *Order & Law*, 80, citing *Roe v. Wade*, 410 U.S. 113, 159 (1973). Rights are not absolute and when there is a 'clash' of fundamental values, the state can assert a compelling reason for choosing one way or the other; in this circumstance, according to Fried, the state enjoys an authority to restrict liberty.

27   Because any state that decided to prohibit abortion could claim to meet the strict scrutiny test by showing that it has a 'compelling' interest for doing this – the protection of human life.

28   Dworkin, 'The Reagan Revolution'.

29   Ibid., 24 n. 7.

30   Fried takes trouble to note that Justice Brennan, in his opinion for the Court, had 'coyly denied going beyond *Griswold*' by ruling that discrimination against unmarried persons was a denial 'of the equal protection of the laws'. (*Order & Law*, 77).

31   Of course, these liberties may be established as constitutionally protected in other ways, for example, access to pornography may be defended under the First Amendment's protection of speech.

32   It may be possible to find legal protection for a woman to secure the termination of a pregnancy under the Fourteenth Amendment, rather than as a Ninth Amendment development based on the recognition of a privacy right. Laurence Tribe, and others, have argued that women must enjoy reproductive freedom if they are to enjoy full equality in the United States today. See Tribe, *Abortion*, 105ff. This is a more promising line of argument but it is different from the privacy defence offered in Blackmun's *Roe* v. *Wade* judgment.

33   They must establish minimal 'rationality', as Justice White requires in his opinions in *Griswold* and *Eisenstadt*; and if they discriminate between categories of individuals, their reasoning will be subjected to a very close scrutiny to ensure that

it does not reflect prejudice. Thus, Fried reads *Eisenstadt* as an uncontroversial Fourteenth Amendment case – extending equal treatment to all – and not as establishing any abstract right to reproductive freedom or privacy.

6 Disagreements Among the Conservatives: *Planned Parenthood of S.E. Pennsylvania v. Casey*

In this chapter I will explore the various conservative positions in dealing with the important abortion case *Planned Parenthood of S.E. Pennsylvania* v. *Casey*. I first consider how Scalia's 'fainthearted originalist' approach is applied in *Casey*. I shall then consider how Charles Fried applies the Harlan approach and compare this to the position actually adopted by Souter, O'Connor and Kennedy in their joint opinion.

Positivism and *Casey*

Rehnquist articulates the position of the positivists. In terms of it, the problem for the Court is to construe the phrase 'liberty' in the Fourteenth Amendment in a manner that is consistent with previous rulings but without endorsing a far-reaching privacy right. Among the liberties Rehnquist is willing to recognize as constitutionally protected are a right to choose whether to send a child to a private school, a right to teach a foreign language in a private school, a right to marry the person of one's choice, a right to procreate and a right to use contraceptives.[1] These liberties have been established in past cases and they are not controversial because they conform with the traditions and expectations of the American people. But Rehnquist wishes to distinguish these recognized privacy rights from liberties such as the right to enter surrogacy contracts, to engage in homosexual sodomy or adult incest, to abort a foetus, to commit suicide, to assist

105

someone to commit suicide, to perform naked in front of a consenting audience. In his view, these liberties should not be protected by the Court (joined by White, Thomas and Scalia) because 'the long-standing traditions of American society have permitted them to be legally proscribed'.[2] Even though these liberties are often of great importance to individuals, among their most intimate and personal choices and central to their dignity and autonomy, the Court should not offer protection. This is because the justices have not been mandated to implement the philosophy articulated by John Stuart Mill in his famous essay *On Liberty*. The reasons why this is so is that the Constitution says absolutely nothing about these particular rights.[3]

The embrace of legal positivism reflects the decision of these justices to remove the Court as far as is practical from policymaking. Of course, judges will continue to make policy as they do in every legal system,[4] but if the positivists on the Court have their way, the role of the United States Supreme Court will come to be more confined so that the discretion the justices enjoy is more like that of judges on courts in other democracies. If this happens, the public should eventually come to see the work of the justices as remote from the more pressing political issues of the day.

Rehnquist, Scalia and Thomas's problem is that they can achieve greater certainty and objectivity in the law only by reneging on the liberal agenda put in place during the Warren–Burger era. Because they confront the liberals at the doctrinal level, they will often have to overrule long-standing precedents and disappoint habitual expectations (because, in their view, the earlier cases are wrongly argued). Because of this, many of their decisions will necessarily be contentious. If Rehnquist, Scalia and Thomas are able to secure majorities on the Court for their agenda (as seems likely) the Court will also be accused of adopting reactionary positions even when it is clear that other branches at the federal level of government or the various state governments are primarily responsible for the outcome. This is because the American people have become accustomed to view the Court as having a special obligation to protect their liberties, even though they often resent its intrusions when it does so. Thus, it will take time for the other branches of government to adjust to the Court's new reluctance to continue as a co-equal policymaker. It will also take time for praise and blame to be focused towards politicians.

There is another serious problem for Rehnquist, Scalia and Thomas. They will not always want to overrule well-established precedents, even when they regard them as a legacy of the Court's past, judicial activism. There are good reasons for hesitation and caution. In the first place, the positivists share the value of certainty in law and acknowledge the importance of *stare decisis*. They accept that they must take into account the practical impact that any important change is likely to bring about. Here, the concern will be for members of the public and administrators who have conducted their affairs according to the rules established by the controversial case in question. Second, even when a precedent is the result of judicial initiatives that have no warrant in any of the acknowledged sources of law, the result may represent a wise revision of untenable arrangements that the framers had set in place. Often the changes would have been occasioned by factual considerations that the framers could not have contemplated, for example, the change from a simple agrarian economy to one as complex as it is today, the change from a union of 13 states to one encompassing 50 states and a population of approximately 249 million. In these circumstances, because the Court facilitated necessary constitutional change, which is now accepted, it may be impractical for the Court to demand a response from the political branches and, in any event, the issues in question may no longer be contentious. Finally, third, the three justices are democrats and they may hesitate to overrule earlier cases because they hope that Congress will take the primary role by initiating changes under Article V of the Constitution (outlining the means of formal amendment) or by enacting laws that would make amendment unnecessary. When this is a possibility, the justices may think it will be better for the Court to defer.

We see, then, that Rehnquist, Scalia and Thomas are not offering a mechanical jurisprudence. Judgment will have to be exercised by the members of the Court and they will often disagree about what to do even when they agree about the relevant legal doctrines. Some of their judgments will seem arbitrary and their own values will inevitably intrude. Nevertheless, it has to be said that they offer a carefully thought-out strategy for change. If their recommendations are followed, the Supreme Court will be removed from the centre of contemporary controversies (where the Warren–Burger legacy has left it) to the side-lines.

Whether this will be an improvement is difficult to say. It depends on whether, when manoeuvred into facing up to unpopular choices (by the strategies adopted by Rehnquist, Scalia and Thomas) politicians will make sensible decisions that are in the long-term interests of the country. It is, of course, absolutely unacceptable for women who seek an abortion to be forbidden or for anyone to be persecuted simply for facilitating this. (This is my own personal view and it may or may not be shared by a majority of the various state legislators elected by the American people.) It is tempting to agree with liberals that the risk of a transgression of liberties is too high to embrace democracy. Why not support the Court's liberal judgment in *Roe* and ignore the legal considerations? The conservative response that abortion cannot be recognized as a constitutional right without at the same time acknowledging that the Supreme Court justices may construe 'liberty' any way they care to is, however, cautionary. This is what *Roe* v. *Wade* represents (according to Rehnquist, Scalia and Thomas) and it is not a result that many Americans feel happy with (as is evident from the fact that they elected Reagan and Bush to reconstruct the Court). On this issue the three positivist justices may be right, it surely is up to the American people to ensure that their rights are properly facilitated. They do not need, at this stage in their history, to fall back into the habit of relying on the judiciary. In any event, a judiciary appointed by Republican presidents may not be as willing to deliver precisely what liberals would like them to. (Those who advocate that the good philosopher be King should realize that the heir to the throne may not embrace as congenial a philosophy!)

The Rehnquist–Scalia–Thomas approach in privacy cases has been severely criticized by Laurence Tribe who argues that, if taken seriously, it will undermine the Constitution's promise in the Bill of Rights. This is so, he tells us, because 'most rights for which people seek vindication in the courts are going to be, at their most specific level, new rights'; thus, the positivist methodology forces us to view all the listed liberties as having little or no application to contemporary problems.[5] In place of the restrictive approach advocated by the conservatives, Tribe argues that the Court should continue to work from abstract rights (for example, the freedom of speech and religion listed in the First Amendment) towards more specific applications (protecting the rights of Indians to practise traditional ceremonies). This kind of jurisprudence does, of course, force the Court to make difficult choices; but, Tribe tells us, this is necessary if the United States system is to remain a constitutional democracy in which the people's liberties are not vulnerable to majorities.

   Tribe's criticisms fail to address Scalia's claim that the Constitution's assumptions about natural law are flawed and reflect a legal theory that is unsuitable for use in a modern legal system. Thus, the conservatives could respond to Tribe by pointing out that he is mistaken in thinking that judicial activism is a good practice. In their view the nine justices on the Court are in no position to make considered judgments on the many policy problems that are presented in the course of adjudication, partly because their case load is so heavy and partly because they lack the special expertise required. Furthermore, they claim that the practice of judicial policymaking is undemocratic and that there are no good reasons why the Court should make choices on behalf of the people. Tribe does not address the claim that the countermajoritarian aspects of the constitutional arrangements, which he finds so congenial, rest on a flawed political theory; but in terms of the conservative view, as we have seen, the system would be better off without the extensive judicial activism characteristic of the recent past.

If extensive judicial involvement in policymaking is a bad practice, as the conservatives allege, why should contemporary jurists feel bound by general commitments made in the light of the discredited beliefs about natural rights prevalent in the eighteenth century? Why not substitute a different conception that reflects modern concerns about democratic accountability? That this is not such an outrageous proposition is illustrated by the practice in other democracies and the conservatives can also point out that the first eight amendments were attached to the Constitution as something of a final compromise – the United States political system was initially designed to work without a Bill of Rights. For the conservatives, the choice is simple: between a system that honours the rule of law and one that institutionalizes the rule of guardians.

The claim made by Tribe about the dire consequences of the new approach is more persuasive. Even at the symbolic level, the cost may be significant for the conservatives clearly intend to authoritatively deny people liberties even when these are strongly supported by liberal political theorists. Thus, it is outrageous that homosexuals are now informed that they have no entitlement to equality because their sexual liberty is not recognized as a fundamental right. Even if it were extremely unlikely that anyone will be prosecuted for engaging in sodomy, the very existence of a law forbidding individuals to pursue their relationships is insulting to homosexuals. Similarly, women are on notice that their liberty to terminate a pregnancy may be overruled and if this happens the action of the Court will be resented even if Congress and most of the states ensure that, in practice, any woman who needs an abortion will be able to secure one at no great cost. As Tribe notes, the promise of equality under the law is not going to be extended beyond the narrow confines of nineteenth century conceptions by the conservatives, so women and homosexuals will know that, institutionally, their fundamental interests are afforded less weight than those of others. This symbolic concern is significant and this is especially so in the United States where so much emphasis has been placed on the importance of fundamental rights within the political culture.

But Tribe once again overlooks the good reasons conservatives have provided for wishing to change the inflated expectations now associated with the Bill of Rights. In their view, these attitudes about the need for constitutional recognition are a relatively modern phenomenon, largely a product of the Warren Court's initiatives, and they argue that it is now time for the American people to look to other branches of government for protection. In any case, cultural expectations are diverse and some religious groups in the community deeply resent the Court's recent activism, which they regard as insulting. The abortion issue is a good illustration of this problem for it is clear that the issue cuts far more deeply in the United States than in other democracies precisely because it has been resolved virtually through judicial fiat. Part of the reason for this is the resentment on the part of 'pro-life' groups that the moral decision was removed from the political agenda. This is not to say that those who feel strongly that abortions are morally wrong would be more tolerant if the decision had been made by the Congress or by a state government; but they may be less resentful if this had been the case, and they would have difficulty showing why their minority view about the issue should prevail. As it is, advocates of the sanctity of life perspective are able to take the high moral ground by arguing that their concerns are afforded less respect than the views of those who adopt a secular approach.

Tribe's warning also involves something of an exaggeration. For one thing, most of the conservatives have told us that they have no intention of applying their judicial methodology in the completely insensitive manner he supposes, but will honour rights that have received solid support from the Court in the past or that reflect core community values; and they are also likely to make some prudent political calculations.[6] It is also evident that the Congress will try to secure framework legislation in support of civil rights. As for opposition to congressional initiatives within the Court, the conservatives are likely to split over whether to uphold legislation that seeks to secure the promise of the Ninth Amendment but the authority Congress enjoys under Section 5 of the Fourteenth Amendment (which provides that it has the 'power to enforce, by appropriate legislation, the provision of this article') has been acknowledged by some of the conservative justices.[7] Whether the Congress will actually be prepared to make good all major shortcomings in the Supreme Court's recent rulings is more questionable, but it is likely that a good number of the liberties Americans cherish will eventually be as well-secured by means of legislation as they are likely to have been by cautious justices exercising judicial review. Of course, this protection falls short of the rigorous scrutiny that would apply if the Court followed the recommendations of Tribe or if the justices exhibited his liberal sensitivity but there can never be any guarantee that this will be the case. Indeed, now that the Court is largely constituted by conservatives, the liberal call for judicial activism that Tribe makes so eloquently is, in practice, self-defeating.

The Harlan Approach and *Casey*

The joint opinion of O'Connor, Kennedy and Souter in *Casey* offers a different interpretation of the competing 'traditional conservative' orientation to the position articulated by Charles Fried that we examined in Chapter 5.

In the case, the three justices must decide whether to uphold five provisions of the Pennsylvania Abortion Control Act of 1982. The Solicitor General as Amicus Curia asked the Court to overrule *Roe* (as the United States government had done in five previous cases) and it was clear that the Court of Appeal had experienced difficulties determining the applicable constitutional principles. As a consequence, the three justices agree that it is necessary to re-examine the 'principles that define the rights of women and the legitimate authority of the state respecting the termination of pregnancies by abortion procedures'. In doing this, they reach the conclusion that it is settled law that the constitution places limits on a state's right to interfere with a person's most basic decisions about family and parenthood and argue that overruling *Roe* would be unjustifiable under *stare decisis* principles. In their view, the right that women enjoy to terminate unwanted pregnancies, protected by *Roe*, cannot be repudiated without serious inequity to the many women who now depend on their being able to control their reproductive lives; moreover, they claim, repudiation of *Roe* would expose the Court to the charge of inconsistency for Blackmun's opinion in support of *Roe* provides good reasons in support of the Court's ruling, citing principles correctly derived from the Court's earlier privacy ruling in *Griswold* v. *Connecticut*.

In reaching this decision, O'Connor, Kennedy and Souter take their orientation from the second Justice Harlan's view that:

> The full scope of the liberty guaranteed by the Due Process Clause cannot be found in or limited by the precise terms of the specific guarantees elsewhere provided in the Constitution. This liberty is not a series of isolated points picked out in terms of the taking of property; the freedom of speech, press, and religion; the right to keep and bear arms; the freedom from unreasonable searches and seizures; and so on. It is a rational continuum which, broadly speaking, includes a freedom from all substantial arbitrary impositions and purposeless restraints, ... and which also recognises, what a reasonable and sensible judgment must, that certain interests require particularly careful scrutiny of the state needs asserted to justify their abridgment.[8]

As if this quotation is insufficient to make the point, they again quote him extensively just one page later:

Due Process has not been reduced to any formula; its content cannot be determined by reference to any code. The best that can be said is that through the course of this Court's decisions it has represented the balance which our Nation, built upon postulates of respect for the liberty of the individual, has struck between that liberty and the demands of organised society. If the supplying of content to this Constitutional concept has of necessity been a rational process, it certainly has not been one where judges have felt free to roam where unguided speculation might take them. The balance of which I speak is the balance struck by this country, having regard for what history teaches are the traditions from which it developed as well as the traditions from which it broke. That tradition is a living thing. A decision of this Court which radically departs from it could not long survive, while a decision which builds on what has survived is likely to be sound. No formula could serve as a substitute, in this area, for judgment and restraint.[9]

These extensive quotations indicate the origins of the three justices' judicial philosophy and its continuity with the work of an earlier generation of justices. As they explain, Harlan's reasoning is adopted by Justice Douglas in his opinion for the Court in *Griswold* v. *Connecticut* in which he identifies privacy as a penumbral right. In their view, it also informs the law of privacy, as the implications of *Griswold* are explored by the Court in many cases, so that now it is settled law that the protected 'liberty' that citizens enjoy affords protection to personal decisions relating to marriage, procreation, contraception, family relationships, child rearing and education.

What is interesting is how (by extensively quoting Harlan) O'Connor, Souter and Kennedy distance themselves from White's reasoning in *Bowers* v. *Hardwick*. They seem to be signalling a willingness to reconsider decisions that some of them have previously joined, such as *Hardwick* and *Employment Division, Oregon Department of Human Resources* v. *Smith* (denying the constitutional right of native Americans to use the drug peyote as a part of a religious ceremony).[10]

Interestingly, as we have seen, Fried does not include any recognition of an abstract right to reproductive freedom in his acknowledgment of a privacy right. He claims that all couples have a constitutional right to protection from intrusion when they are intimate in their homes but he does not argue that governments may not forbid the distribution of contraceptives or that they must disseminate advice about contraception. Thus, in his commentary on *Eisenstadt* v. *Baird*, he praises Justice Brennan for declining to identify a fundamental right to obtain contraceptives and criticizes him for suggesting, as he does in a subsequent case, that *Eisenstadt* demonstrates a 'constitutional protection of individual autonomy in matters of childbearing'.[11]

Assessing the Use that O'Connor, Kennedy and Souter Make of the Harlan Approach in *Casey*

As we have seen, O'Connor, Souter and Kennedy seek to retreat from judicial activism but are not persuaded that a wholesale retreat from the liberal agenda is necessary. Thus, they will sometimes prefer to secure their own agenda, hoping for support from the moderate justices, such as Blackmun and Stevens. (This kind of coalition resulted in a majority in only five of the 53 close 5–4 decisions in the 1991–93 terms.)

In any event, as their disagreements with Charles Fried indicate, the jurisprudence that O'Connor, Kennedy and Souter embrace offers no certainty about future developments. Central problems, for them, must be to decide (a) what controversial precedents are binding and, (b) when they do decide to uphold a case such as *Roe*, what this commits them to in dealing with similar problems when these arise.

With regard to the first problem, they are moved by the considerations I outlined in describing the attitude of Scalia and Rehnquist to *stare decisis*. But they are much more reluctant to overrule. For example, in *Casey*, they tell us that the fact that women have been encouraged by the ability to control their reproductive lives (afforded by *Roe*) to participate more fully in the economic and social life of the nation is in itself enough to caution against overruling the decision. They also place some weight on political considerations and the implications these may have for the standing of the Court. Thus, they worry about overruling *Roe* because they fear the inevitable efforts to thwart the implementation of such a controversial decision (precisely the kind of political responses that would encourage Scalia and Rehnquist to place the issue back in the political arena!). Their preferred strategy for retreating from the past is to offer a narrow interpretation of what they accept as the holding in controversial cases. Thus, O'Connor's notion that *Roe* does not require the Court to submit the regulations impacting on abortion to 'strict scrutiny' is not regarded as a controversial overruling of precedent (even though most of the post-*Roe* abortion decisions must now be regarded as overruled, for example, *Planned Parenthood of Central Missouri* v. *Danforth, Akron* v. *Akron Center for Reproductive Health, Doe* v. *Bolton, Thornburgh* v. *American College of Obstetricians and Gynecologists*[12]). Instead of the 'strict scrutiny' requirement that was applied by the Court in these cases, the justices choose to use a more permissive 'reasonable restraint' standard, which O'Connor began to articulate in her opinion in *Webster*. (In terms of it, the Court need only inquire whether or not regulations place substantial obstacles in the way of women who seek an abortion.)

This brings us to the second problem that O'Connor, Souter and Kennedy must face. When they choose to uphold a precedent (conceding that a case was wrongly argued in the first instance), they must decide how much weight to place upon its underlying doctrines in developing the law in future cases. Here, the conservatives are on a slippery slope for while they are willing to live with some of the implications of the doctrines articulated by the Court (for example, they approve the reliance in *Roe* on rulings that prevent states from imposing unwanted sterilization or from requiring minors to undergo an abortion procedure) they may be very reluctant about others. For example, O'Connor and Kennedy both joined White's opinion in *Hardwick* but this decision is clearly inconsistent with *Casey*. Once they recognize a commitment to an abstract liberty principle, they must surely be intolerant of many violations by state governments that they had previously thought lay outside the scope of the Court's authority to resist. Their problem, in short, is that once *Roe* is accepted as good law, anything goes.

This problem is serious for the three justices go out of their way to praise Douglas's reasoning in *Griswold* and they articulate approval for abstract, general principles of political morality in thinking about abortion. Indeed, O'Connor, Souter and Kennedy are committed to recognizing a general liberty principle which, they tell us, protects:

> the most intimate and personal choices a person may make in a lifetime, choices central to personal dignity and autonomy … [implicating] the right to define one's own concept of existence, of meaning, of the universe, and of the mystery of human life.

It is difficult to reconcile *Hardwick* with this new doctrine. But many other recent judgments must also be questioned.[13] Consistency surely requires that all attempts to contain the reference to 'liberty' in the Fourteenth Amendment must now come under scrutiny. Indeed, it is difficult to see how O'Connor, Souter and Kennedy are going to hold a firm line against liberals like Dworkin who advocate further developments in the name of 'liberty'. Why not recognize a right to commit suicide? What about a right for doctors to assist those who are chronically ill to end their lives? If the justices eventually concede that the taking of drugs in a religious ceremony is a matter of intimate personal choice of fundamental importance to the individuals concerned, can they distinguish recreational uses of drugs? In all these cases, the liberty in question involves a matter of very great importance to the individuals concerned. Even the taking of recreational drugs can be asserted as a liberty of vital concern in some circumstances, for example, musicians and artists who wish to stimulate their sensibilities may be able to make out such a case. The problem O'Connor, Kennedy and Souter face, here, is that once they enter into a dialogue about rights on the terrain marked out by Professor Dworkin, their usual conservative responses are bound to seem ungenerous, even reactionary and their opinions must also seem arbitrary, in contrast to the masterly development of fundamental political principles advocated by Dworkin's fictional 'Justice Hercules' and by prominent liberal writers, such as Professor Tribe.

Nor are the problems confronting the traditional conservatives confined to the Liberty Clause. If relevant philosophical principles may be deduced from the development of case law, as O'Connor, Souter and Kennedy seem to acknowledge in *Casey*, there is no reason why the Fourteenth Amendment's protection of equality should not be developed in a similar way to the Liberty Clause. If this is so, the conservatives seem to have embraced John Rawls's *Theory of Justice* as well as John Stuart Mill's *On Liberty*, forfeiting all grounds for objecting to the precedents that were set when Justice Brennan could find a majority to support his innovative jurisprudence.

Conclusion

As I have shown, the conservatives are divided. I distinguished the two main orientations on the Court which I called 'fainthearted originalism' and 'traditional conservatism'. My purpose was to examine each of these by considering the opinions of the justices in the most recent abortion case.

It is clear that 'fainthearted originalism' as it is embraced by Rehnquist, Scalia and Thomas is very well-suited to achieving the conservative agenda. By agreeing to defer to other branches of government unless there is some unambiguous, constitutional mandate not to, these three conservatives are committed to a very different form of legal reasoning from that which liberals recommend. Although their position often forces them to adopt politically unpopular positions (as they do in *Hardwick*) the three justices have been prepared to face their critics without retreating. Nor have they been unwilling to overrule past cases when these seem to rely on abstract philosophical principles. The strengths of 'fainthearted originalism' arise out of the coherence it provides for the justices are usually able to explain precisely how they reach their decision and they cite only recognised sources of law. The orientation has the added advantage of intellectual pedigree for legal positivism is an approach that has been adopted by jurists for a very long time in Europe (mostly by those on the left of the political spectrum!).

The main problem 'fainthearted originalists' face is political. There is strong support for the powerful interest groups who wish to secure the role that the Supreme Court has played in safeguarding the rights of Americans. These lobbyists and intellectuals are often able to ensure that the work of these conservative justices is widely regarded as a form of reactionary politics. Nevertheless, the 'fainthearted originalists' have good reasons for trying to move the United States political system more towards the successful European models in which legislators must make the most important social choices; and they are likely to persist in this endeavour despite the criticism.

Those justices I have labelled 'traditional conservatives' are much more cautious and do not think it wise for the Supreme Court to adopt a confrontational stance by overruling important precedents when these have come to be accepted. To this extent, they are more sensitive than the 'fainthearted originalists' are to the charge that the conservative resolve to retreat from activism is itself a form of activism. Thus, they choose to place more weight on the rule of *stare decisis* within their deliberations. Instead of embracing legal positivism, they have sought roots in the work of the second Justice Harlan whose dissenting voice during the Warren years is widely respected.

After examining this philosophy, I reached the conclusion that it requires more careful application than is evidenced in the *Casey* opinion if it is to provide a coherent way forward for the conservatives. The problem with this opinion is that the 'traditional conservatives' do not seem to notice how much of their own position they must abandon when they embrace abstract philosophical ideals and principles. In their efforts to defend *Roe* v. *Wade* as a development from *Griswold*, O'Connor, Kennedy and Souter correctly notice that it is necessary to reach for abstract principles; but they do not see that in doing this, they necessarily enter a terrain that is dominated by philosophical speculations – precisely what the conservatives tell us they hope to avoid. This failure, in the joint opinion in *Casey*, must be compared to the approach adopted by Charles Fried who recommends the overruling of *Roe*. I have shown that Fried's reasoning is the more compelling. If the case law approach, exemplified in the second Justice Harlan's work and embraced by both Fried and the 'traditional conservatives' on the Court, is to be developed without falling back on abstract philosophical principles, it is necessary to overrule *Roe*. Fried not only offers a better interpretation of Harlan's method of legal analysis but his recommendation is much more consistent with the conservative belief that judges should try not to read their own values into the law.

The fact that some of the conservatives on the Court have embraced 'traditional conservatism' rather than 'fainthearted originalism' as their preferred orientation does not mean that we are likely to see frequent divisions among the justices. In the hands of a practitioner as skilled as Fried, 'traditional conservatism' will be likely to result in a significant retreat from the Warren–Burger legacy and, in most cases, the justices who endorse the approach will concur with the result reached by justices who embrace 'fainthearted originalism'.[14] There will be some disagreements (for example, over *Hardwick*) but there are no reasons for thinking that the 'traditional conservatives' on the Court do not themselves view *Casey* narrowly, even as a necessary aberration that has resulted more from their desire to act expediently than from the cogency of their arguments.

Notes

1   Rehnquist cites *Meyer* v. *Nebraska* 262 U.S. 390 (1923), *Pierce* v. *Society of Sisters*, 268 U.S. 510 (1925), *Loving* v. *Virginia*, 388 U.S. 1 (1967), *Skinner* v. *Oklahoma ex rel. Williamson*, 316 U.S. 535 (1942), *Griswold* v. *Connecticut*, 381 U.S. 479 (1965), *Eisenstadt* v. *Baird*, 405 U.S. 438 (1972) as precedents which should not be overruled.

2   Scalia makes this point even more forcefully than Rehnquist, 1992 U.S. Lexis 4751 (Scalia, joined by Rehnquist, White and Thomas).

3   Id.

4   See Aharon Barak, *Judicial Discretion* (New Haven, Conn.: Yale University Press, 1989) for an interesting account of why this is necessarily the case, and for suggestions about what judges should do about it.

5   Laurence H. Tribe, *Abortion the Clash of Absolutes*, (NY: W.W. Norton), 96–101.

6   The justices will respect *stare decisis* because, as White explains, '[T]he rule of *stare decisis* is essential if case-by-case judicial decision-making is to be reconciled with the principle of the rule of law...' (dissenting in *Thornburgh*, 90 L.Ed 2d, 1986 at p. 810). As for the conservatives' political prudence, my claim is more speculative. Nevertheless, they are likely to uphold politically motivated rulings such as Justice Powell's compromise formula in *Regents of California University* v. *Bakke* (438 U.S. 265, 1978) when the consequences of not doing so will involve the Court in heated political controversy.

7   *Fullilove* v. *Klutsznick* 448 U.S. 448 (1980).

8   Quoted in *Casey*, 1992, Lexis, 4751 at p. 5, citing *Poe* v. *Ullman* 367 U.S. 497 (1968) at p. 543 (Harlan, J., dissenting from dismissal on jurisdictional grounds).

9   Ibid., at p. 542.

10   110 S. Ct. 1595, 1990.

11   Charles Fried, *Order & Law: Arguing the Reagan Revolution* (NY: Simon & Schuster, 1991), 77, quoting Brennan's judgment in *Carey* v. *Population Services, Intern.*, 431 U.S. 678, 687 (1977).

12   *Danforth*, 428 U.S, 52, (1976); *Akron* 462 U.S. 416 (1983); *Bolton*, 410 U.S. 179, (1973).

13   Besides *Hardwick* and *Oregon* v. *Smith* 110 S. Ct. 1595, 1990, (the peyote case) mentioned earlier, we may have to include *Michael H.* v. *Gerald D.* 491 U.S. 110, 1989 (rejecting the asserted liberty interest of a biological father to see his child). It is interesting that Kennedy and O'Connor's criticize Scalia's methodology in his opinion for the Court in this case, although they concur with the outcome.

14   See for example, *Oregon* v. *Smith*. Fried also supports Scalia's opinion for the Court, see *Order & Law*, p. 219, n. 27.

7　Dualist Jurisprudence: Ackerman, Meiklejohn and Ely

In this chapter, I begin my review of various dualist theories that directly confront the conservative approaches I have delineated, examining the arguments of leading writers, such as John Hart Ely, Bruce Ackerman, Ronald Dworkin, Laurence Tribe and Michael Dorf. All these writers are 'liberals' (in the American sense of this term). By examining their work, I try to understand why most constitutional dualists invest so much in the achievement of judicial victories; and why they harshly judge the Rehnquist Court conservatives for preferring to place their trust in a revitalization of representative institutions. I am interested in why liberals in the United States are so outraged by the thought that justice will have to be pursued in the political arena.

Dualists try to reconcile the United States commitment to accountable government with a situation where a group of nine judges make unreviewable policy, often exercising a veto over what legislators can do. They attempt to reassure us that their orientation is not hostile to the ideals of democrats by showing why the American people ought to allow that state and federal parliaments can and, in some cases, should be frustrated by five individuals who have not been elected to office.

Ackerman's Dualism

One approach that I explore in this chapter is provided by Bruce Ackerman in an ongoing work that he calls *We the People*.[1] According to him, democracy in the United States is sustained in a few periods of heightened political participation when, as he puts it, citizens act as 'we the people'; on these occasions a process of 'higher lawmaking' occurs in which the people, acting as citizens engaged in a process of thoughtful and sustained deliberation, negotiate the terms under which their future will be shaped. These periods of engaged 'higher lawmaking' are not sustained for more than a few years so, for most of the time, most people are not lawmakers. Elites act on their behalf. Ackerman approves of this dualist conception of citizenship because he thinks the public is justified in devoting only a small part of its energies and time to politics.

An example that, by analogy, helps to make sense of Ackerman's concern is the case of a susceptible consumer who, understanding her own weakness for purchasing unnecessary items on credit, decides to destroy her credit cards. Ackerman views judicial review as serving a similar function. It provides a mechanism for upholding the more considered judgments that have been endorsed by the community through citizens when acting as 'we the people' against the ill-considered moods of the temporary coalitions that emerge after routine elections. He claims constitutional restraints serve in the same way as the missing credit card – allowing further time for reflection – by requiring the judgment of a government to be reconsidered after more careful thought and analysis on the part of the people. According to Ackerman, then, the various governments who achieve power in a democracy usually enjoy a very restricted mandate to act on behalf of the people.

Ackerman also attempts to reassure us about the role of the Supreme Court in the United States, arguing that the countermajoritarian issue is conjured up by a misunderstanding of what is actually involved in judicial review. In his view, the Supreme Court can and should serve to reinstate the considered judgments of 'we the people' against the less well-considered wishes that are expressed when the electorate selects those who are to form a government. He claims that it is a mistake to assume that the political party that wins at an election is automatically entitled to govern without restraint or to act in the name of 'we the people'. It must honour the agreements that the people have reached in the past during periods of 'higher lawmaking'.[2] Although such a party in power may make some decisions, as the temporary governing authority, it may not presume to act on behalf of 'we the people' and cannot alter constitutional arrangements as these are reflected in written texts, case law, and conventions. In his view, these constitutional devices, by placing restraints on temporary governing majorities, allow the considered judgment of the people to prevail.

Normal v. Constitutional Lawmaking

Crucial to Ackerman's case is the distinction he makes between normal politics and 'higher lawmaking'. The former is characterized by apathy, ignorance and selfishness on the part of most people; the latter by the acumen ordinary human beings display when they 'define, debate, and transform their received political tradition'.[3] Normal politics is an on-going struggle for influence in which a vast number of professional lobbyists (representing mostly wealthy interest groups) participate eagerly in the lawmaking process usually to gain private benefits for their clients – meanwhile, most citizens are so preoccupied with their private affairs that they have very little time to observe this not so edifying pageant. Indeed, a great number of them cannot even muster enough enthusiasm for public affairs to vote when elections are called; and even those who do vote usually exhibit very little comprehension of the policy positions adopted by the contending parties and candidates.

Normal politics, as Ackerman envisages it, is not very inspiring. Although a few citizens do participate actively 'organising and agitating for large projects of political renewal and redefinition', most do not.[4] But he does not worry about this. He thinks it good that most people are free to devote their energies to non-political matters, pursuing various chosen projects that do not often involve placing much value on participation in the public life of the nation. According to him, most are actually better off pursuing careers, playing golf, going on dates, making money, writing books, or entering into religious life, than they would be worrying about political affairs or trying to secure significant social change. He thinks it a wonderful feature of a constitutional democracy, of the kind that prevails in the United States, that most people do not fear the state and can give their private concerns priority in their lives. As he sees it, this opportunity is a privilege only afforded to those who live in the kind of society in which most of the really important political decisions have been reserved as constitutional matters. The United States is a society of this kind. Once the will of 'we the people' is established (embodied in clauses attached as amendments to the Constitution, recognized in case law as binding precedent, or honoured as part of traditionally recognized conventions), the American people are free to retire from involvement in politics. They can be secure in the knowledge that the Supreme Court is honour-bound to uphold their liberties and to secure fundamental values until such time as they, acting once more in the role of 'we the people', choose to engage in another period of constitutional deliberation so as to make another authoritative and binding declaration.

How does 'higher lawmaking' proceed? This is a complex undertaking that, in the United States, can involve different tracks. The Constitution itself envisages at least two in Article V that set the benchmark that other procedures must aspire to meet. First, there is the possibility of constitutional amendment if two-thirds of the state legislatures call for a convention in which delegates are authorized to consider fundamental principles and recommend changes for ratification by three-fourths of the states (this procedure has never been used); second, Congress can make recommendations by a two-thirds vote in both houses and these can then become amendments if ratified by three-fourths of the states.

Besides formal amendment, most constitutional scholars agree with Ackerman that the Constitution has been amended by the Supreme Court in its capacity as the final judicial authority. This last-mentioned procedure is, of course, controversial because it avoids the necessity of working through the processes envisaged under Article V, and constitutional change can take place even when widespread popular support has not been manifest. This kind of change is also questionable because the members of the Supreme Court seem to be unbridled by legal norms. Indeed, the broad discretion they enjoy often seems to enable them to construe the Constitution any way they deem desirable. Conservatives claim that this state of affairs encourages the justices to cheat the public by acting in a manner that betrays the vow that each of them must make to uphold the Constitution.[5] Although most other scholars concede that judicial adaptation of the Constitution takes place, they are less apologetic; but there is no agreement about how much judicial rewriting of the Constitution should go on, nor about the circumstances in which the justices are justified in redefining the terms on which the public life of the nation must be conducted.

Ackerman spends a good deal of time re-examining the informal amendment process. He is concerned to disentangle the mystery that surrounds the judicial penchant for redefining the terms of political life, and seeks to challenge conventional wisdom by offering arguments to legitimate the Supreme Court's role that go beyond an appeal to expediency. According to his dualist understanding, the justices do not necessarily act illegitimately when they amend the Constitution because, very often, their endorsement of change comes after the will of 'we the people' has already become manifest. The Constitution is not just what the nine justices say it is because they often serve as the mouthpiece of 'we the people' and, as such, can claim democratic authority. According to Ackerman it is the proper responsibility of the Supreme Court in the United States to transform proposals for change that have been endorsed during times of political renewal into constitutional form.

But Ackerman does not allow that everything that the justices seek to accomplish necessarily embodies the kind of democratic authority he recognizes. In particular, he disapproves the rewriting that has been actively pursued by the Rehnquist Court because he alleges that they have less of a mandate for this than the Warren Court enjoyed to make the changes that it accomplished. Ackerman explains that the judicial role, consolidating change, should come only after three stages in the public deliberation about fundamental reform are already complete. First, there must have been some signal that important change is under consideration (this requirement is met when a President mobilizes support for policies that would require constitutional amendment);[6] second, there must have been considerable involvement by Congress (this requirement is met if it endorses legislation that is clearly intended to support the President's constitutional plans); finally, third, there must have been a prolonged period of mobilized popular engagement in which ordinary citizens are afforded an opportunity to express their support or opposition.[7]

Difficulties with Ackerman's Account of Higher Lawmaking

The sharp contrast Ackerman draws between 'higher lawmaking' and 'normal politics' and legitimate and illegitimate constitutional amendment is not very plausible.

Consider the role he allocates to citizens. According to his characterization, we must suppose that the American people have acted as Clark-Kent-like citizens for most of the 200 year history he surveys (most are passive about politics and largely preoccupied with private matters); yet these same citizens emerge in rare periods as Superman-like citizens (public-minded, engaged and idealistic) to address complex constitutional problems with energy, acumen and integrity. Ackerman himself alerts us to an inherent problem with this account for it is difficult to reconcile both characterizations. How can the American people be both passive and active? As he notes, there are many active citizens who participate during normal times, sacrificing money and time to secure significant political goals.[8] We find, in normal times, that the people are somewhat active and somewhat passive and that different sections of the public are mobilized at different times. (For example, some Americans responded to the abortion case *Roe* v. *Wade* by participating actively in the debate that followed, but most of those who favoured a right for women to choose did not; some Americans participated actively in the protests against the Vietnam War but many Americans who supported the war remained largely passive; many Americans called for death-sentences in cases involving murder in some circumstances but many who opposed capital punishment remained passive.) Thus, we must surely question the accuracy of the active/passive stereotype. There are no good reasons for assuming that generally passive people who in normal times can barely devote enough time to read a serious newspaper are so motivated in formative moments that they com-

prehend complex and abstract issues that relate to constitutional law.
If they are passive and ignorant most of the time, why should we
suppose that this will change or did change in the periods that
Ackerman delineates as special?

Ackerman tells us that the line between normal and 'higher lawmaking' must depend on showing whether a reform movement, led
by a President, is successful in forcing its agenda to the centre of
political concern, 'to make normal politicians/statesmen treat *its* questions as *the* critical questions they *must* answer if they hope to represent the People'.[9]

There have been times in which a reform agenda has been placed
at the centre of the on-going political struggle between contending
parties in the United States, and Ackerman is correct to identify the
New Deal period after the 1936 election as one of these (the period
following the election of Reagan in 1980 was another but he refuses
to recognize this). But to satisfy the criteria he sets out for 'higher
lawmaking', Ackerman also needs to show that ordinary citizens are
actively involved in the process. He needs to demonstrate that the
attention of ordinary citizens is qualitatively different during the
times of constitutional change he identifies than during normal times
(thus, according to him, the period following 1936 was qualitatively
different from the period following 1980). To succeed in distinguishing 'higher lawmaking', he must also provide evidence that some
policy proposals are projected in such a way that they are scrutinized
more closely by the people (with as much seriousness as they usually
devote to their private concerns, for example, when buying a house
or a car). But he provides little evidence that there are greater numbers of active citizens during the periods of constitutional change
that he identifies or that citizens in these times pay closer attention to
the proposals placed before them by elites than citizens in other
periods. Nor is there evidence that a mobilized electorate is necessarily more attentive and better informed. Far from it. We know that
highly mobilized electorates during wars or depressions are often
the most gullible and pay the least attention to detail, often showing
very little concern for moral principles. In any event we find that
Ackerman provides little evidence about popular perceptions or participation. Although he claims to document authority from 'we the
people', we find that the participants in Ackerman's history are all
members of the elite (presidents, members of Congress, judges, leaders of the contending parties and interest groups). 'The people' merely
endorse initiatives made by the elites at elections. But this is what
happens in normal times as well. Thus, his distinction between normal participation and periods of heightened active involvement in
political life by citizens is spurious – to establish his case he exaggerates the political passivity of the people in normal times and

mischaracterizes the nature of their involvement in the so-called engaged periods.

Ackerman's treatment of the contrast between the Roosevelt and Reagan periods illustrates some of these problems. He tells us that the process of interbranch struggle and popular mobilization made the election of Roosevelt in 1936 decisive because the New Dealers could plausibly claim a massive mandate from the people. Because all three branches of government finally co-operated with President Roosevelt, Ackerman tells us his 'higher lawmaking' initiative proved triumphant; the only task that remained was for the Supreme Court to synthesize the changes agreed to by 'we the people' in a coherent re-reading of the Constitution. Ackerman obviously approves the changes that the Roosevelt coalition succeeded in securing. His problem is that other presidents will also claim mandates, sometimes for imposing changes that he thoroughly disapproves of. The Reagan victory in 1980 and the subsequent legislative success that followed in his first term is a case in point. Supporters of Reagan's agenda can claim that his electoral success represented a substantial mandate, lifting his initiative to the level of 'higher lawmaking', because the policy changes that he proposed were endorsed by Bush in 1988 when he secured an overwhelming victory (giving the Reagan agenda for change three successive presidential victories in which the Republicans secured popular majorities in more than 30 of the 50 states). More significantly perhaps, when President Clinton ran in 1992, he did not confront the Reagan issues (quotas, crime, religious values, patriotism and taxes[10]), preferring to focus exclusively on the state of the economy.

One unambiguous element of the Reagan agenda was the displeasure he signalled about the role of the Supreme Court and the federal judiciary generally in the period following the appointment of Earl Warren as Chief Justice. Reagan (like Nixon who also secured a massive endorsement partly by running against the Warren Court, in 1972) addressed this issue by indicating that he would appoint justices who would adopt a much more disciplined approach. He made very clear that he wanted to allow the more accountable branches of government a greater freedom to set public standards and to pursue policies endorsed by the people. Not all of Reagan's agenda required the securing of constitutional changes of this kind. But he was largely successful in getting this specific change secured.

Ackerman will not allow that Reagan initiated a successful process of 'higher lawmaking' in transforming the role of the Supreme Court and in limiting the reach of the Bill of Rights, but he is surely required to do this by the nature of his argument. If landslide victories of both Nixon and Reagan did not secure a proper mandate for this one aspect of Reagan's agenda (that is, his promise to transform the

Supreme Court), it is difficult to see how Ackerman can plausibly claim that the Warren Court justices could call on the democratic authority that Roosevelt enjoyed.

Ackerman explains why he thinks that Reagan failed to obtain a proper endorsement from 'we the people' but his argument is unconvincing. First, he cites Reagan's failure to secure the appointment of Judge Robert Bork to the Supreme Court as a serious rejection of his agenda by Congress.[11] But this event was merely a minor setback that resulted partly from the weakening of the President's popularity following the exposure of the Iran–Contra issues, and partly from the fact that Bork presented as an extremist who also seemed arrogant about his abilities and values. (Reagan the populist had enormous difficulty selling an unashamed elitist and Bork's television profile was appalling.) At the most, the rejection of Bork may conceivably be read as calling into question those who would advance an uncompromising adherence to originalism as the correct way of interpreting the Constitution (for example, overruling *Brown* and *Griswold*). But as we have seen not even Bork believes that the Court should always uphold the framers' intentions, regardless of the consequences. Ackerman also seems to want to have things both ways by claiming that the rejection of Bork should count as a refutation of Reagan's mandate and that Reagan's success in securing the confirmation of all his other very conservative appointees should not count as an endorsement of his view that judges should be more deferential to the wishes of the people.[12] (But O'Connor and Kennedy are very supportive of the Reagan agenda, yet they do not embrace originalism.) Ackerman also questions whether Bush's victory in 1988 should be counted as a confirmation of the popular support for Reagan's agenda.[13] He claims that George Bush and Michael Dukakis were moderate candidates who recommended no new constitutional principles; in his view, 'both were intelligent and decent men who promised competence and prudent adjustment of preexisting values (though Bush would make his trade-offs in a somewhat more "conservative" way than would Dukakis)'.[14] But this account is completely misleading about the issues that motivated the electorate in 1988.[15] Does Ackerman not remember the Willie Houghton advertisement or Dukakis's fumbling attempts to explain why his association with the American Civil Liberties Union should not be held against him. Why did Bush change his stand on abortion and tell everyone that he was going to appoint conservative judges? Bush said that the campaign would be about ideology and values, not about competence; Dukakis said that the campaign should be about competence. But the Republicans set the agenda and this is why Bush won. Of course, it is true that the 'preppy' George Bush was an unlikely person to lead a populist movement and Ackerman is correct to note that he was uncomfortable in the role – the fact that he could not sustain his part convincingly is one of the reasons why he ran so badly in 1992. But Ackerman's reading of the 1988 election is hardly persuasive.

The Role of Supreme Court Justices

Now consider the role attributed by Ackerman to Supreme Court justices in 'higher lawmaking'. Although ill-equipped as historians, the justices must agree on an appraisal of the past because, as he sees it, they are morally and legally bound to uphold the intentions of 'we the people'. According to Ackerman, the constitutional crises that arise in periods of heightened turmoil, when large numbers of people participate in 'higher lawmaking', are ultimately resolved when the Supreme Court justices reach agreement to recognize new legal norms, forging a synthesis between the past and the present.[16]

A first problem we must face in assessing Ackerman's account is that there is an extraordinary lack of consensus among Supreme Court justices in the United States. They seem to be incapable of securing any consensus among themselves about the sources of law and many younger members of the legal profession have now reached the cynical conclusion that what counts as 'law' in the United States is simply what can gain the vote of five justices who are free to make their own values decisive. The Warren–Burger Court was highly politicized and this legacy continues through to the present. Not surprisingly, many judgments are supported by the narrowest of margins with the justices dividing along political lines. It is simply a fiction to suppose that a successful synthesis informing the work of the Warren–Burger period has ever been forged. Although intellectuals such as Ronald Dworkin and Laurence Tribe have provided coherent theories which have influenced particular members of the Court, it is extraordinary that the United States political system has been able to function even though its most senior judges disagree about how to recognize what constitutes law in the system.[17] Luckily, subordinate courts usually agree that what the Supreme Court says is *the law* and must prevail[18] – even so, judges often have great difficulty determining what they are supposed to do in many cases.

Ackerman seems to suppose that there is some kind of norm that informs the work of the Supreme Court in normal times. But his own analysis demonstrates the problem for he has difficulty persuading us that his understanding of what 'we the people' have said on matters of fundamental importance is compelled by the historical evidence; and he also has difficulty explaining what 'we the people' intend to accomplish through the various agreements he identifies. Here, the most controversial issue is how Ackerman understands the mandate that he claims the Supreme Court now enjoys – thanks to Roosevelt and Reconstruction – to expand the meaning of the Bill of Rights. He wishes to argue that the Supreme Court is entitled to recognize unenumerated liberties and privileges even though there is no evidence that 'we the people' ever considered these issues carefully; nor does there seem to have been a time (apart from 1980 when Reagan suggested the need for reversing what he took to be the mess that unbridled activism has made of the United States system) when the American people actually considered the role allocated by Ackerman (and other liberal dualists) to the nine Supreme Court justices in the modern period. Most of the specific rulings of the Supreme Court on civil rights are highly contentious and have been systematically rejected by the American people whenever they are asked relevant questions by pollsters. The American people have also shown their opinions by their sustained support for conservative candidates (both Democrat and Republican). Thus, it is difficult to see how Ackerman can support his case that the Warren–Burger justices have been acting in the name of 'we the people'.

At this point we confront a difficulty that arises in all theories that make use of history – the problem of certainty. Ackerman does not require 'we the people' to speak with precision or even to list its commands. On his understanding of a constitutional amendment, certainty about what is intended takes time to achieve and, for him, it is the justices of the Supreme Court who are responsible for providing definitive answers. They determine what 'we the people' intend when they have acted in ways that are alleged to have altered the Constitution. It is the justices, not the people, who must learn to articulate and apply the new rules for recognizing what is to count as the law of the land. Yet it is the people and not the justices who are supposed to enjoy authority!

Finally, it is worth noting that it is one thing to articulate a constitutional theory to justify the judicial review exercised by the Warren Court, quite another to show that actual members of the Court have been informed by it. Ackerman needs to show that his account of constitutional history throws new light on what the Warren–Burger Court justices were in fact doing. But we find that Ackerman cannot show that the justices, or even the community of scholars that reviews the work of the judiciary, have been influenced by his dualist account – or anything like it. Although many judges claim that they enjoy an authority to discover unenumerated liberties that are implied and that the Constitution's meaning evolves, no practitioner can be found who has openly declared that 'we the people' may alter the Constitution in the manner that Ackerman describes. Most liberal constitutional theories explicitly acknowledge that their approach is countermajoritarian and most would not pursue the kind of historical analysis that Ackerman thinks essential. Nor do conservatives. Modern Supreme Court justices, for example, do not worry whether Roosevelt or Reagan enjoyed a mandate to change the Constitution through appointments or in other ways. For example, when Souter, O'Connor and Kennedy decided to uphold *Roe v. Wade* they do not launch into an historical exploration of the Reagan–Bush electoral mandate. 'Did he appoint us to do this?' is not a question they think it proper to ask; rather, they pretend to be relying on legal arguments based on a commitment to the doctrine of *stare decisis*, and they deny that they are responding to the political agenda of a popular leader who may or may not have mobilized enough of the people on the issue of abortion to claim a mandate.[19] Of course, Ackerman's concern about democratic accountability may have served as a background assumption that may have helped some members of the judiciary to accommodate changes, but reference to 'we the people' does not feature as part of the official explanations that judges have provided to legitimate their decisions.

Assessing Ackerman's Political and Constitutional Theory

More troubling than his historical problems is Ackerman's complacency about the alleged passivity of citizens during normal times, which relates to the way that he characterizes and evaluates normal politics. He envisages the American political system as caught up in a kind of perpetual gridlock in which competition between elites ensures that each faction is blocked from doing much good or harm. In normal times no group seeking a mandate is able to project its agenda as *the* fundamental issue that the nation must face up to, so the electorate is necessarily confused by numerous conflicting concerns. This allows only moderate changes to occur and it is not surprising that most of the people find politics boring.

Let us concede that most people in the United States, for most of the time, have little idea of what matters of importance are being discussed in Congress or how they would like them to be resolved, and that presidential elections are confusing because the contestants resort to sound-bites, misleading promises and negative advertising. Even so, we cannot help noticing that a great deal is at stake during normal times. But Ackerman ignores this. Indeed, he seems to view politics through the confining lenses of a constitutional scholar, failing to see why, as a professed democrat, he should be as concerned when the people delegate responsibility for resolving issues such as those relating to poverty, to welfare and to the management of the economy as he is when elites make constitutional choices on their behalf. Another matter of normal politics that citizens in the United States cannot afford to ignore is the international role that their society plays. Once again, we find that Ackerman's complacency about citizen apathy in normal times is a problem. Surely he is unhappy to leave important concerns relating to matters such as world order, the environment, and peace, to a group of elites who are largely unaccountable to the people.

Ackerman's dualist account is also questionable as a constitutional theory because it is a species of originalism.[20] It matters to Ackerman that, as he believes, the American people have spoken on issues of constitutional importance. However, Ackerman's commitment to originalism differs from that of conservatives who, as we have seen, are interested in securing an objective source for constitutional law so that certainty can be achieved and the subjective judgments of the various individuals appointed to the Supreme Court are not determining. Conservative constitutional theorists want to remove judges from involvement in the political processes of the nation and they do this by declaring that judges should be bound by clear rules agreed to in the past (the plain meaning of the words used, read in the light of the established intentions of the framers should prevail). They do not claim that the determining norms are good or just, simply that there is no other objective source for law. In contrast, Ackerman is far less concerned about certainty as a legal ideal and has no intention of removing judges from the political process. His primary consideration arises as an issue of political philosophy – he wants to dissolve the countermajoritarian issue by showing that judicial lawmaking reflects the considered wishes of 'we the people'.

A problem that he faces (which the conservatives do not) is why anyone should think that past judgments by 'we the people' should be binding on present generations. Why should we consider ourselves obligated? Ackerman takes his stand as a democrat arguing that we are bound because 'higher lawmaking' reflects the will of past generations who have addressed issues on our behalf. But even if this were true (and it is not in the United States) it is unconvincing as a proposition of political philosophy. There is no reason why, for example, President Clinton should feel bound to honour the achievements of the Reagan period. He embraces a different agenda and enjoys a different mandate and his lawmaking must be accredited with as much credibility as that of other presidents. Ackerman's attempt to privilege Roosevelt's legacy and to persuade us that the Warren–Burger Court was securing the 'higher lawmaking' of 'we the people' must be rejected.

Moderate Dualism: Meiklejohn and Ely

Before concluding this chapter, it will be useful to look at some less ambitious (more successful) attempts at finding a reconciliation between the practice of judicial review and the American commitment to democracy.

One problem with the practice of judicial review, as we have seen, is that it seems to be undemocratic. Why should judges be able to overrule the considered policy choices of democratically elected governments? Legislators are accountable and can claim to represent sections of the electorate, but judges are not. One answer to the 'countermajoritarian issue' relating to judicial review is that it may sometimes be necessary for judges to facilitate fair elections. If a government uses its authority to try and avoid accountability, judges may need to act as umpires of the democratic system to prevent this. The term 'representation-reinforcing review' refers to this line of argument. Some theorists claim that the Constitution sets out fair rules for representative government – it establishes how choices about competing substantive values may be made democratically. In terms of this reading, the Constitution aims to ensure that there is an open and informed discussion of political issues and that those who act on behalf of the American people are genuinely representative. Thus, when judges act in the name of the Constitution, according to this reading, they cannot be accused of violating democratic values.

One writer who has used the representation-reinforcing rationale in an interesting way is Alexander Meiklejohn. In his essay *Free Speech and its Relations to Self-government*, Meiklejohn claims that the First Amendment to the Constitution should be read as a protection for all communications that contribute to rational deliberation on matters of public policy; but other categories of expression are not necessarily protected. This limited view of the First Amendment reflects the Schumpeterian conception of democracy (as competition for the right to govern between rival elites[21]) which many American theorists in the 1950s and 1960s embraced.

But this conception of the meaning of the free speech protection in the United States Constitution has never been accepted. The First Amendment has always been read as reflecting broader concerns about the importance of freedom in discovering truth or in encouraging artistic expression. Moreover, emotional appeals are far more important in conveying messages than Meiklejohn allows – indeed, the ability to amuse, shock or horrify may be more necessary in conveying a political message than its cognitive content.

Nevertheless, Meiklejohn's analysis has sometimes provided guidance when difficult choices have had to be made (for example, in delineating the power of governments to regulate commercial speech, libellous speech, offensive speech, and obscene speech). In this regard, the Supreme Court has found Meiklejohn's identification of a primary function of the First Amendment (to keep the government from legislating to secure itself in office or to silence critics of its policy agenda) useful. Indeed, many of the Court's doctrines assume a balancing process in which various categories of speech are ranked according to how they contribute, in a reasoned way, to the public discussion of political issues – the less cognitive the mode of communication, the lower the ranking; the less relevance to the subject of politics, the lower the ranking. Thus, when words are of the kind which are of 'such slight social value as a step to truth that any benefit that may be derived from them is clearly outweighed by the social interest in order and morality' the Supreme Court has tended to defer to legislators, recognizing traditional limitations on freedom.[22] But the justices do not defer to legislators when the harm in question arises because of the particular message being conveyed; in these circumstances, the Court has recognized that the 'hazards of political distortion and judicial acquiescence are at their peak'.[23]

Another influential theorist who has used the representation-reinforcing rationale is John Hart Ely. Ely's objective is to provide a convincing defence of the work of the Warren Court by describing its role as analogous to that of a referee. In his view, the justices have not often imposed their personal values, nor have they attempted to act as surrogate representatives who are authorized to identify the fundamental values of the people, displacing state governments. Rather, the Supreme Court under Chief Justice Earl Warren's leadership, took responsibility for detecting malfunctioning of the system of representation that occurs, according to Ely, when

> (1) the ins are choking off the channels of political change to ensure that they will stay in and the outs will stay out, or (2) though no one is actually denied a voice or a vote, representatives beholden to an effective majority are systematically disadvantaging some minority out of simple hostility or a prejudiced refusal to recognise commonalities of interest, and thereby denying that minority the protection afforded other groups by a representative system.[24]

This judicial role is justified, Ely tells us, for the judiciary needs to 'clear the channels of political change', and it must also scrutinise statutes to ensure that those who are unable to use the political process are not subjected to disproportionate burdens or excluded from benefits. In terms of Ely's understanding of the representation-reinforcing rationale, then, the judiciary has a duty to protect the politically weak when they are ignored, isolated or oppressed by governments.[25]

Dualist Jurisprudence 133

Ely's dualism must be deemed moderate because one of his reasons for articulating the representation-reinforcing rationale is to limit judicial discretion. In his view, judges are equipped by their training to make judgments about procedures – keeping the players to fair rules – but they are not better than others as policymakers. Thus, he seeks to articulate a theory of judicial review that is concerned primarily with policing the policymaking processes. Far from wishing to empower unelected judges to make policy, he concedes that judicial review presents a serious difficulty precisely because 'a body that is not elected or otherwise politically responsible in any significant way is telling the people's elected representatives that they cannot govern as they'd like'.[26] In his view, judges have no authority to overrule just because they dislike what the legislators have done.[27] If they exercise review, according to Ely, they should be able to show that this is necessary to preserve the competitive processes that make it possible for the elected representatives to claim their authority to govern in the name of the people.

The conception of democracy that seems to inform Ely's view is also derived from Schumpeter (in that he envisages competition between rival elites for the right to govern) but he offers a slightly more egalitarian vision than Meiklejohn. For example, he thinks it important that all votes be counted equally and that sections of the community are not excluded from the ballot. As his analysis demonstrates, even a narrowly conceived Schumpeterian democracy is not easy to realize or sustain. If the public are unable to distinguish lies or gross exaggerations, if sections of the population who would support one group of elites are excluded from the ballot, if electoral districts are drawn unequally so that competition is unfair, if communications are monopolized or some speakers enjoy an overwhelming advantage in conveying their messages, the point of holding elections may be undermined.

A problem for those who make use of the representation-reinforcing rationale is that there is no clear indication of what the framers had in mind when they made their commitment to democracy and a considerable amount of unfairness was built into the system that they endorsed (for example, the states were entitled to draw electoral boundaries as well as to supervize any elections that were to be held; seats in the Senate were allocated in a manner deliberately designed to favour states with smaller populations; the President was elected indirectly; large numbers of people were excluded from the ballot). It would be totally unacceptable for the Supreme Court to declare today that all these arrangements are now anomalous and may be changed without formal amendment under Article V (for example, that California should be allocated two more Senate seats); yet the Court has successfully restricted the right of the states to draw their district boundaries in a manner that favours rural voters and it closely supervizes elections to prevent discrimination that adversely affects minorities.

When we look beyond numbers and procedural arrangements we must acknowledge that many inequalities affecting the ability that citizens enjoy to influence public affairs prevail, making the system of democracy in the United States inherently unfair. Wealth is easily translated into political power and those who are well educated, articulate or famous also have special advantages. More significant, those who can gain access to the media have an overwhelming advantage. Yet it would be anomalous for the Supreme Court to rule that Jane Fonda, Barbra Streisand and Arnold Schwarzenegger are each forbidden to use the public figure status each has acquired as an entertainer to assist their favoured political candidates, or to stand for office themselves. It would also be anomalous for the Court to start supervizing television in the name of fairness to ensure that everyone has a fair chance to influence the electorate. Yet it has ruled that public corporations and unions may not engage in political speech because this makes unfair use of resources that citizens have allowed them to acquire for other reasons. More significant, gender differences are important in determining social roles, partly because of discrimination, and this has meant that less women than men are elected to public office. Should the Supreme Court now declare this inequality anomalous and require that 50 per cent of Senate seats be allocated to women?

Ely denies that this kind of judicial activism is proper because, on his conception of the representation-reinforcing role, the Court is only entitled to secure fair procedures. It enjoys no mandate to secure substantive justice. But it is difficult to see how the representation-reinforcing rationale can be contained in this way. Thus, a question we must ask of Ely and others who think that the rationale can be used to constrain the role of a constitutional court is how they decide on the appropriate conception of democracy that the court is required to facilitate. Why not ask judges to secure full political equality so that each individual has a fair chance to influence the outcome of elections? Why not require judges to review elections to see whether politicians have misled the people? It would seem that there is no non-arbitrary normative response that can be given to this line of questioning.

This said, it must be allowed that the representation-reinforcing rationale offers the most coherent reconciliation between dualist and monist approaches that is available. Moreover, a constitutional court can choose to confine itself to recognizing only those facilitating liberties that have been afforded in a society's past. To the extent that a conception of democracy is genuinely discernible as traditionally accepted within a community, a constitutional court is surely justified in upholding it against those who are trying to cheat their way back to office. This is why there is some justification, even without the listing of rights in a charter, for a constitutional court to recognize protection for political speakers and a right to freedom of association. The representation-reinforcing rationale becomes less acceptable when controversial judgments are made (for example that genuine democracy requires that all citizens enjoy an effective and equal school education or that women are entitled to funded child-care). These judgments would be controversial precisely because it cannot usually be shown that fully-funded schooling or childcare had been traditionally recognized as a requirement for fair participation in a particular democracy.

The Issue of Illegitimate Discrimination

Ely's claim that a constitutional court must protect groups when they are disadvantaged politically because of prejudice that makes it difficult for members of the group to combine with others in the pursuit of common interests is also one that needs to be interpreted very narrowly. He clearly has in mind the landmark civil rights case *Brown* v. *Board of Education* in presenting this argument. He wishes to show that the Supreme Court was justified in ruling that school authorities must desegregate southern schools with 'all deliberate speed' even though the framers of the Fourteenth Amendment had never intended to question the widespread practice of segregation that prevailed in many parts of the world at that time.[28] The *Brown* ruling was also in conflict with *Plessy* v. *Ferguson*, a longstanding precedent, and this raises the question of whether it was proper for the Court to reverse itself when Congress had not taken any action to signal its resolve to see this done.

Ely's analysis offers an easy way around these problems. The justices did not defer to southern legislators or to Congress in *Brown* v. *Board of Education* because they knew that the southern whites were deeply prejudiced against the descendants of former slaves; and they also knew that the southern block of representatives and senators held strategic positions in the relevant committees in Congress. As Ely claims, the Warren Court's decision in *Brown* seems reasonable to us today because it is clearly intended to protect a group that had little capacity to make use of the representative system. So long as white southerners monopolized all political power in their region, Congress was unlikely to protect African Americans.

Ely's line of argument does serve to provide a reasonable rationale for the initiative taken by the Warren Court in *Brown*, but it is difficult to apply in many other circumstances. As Ely points out, almost every group that loses in political life can be regarded as a 'discrete and insular minority'.[29] Consider the conflict between those who ask for more funding for AIDS research and other programmes to combat the spread of the disease and those who ask that more be provided to help combat breast cancer. If substantially more funding is provided to research AIDS, groups representing women may claim that they have been discriminated against unfavourably as a 'minority' (they lost in getting funding for their cause) and they may also claim that they are 'insular' (unable to secure the political momentum to defeat the discriminatory allocation of medical research funds); on the other hand, if the priorities are reversed and most of the funding goes to combat cancer, it will be the gay groups that will complain that they represent an 'insular' community that is unable to ensure that it does not suffer discrimination. Other groups may also regard themselves as disadvantaged politically. What of those whose disease is so badly understood that there is little public sympathy for their plight, for example, the intellectually disabled and the mentally ill? Nor do these cases exhaust the groups who are likely to emerge to ask the Court to defend them from government prejudice and oversight. (Consider the government initiatives to help farmers who suffer from a natural catastrophe, such as floods, in comparison to the unemployed who are offered only token assistance; or consumers who argue that governments ignore their interests to favour manufacturers and those who market their products. Are consumers a 'discrete and insular minority'?)

Ely argues that we should see whether a government targets its programmes in illegitimate ways and provides us with a number of tests for reaching this conclusion. We should be cautious when a legislative majority (a) is motivated by callousness towards the interest of a particular group (indicated by the fact that the group in question is the 'object of widespread vilification');[30] (b) relies on generalizations 'whose incidence of counter-example is significantly higher than the legislative authority appears to have thought it was';[31] (c) sets out different rules (usually through prejudicial administration) for others than it does for itself.[32]

But this narrowing of the reasons that may lead to political vulnerability seems arbitrary. What matters, after all, are prejudicial outcomes that impact in a serious way on a vulnerable group. It does not seem to matter what motivates the legislators who allow this to happen or bring it about.

Consider a recent controversy relating to the closure of a secondary college in Melbourne (Australia). In this case, a feminist lobby group in the State of Victoria's education department demanded the opening of an academically orientated high school reserved for girls. The idea that motivated this initiative was the desire to encourage

more girls to pursue scientific careers. Steps were taken by the government to establish a suitable school with the necessary computers,
science laboratories and skilled teachers. (What we are talking about,
here, is an enormous subsidy to middle-class parents.) To get the
resources for the school in a time of budgetary constraint, the government closed a co-educational school that was serving a poor community. The girls from this school were able to apply for enrolment
to the new school but the disadvantaged boys, whose school was
now closed, were relocated to more distant schools. It is hard to say
whether these boys are a politically vulnerable minority, according to
Ely's criteria. No false stereotypes were used in making the policy
decision to close their school and none of the education department
bureaucrats who advocated the change was maliciously motivated
or prejudiced. They simply cared about affirmative action for girls.

It is difficult to see how Ely can allow us to ignore this kind of
discrimination. Yet he must do so if he is to ensure that courts,
relying on his theory, are not going to displace legislators.

Similar examples could be taken from recent experiences in the
United States. For example, in most universities unaccountable older
male bureaucrats go along with feminists in seeking to secure the
advancement of women in academic careers. Their sentiments in
seeking out qualified women for appointments and promotions are
admirable but, when women are advanced affirmatively, younger
males are inevitably discriminated against. Nor are the younger men
able to defend themselves through the representative process. Is this
a case of 'benign' discrimination as Ely claims (because the older
males must be presumed to have no prejudice against the advancement of younger men) or are the younger men vulnerable as an
'insular minority' in a competitive profession? The fact that young
women now have an influential lobby working for their advancement in many organizations, whereas young men do not, does not
seem to bother Ely.

No doubt Ely has good responses to these kinds of questions. He
has certainly provided the best account that there is of the 'suspect
category' doctrine. But his line of argument is vulnerable for other
reasons and these are also of significance.

Historical Relevance

First, there is the question of whether the representation-reinforcing
rationale on which he relies was actually intended by the framers.
There is no evidence that it was and a lot of evidence that shows that
the framers were not very egalitarian in their approach to democracy
(thinking it quite appropriate to exclude large numbers of citizens
from the franchise and to rely on very indirect and unfair procedure

for electing the President and the Senate). Even conceding Ely's point that the framers' original intentions are not the only significant guide as to how to read the Constitution, and that subsequent amendments added to the Constitution that extend the franchise to women and to previously excluded minorities, as well as conventions that make presidential contests fairer that are now honoured, do establish a national concern for political equality as a fundamental value in the United States, we may still ask whether this concern for representational fairness actually informed the work of the Warren Court.

Ely can claim that if the representation-reinforcing rationale was not acknowledged by the Warren Court justices, it should have been; but he must concede a great deal to opponents in allowing this, for when we work through past decisions we find that many of the justices rely on quite different considerations and their rulings cannot easily be accommodated by Ely. Ely concedes, for example, that *Roe* v. *Wade* cannot be defended. But other cases that liberals might like to defend are also vulnerable, such as most of those that relate to law and order and many that impact on freedom of speech (for example, *Miami Herald Publishing Co.* v. *Tornillo*[33] and all those cases dealing with forms of communication that are not relevant in assessing rival political claims, such as *Stanley* v. *Georgia* and *Miller* v. *California*[34]). More significantly, Ely must often stretch his line of argument to breaking point to get the results he desires.

The Death Penalty Controversy: Eighth Amendment Jurisprudence

Consider the 1972 capital punishment case *Furman* v. *Georgia* that Ely discusses at some length. Here, the Court is forced to address the issue of whether capital punishment is unconstitutional, and because he strongly supports the outcome in the case, Ely is concerned to show that it can be reached using the representation-reinforcing rationale.

For many, the issue of capital punishment is of enormous symbolic importance because it goes to the heart of how citizens in the United States view their society. Should it take its place as a leader among civilized nations or will it remain a pariah, as one of the very few democracies that still asks its officials to perform a barbaric act. Apart from the nation's standing in the world, civilized people must oppose the use of death sentences as a form of retribution or as deterrence – the practice is reprehensible and should not be tolerated because it serves no significant purpose. The constitutional issue posed by the practice of capital punishment in the United States is whether the various state governments are entitled to demand the termination of a human life as retribution for a crime. Surely we can agree that it is unthinkable that a civilized community should do this? But it would seem that the states have a legal right to set sentences so long as they do not violate the Eighth Amendment that prohibits the imposition of 'cruel and unusual' punishments. A problem is, of course, that death sentences have not been unusual in the United States and it is controversial whether they should be regarded as 'cruel' in the required constitutional sense.

In their opinions supporting the ruling in *Furman*, Justices Brennan and Marshall see the death penalty as a form of barbarism that needs to be forbidden even when every procedural protection has been afforded. This is why they are prepared to accept that capital punishment is a violation of the Eighth Amendment. But they were unable to persuade five members of the Supreme Court to accept this view.

Ely is sensitive to the countermajoritarian tenor of the Brennan–Marshall line of argument. Large numbers of people in the United States are not liberals and they think it appropriate for the state to demand a life as retribution when a murder has been committed in aggravating circumstances. Thus, many state governments have imposed death sentences as a last resort in dealing with the most heinous crimes. In the light of this evidence, Ely thinks that it is inappropriate for Brennan and Marshall to appeal to community standards – their judgements do not reflect the sentiments that are actually manifest in the community and, in his view, they have no mandate to speak for the people. Instead of appealing to community standards, Ely recommends that the practice of capital punishment be prohibited on procedural grounds. As he explains, it is virtually impossible to ensure that prejudice does not influence the exercise of discretion when the highest penalty is at stake. Even if mandatory death sentences are imposed for certain categories of killing, juries and prosecutors will inevitably find ways of not imposing the sentence in many circumstances – for example, by refusing to lay the appropriate charge or by refusing to convict individuals who face the death penalty. Thus, according to Ely, the imposition of the death sentence will necessarily fall most heavily on individuals who are from sections of the community that are regarded as deviant or whose personality or looks set them apart. This is why he argues that a representation-reinforcing constitutional court would be justified in forbidding it. Capital punishment in practice is constitutionally suspect, according to him, because it involves a circumstance where we (those who enjoy political influence) impose outcomes on others (those groups in the community whose members are sentenced to death) that we are not prepared to impose on people like us.

It is for this reason that Ely approves the outcome in *Furman* v. *Georgia*. As he shows, a plurality of the Court in this case (Justices Douglas, Stewart and White) came close to accepting his view that, in a criminal justice system that is constructed so that 'people like us run no realistic risk of punishment, some nonpolitical check on excessive severity is needed'.[35] Unfortunately, *Furman* did not stand for this proposition for the same plurality of the Court held that capital sentences may be imposed so long as juries are appropriately guided and all reasonable efforts are made to avoid arbitrariness in sentencing. Thus, the procedural argument relating to fairness, offered in *Furman*, provided nothing more than a very temporary safeguard.

Of course Ely complains about this. According to him:

> Death being the ultimate and irreversible penalty, one can at least strongly argue that a 'prophylactic equal protection' holding that capital punishment violates the Eighth Amendment is appropriate. It is so cruel we know its imposition will be unusual.[36]

This argument confuses two different conceptions of 'procedural fairness'. We can surely all agree that the utmost effort must be made to ensure that those who are accused of a capital crime have an opportunity to dispute the evidence brought against them – the trial procedures must not give the prosecutor any advantage – but this does not imply that prosecutors and juries cannot be influenced by factors such as the way a person dresses or whether they are attractive or look menacing. Prejudice of this kind will have an influence on any trial that must rely on human appraisal. Nor is the harm of this kind of discrimination against an individual so serious – they are not being sentenced for something that they did not do. Unless a criminal trial can be conducted in a purely mechanical way, it will involve arbitrariness of one kind or another, whether capital sentences are in prospect or not.

If Ely has his way and the Supreme Court comes to endorse his interpretation of the Eighth Amendment, it would indeed be lucky for first-degree murderers who have killed in aggravating circumstances that Americans are so sensitive to the advantages that go along with race and class. But the kind of arbitrariness that worries Ely is so common in the law (consider the fortunate fate of the police who battered Rodney King) that one must question why Ely thinks it becomes an important countervailing value only in cases in which the accused faces death. Why is it so bad that those who are correctly sentenced for their crimes are not treated in exactly the same way? We know full well that juries and prosecutors are inevitably prejudiced in all criminal cases, yet we do not think that this human fallibility necessarily calls the criminal law into question. We also know that 'white-collar' criminals are more likely to get lighter sentences in the United States, and that those from minority groups are more likely to be convicted and to suffer more severe penalties. This arbitrariness is unfortunate and every effort should be made to avoid it, yet we do not complain of a mistrial unless the procedure is distorted (for example, a judge may mislead a jury because of his or her sympathy or hostility for the accused).

Ely tries to explain why unavoidable arbitrariness in the administration of the criminal law is so much more despicable when the death penalty is involved. As he shows, there are good reasons why we should expect that this kind of arbitrariness will be likely when a death sentence is in prospect. But subjective judgments are at play in every trial and Ely does not show that capital cases are markedly different from others.[37] The plea-bargaining that goes on in the offices of prosecutors throughout the United States relating to all criminal charges is something extraordinary by world standards and these negotiations greatly favour those who can afford to pay good lawyers to speak on their behalf. To distinguish capital cases, Ely must allow that there is something so barbaric about the death sentence that this kind of arbitrariness, although tolerable in criminal trials, cannot be allowed.

Most of us will agree that the death penalty should not be a prospect – no matter what the crime. Thus we will be persuaded to agree with Ely. But this is a moral judgment that brings us back to the position taken by Justices Brennan and Marshall. Do judges have a legal right to impose enlightened moral judgments of this kind on behalf of the people? Ely admits that they do not, so his argument cannot rely on a judgment of this kind. We must conclude, then, that Chief Justice Burger (speaking for the conservatives) was justified when he insisted (as Burger does in his dissenting opinion in *Furman*) that what is to count as a community standard is something that must be determined by legislators who are better placed to reflect public sentiments. On this understanding, Brennan and Marshall have no special claim to have their moral judgments embodied in the law and their judgment in *Furman*, however understandable, is defective because it is clearly countermajoritarian.

Conclusion

In this chapter I have considered the views of major writers who attempt to reconcile the work of the Supreme Court under Warren and Burger with a commitment to democracy that they take to be fundamental. Both Ely and Ackerman argue that we do not need to view the work of the Court as necessarily countermajoritarian.

The differences between Ely and the Rehnquist conservatives are not substantial. Even though he sets out to defend the Warren–Burger-

Court legacy and they are intent on dismantling it, Ely and the conservatives are both genuinely troubled by the countermajoritarian issue. Ely is as interested as the Rehnquist conservatives in securing democratic accountability and a clearer delineation between law, philosophy and politics. Ely must also allow that a good deal of the Warren–Burger legacy is indefensible on his rationale (in the narrow procedural form that he presents it). Certainly it is possible to present a more conservative version of the representation-reinforcing rationale. There is, then, a convergence on the middle ground that President Clinton would be wise to reinforce by nominating John Hart Ely or an Ely-style liberal to the Supreme Court when next he has an opportunity.

Ackerman's differences with the conservatives are much more profound because he is a dualist. But he fails to sustain the distinction that he makes between normal and 'higher' lawmaking. Although he claims democratic authority when recommending the privileging of 'higher lawmaking', we find that he arbitrarily rules out of consideration President Reagan's claims to have successfully accomplished constitutional change; also, the way that he delineates the role of Supreme Court justices in the United States system virtually sets them up as privileged lawmakers, even though they often act contrary to the wishes of the people. According to Ackerman it is the justices who must determine what 'we the people' have said, and it is the justices who must declare what new constitutional rules need to be recognized after a revolutionary period. But, as we have seen, Ackerman cannot sustain the distinction he makes between normal and 'higher' lawmaking and his theory is also defective as a version of originalism.

Notes

1   Bruce Ackerman, *We the People: Foundations*, vol. 1, (Cambridge, Mass.: Harvard University Press, 1993).
2   Ibid., 266–94.
3   Ibid., 235, 204.
4   Ibid., 270.
5   Robert Bork, *Tempting of America: the Political Seduction of the Law* (NY: The Free Press, 1990).
6   Ackerman, op. cit., 273–4.
7   Ibid., 266.
8   Ibid., 270.
9   Ibid., 271.
10   Clinton outbid the Republicans on crime and taxes, promising to be tougher than Bush on crime and to reward middle-class Americans with lower taxes; on racial quotas, Bush let him off the hook by signing the Civil Rights Act; on social issues, Clinton embraced many of the Reagan policies (for example, distinguishing

working Americans as 'deserving' poor and the unemployed as 'undeserving'). He differed from Republicans on abortion but opinion polls showed that the momentum had shifted because of the Supreme Court's threat to overrule *Roe* v. *Wade*. As for his promises to gay groups and the people of the inner cities, he promptly broke these when he was faced by opposition. This adoption of many of Reagan's themes is one reason why Clinton won the election, and his willingness to act expediently, for example, refusing to continue with the nomination of Lani Guinier to the Justice Department when she became identified as an advocate of racial quotas, is why he is still acceptable as a national leader to so many Americans.

11   Ackerman, op. cit., 51.

12   Ibid., 52, 53.

13   Ibid.,113.

14   Ibid.

15   For a more balanced account, see Joshua Muravchik, 'Why the Democrats Lost Again' in *Commentary* (Feb. 1989), 13–22.

16   Ackerman, op. cit., pp. 288–90.

17   H.L.A. Hart, *The Concept of Law* (Oxford: Oxford University Press, 1961). The members of the United States Supreme Court do not share what the philosopher H.L.A. Hart calls 'a rule of recognition'. In recent years the Court has been divided 5–4 in a systematic way reflecting fundamental disagreements. Has this been a normal period?

18   But this is not always the case. Divisions on the Supreme Court sometimes encourage subordinate courts to take sides; see Clarence Thomas's opinion for the Appeals Court in *Lamprecht* v. *F.C.C.* 958 F.2d 382 (D.C. Cir. 1992) esp. 393–8, which follows the minority opinion of O'Connor in *Metro Broadcasting* deliberately ignoring the majority opinion written by Brennan.

19   See their joint opinion in *S.E. Pennsylvania* v. *Casey*.

20   As such, it suffers from all of the problems that I have listed in considering the doctrines of conservative writers such as Edward Meese and Robert Bork.

21   Joseph A. Schumpeter, *Capitalism, Socialism and Democracy* (London: Allen & Unwin, 1970), 269, claims 'the democratic method is that institutional arrangement for arriving at political decisions in which individuals acquire the power to decide by means of a competitive struggle for the people's vote'.

22   Thus it has allowed the restriction of defamatory, obscene, insulting and offensive speech. The quote is from *Chaplinsky* v. *New Hampshire* (1942) (recognizing 'fighting words' as falling outside First Amendment protection); see also *Roth* v. *United States* (1957) (obscenity); *Beauharnais* v. *Illinios* (1952) (defamation).

23   Alexander Meiklejohn, *Political Freedom: The Political Powers of the People* (NY: Oxford University Press, 1965) at 111.

24   Ibid., 103.

25   This argument is foreshadowed in a footnote in Justice Stone's opinion for the Court in *United States* v *Carolene Products* Co 304 U.S. 144, 152–53 n. 4 (1938). See John Hart Ely, *Democracy and Distrust: a Theory of Judicial Review* (Cambridge, Mass.: Harvard University Press, 1992), 75–7.

26   Meiklejohn, op. cit., 5.

27   Despite his own sympathies for women who do not wish to continue with a pregnancy, Ely questions the controversial abortion decision *Roe* v *Wade* (in which the United States Supreme Court settled a moral dispute on a matter of fundamental importance).

28   Segregation was practised in Washington DC and in most other states, throughout the British Empire, and in all other parts of the world where European powers such as France, Germany or Italy enjoyed hegemony.

29   Ely, op. cit., 151–3.

30   Ibid., 153.

31   Ibid., 157.
32   Ely illustrates this by considering the case of capital punishment that he thinks should be ruled out of consideration in the United States by the Supreme Court on equal protection grounds. As he shows, it is difficult to find procedural restraints that will ensure that everyone will be treated equally because, ' there is a very effective series of buffers at work here, protecting those who make the laws and others like them from the harshness of their application', Ely, op. cit., 176.
33   *Miami Herald Publishing Co.* v. *Tornillo*, 318 U.S. 241 (1974).
34   *Stanley* v. *Georgia*, 394 U.S. 557 (1969); and *Miller* v. *California*, 413 U.S. 15 (1973).
35   Ely, op. cit., 173.
36   Ibid., 177.
37   Ibid., 176.

8 Ronald Dworkin v. Cass Sunstein: First- and Second-Wave Liberalism

In this chapter I will be concerned to assess some of the views of Ronald Dworkin and Cass Sunstein. The former is perhaps the most influential critic of approaches adopted by the conservatives and offers arguments to defend the activism of the Supreme Court during the Warren–Burger period. The latter is one of the few liberal writers who shares the conservative view that the United States political system would work better if the Supreme Court were to adopt a less interventionist role. We may see Dworkin as a first-wave liberal concerned to tell us why the work of Justice William Brennan must be applauded; whereas Sunstein is a second-wave liberal critic of the Rehnquist Court who tells us that Rehnquist, Scalia, O'Connor, Kennedy, Souter and Thomas are abusing their authority. The first-wave (including Ackerman and Tribe) are optimistic about judicial leadership. In this, their perspective reflects their approval of the work of the Supreme Court when a majority of the justices followed liberal intellectual leadership. But the nostalgia of these liberals seems somewhat behind the times, given the fact that the Rehnquist Court now displays a manifest hostility to philosophical jurisprudence and refuses to impose liberal ideals. The kinds of arguments that would have appealed to Justice Brennan are certainly not likely to be taken up by anyone who wishes to argue a case successfully before the likes of Rehnquist, Thomas and Kennedy.

Judicial activism is fine when your side is calling the shots but terrible when the Court is ruling to frustrate what you regard as progressive attempts by legislators to secure changes. Judicial activism can favour progressive policies but it can also serve as a barrier to such change, entrenching liberties that make it difficult for governments to regulate property and to secure political equality or justice. When conservatives dominate the Supreme Court, liberals often advocate judicial restraint; when liberals dominate, conservatives advocate restraint. Thus, before President Franklin Roosevelt's New Deal, during the first three decades of this century, the Supreme Court was able to frustrate attempts by state governments to regulate the labour market and invalidated legislative attempts to secure a minimal welfare state. Naturally this judicial policymaking was deeply resented by liberals. During the period of liberal dominance under Warren and Burger, in contrast, it has been conservatives who complain about judicial interventions and resent activism by judges.

Ronald Dworkin on Conventionalism

Before considering Sunstein's second-wave liberalism, let us review Ronald Dworkin's critique of the work of the Rehnquist conservatives and the reasons he provides for praising Justice Brennan. Why is he so keen on judicial activism and so hostile to judges like Scalia and O'Connor who hope to discipline their work?

The Critique of Conventionalism

Dworkin challenges those who recommend the goal, derived from Bentham's critique of Blackstone, of ensuring that legal reasoning is not confused with moral reasoning or theology. His first target is the work of the British philosopher H.L A. Hart whose book *The Concept of Law* represents, for Dworkin, one of the most sophisticated defences of the Benthamite theoretical orientation that is generally referred to as legal positivism. Dworkin accuses Hart of misrepresenting the actual arguments used by judges in many cases by failing to properly understand how and why they so often appeal to moral and political principles. According to Dworkin, Hart's understanding of 'law' as constituted by primary and secondary rules forces him into the absurd situation where he must describe a great number of the arguments that go on in courts as not, strictly speaking, arguments about law at all. This implication greatly troubles Dworkin because, coming from the United States, he is very sensitive to the fact that many of the cases before the Supreme Court, especially those dealing with the various liberties listed in the Bill of Rights or the unenumerated liberties recognized as protected by the Court, are finally resolved by an appeal to abstract moral principles. If Hart's account of 'law' is correct, according to Dworkin, the Supreme Court justices, during the Warren–Burger period, were most often acting as surrogate legislators, making policy choices on behalf of the American people without any constraining guidance from the law.

Not surprisingly, Dworkin rejects this description of the Supreme Court's work (attributed to Hart) and devotes his scholarly and analytical skills to developing an alternative account of judicial reasoning that places much greater emphasis on the importance and relevance of abstract principles and appeals to political morality. One result of this sustained work is his book *Law's Empire* in which he argues that most of the landmark rulings of the Warren–Burger period, including *Brown* v. *Board of Education,* can be justified by appealing to abstract co-ordinating political principles that show the American system as promoting 'a kind of equality among citizens that makes their community more genuine and improves its moral justification for exercising the political power it does'.[1] More significantly, he launches an attack against those justices on the Court (and their supporters) who remain attached to Hart's way of thinking. According to him, conventionalist approaches to law of the kind embraced by the likes of Scalia (who, as we have seen, adopts a version of legal positivism) offer an indefensible conception of legal practices in the United States.

Let me present Dworkin's argument more systematically before I consider some of the objections that can be directed towards his account.

Dworkin's point of departure is his view that legal theorists must offer what he calls a 'constructive' interpretation of the legal practices in their community. He requires that they impose 'purpose' in order to render these practices 'the best possible example of the genre to which they belong'.[2] According to this understanding of the judicial task, the legal theorist must first situate herself within a given community by accepting its shared legal practices as her own; she is then in a position to offer an account of why practices of that general kind are worth participating in, if they are; finally she may recommend reform in the light of her understanding of how such a system can be justified.[3] Significantly, as a participant within the legal practices, the theorist will also be able to engage other theorists in her community, comparing their recommendations and interpretation of the shared practices with her own; the goal is to discover which interpretation is, on balance, better than the others, and to promote its requirements.[4]

Dworkin is clear about what he takes to be the purposes of legal practices in the United States:

> Our discussions about law by and large assume, I suggest, that the most abstract and fundamental point of legal practice is to guide and constrain the power of government in the following way. Law insists that force not be used or withheld ... except as licensed or required by

individual rights and responsibilities flowing from past political decisions about when collective force is justified.[5]

What is crucial here is what Dworkin counts as a justification for the
use of force. Does he mean that force should be constrained by the
rules that police and other officials in the system conventionally
follow? Or is he suggesting that conventional rules cannot be counted
as establishing rights unless they are capable of being justified as
appropriate in the light of some underlying political theory presupposed by the system? If this more demanding requirement is intended, and it seems to be what Dworkin is claiming, he is suggesting that arguments about 'the law' in the United States must be
evaluated by how well or badly they are accommodated within the
best available political theory. Many arguments will count as 'legal'
but some will be better than others because they offer better reasons
in delineating when and explaining why coercion is sometimes necessary. He also argues that rival conceptions of law can be distinguished and assessed by the reasons they provide for requiring that
force be constrained by past political decisions. In other words, they
should be assessed in the light of an evaluation of the adequacy or
failings of the political theory that they presuppose.[6]

Accordingly, in assessing legal positivism in the United States, we
must first comprehend what its advocates take to be their justification for requiring that force be licensed by past political decisions,
according to procedures that are conventionally regarded as legitimate. This is a matter of articulating the underlying political philosophy that presents the orientation in its best possible light. The
positivists (those Dworkin describes as embracing conventionalism)
are required, in the light of Dworkin's standards for assessment, to
present their conception as an interpretation of the legal practices in
the United States that shows why they think that it is better for
judges to seek objective sources, respecting settled legal conventions
about when force is appropriate, rather than rely on any policy evalu-
ations they may personally think relevant or on judgments reflecting
a political morality that relies on some conception of justice.

Of course, the Rehnquist conservatives have not explicitly addressed
this issue so Dworkin must find arguments to suggest on their behalf. But he has difficulty finding reasons that sound convincing
partly because he seems to assume that they cannot embrace utilitarian arguments (as Bentham and Hart do).[7] In any event, Dworkin
offers the following argument (as a possible answer that conventionalists might give as to why past politics should be decisive in delineating present rights in the United States): it serves the ideals of
certainty and predictability by protecting settled expectations of what
will be regarded as legally binding. Dworkin does not explicate these

virtues, although he allows that they are associated with other ideals of the 'rule of law', such as the prohibition against retroactive punishment and the commitment to procedural fairness.

This is a very unsympathetic presentation. One suspects that it has been carefully designed to allow Dworkin to let fly a number of well-directed body blows. Nor are we disappointed. First, he questions the assumption that protecting expectations is such an important value that it must be advanced at the cost of other considerations such as justice or efficiency. Second, he shows, to his own satisfaction, that the goal of achieving certainty in law is unrealizable in practice, except at a social cost that not even conventionalists would be prepared to pay (except in the area of criminal law).[8] As he explains, conventionalists in the United States actually pursue a policy of balancing the competing claims of predictability and flexibility because they wish to allow courts to make policy choices and to uphold justice in circumstances where the accepted conventions are indeterminate. Third, he tells us that because conventionalists are not prepared to pursue certainty at any cost, they are no better placed than any other lawyers in dealing with most of the cases that come before the courts because a reference to accepted conventions will be insufficient to dispose of most legal conflict. Judges will need to make judgments, they cannot expect to rule mechanically. In most cases they will have to deal with competent lawyers who do not agree, so the issues before them will reflect genuine uncertainty. Nevertheless, arguments will be presented to establish legal claims on both sides of the dispute. These (rather than the more technical considerations favoured by conventionalists) are the stock-in-trade of advocates and judges, according to Dworkin. His point is that the conventionalist is no better situated to secure certainty in the outcome than anyone else. Indeed, in a large number of cases, she will be at a disadvantage if she openly declares that there is no relevant 'law'. Finally, fourth, a consideration that troubles Dworkin about conventionalism is its inability to facilitate change; according to him, the recommendations that can be made in the light of conventionalism seem to allow for too little flexibility, especially in the area of constitutional law.

Assessing Dworkin's Challenge

Let me now consider possible responses by someone who wished to defend conventionalism.

Conventionalism can be presented as a reformist agenda. In this endeavour, it need not aspire to offer a comprehensive interpretation of a legal system, let alone a theoretical justification about when coercion by the state may be regarded as morally legitimate. A reformist may even acknowledge, as Scalia does, that the system is incoherent and that reform will have to be 'fainthearted'. All that is required from a conventionalist in the United States today is a commitment to minimize the extent to which judge's rely on their personal convictions and moral values when making decisions.[9] A slogan for such a reformist might be – 'Legal conventions should count for more than they do now'; another possibility is – 'More policy choices should be made by legislators, less by judges'. This reform ambition may be embraced more or less cautiously, depending on how much change from the present practice is regarded as desirable.

If we view conventionalists as reformers, we may also allow that they may seek to justify their programme using arguments that are external to law. For example, a conventionalist could agree that a rival judicial theory (say, the position advocated by Dworkin) would result in better consequences if it were applied by judges who are enormously skilled and wise, but argue that attempts to apply the theory in the United States would prove disastrous in practice because of the human failings of the individuals appointed as members of the judiciary. Ordinary members of the legal profession are highly likely to make serious errors of judgment and will be inclined to impose their own values, misusing the theory.[10]

A conventionalist could adopt a version of the sceptical position that Dworkin describes as pragmatism. According to this view, judges should follow whichever method of deciding cases they think will produce the best community for the future. This theory is difficult to refute so long as we agree that every judge will act wisely and with integrity. But the conventionalist would claim that this fortunate circumstance is highly unlikely. Indeed, she could claim that the goals of pragmatism would be better served in the United States if all judges agree to restrain themselves by accepting that the prevailing legal conventions are binding. On this conception, 'law' as defined by legal positivists is embraced as a regulative device – to control judges who would otherwise abuse or misuse their authority. Our conventionalist could justify this strategy by arguing that (given the fact that the judiciary is not constituted by expert philosophers like Dworkin's fictional Justice 'Hercules'[11]) more good will follow if all members of the judiciary consider themselves constrained by publicly recognized norms (referred to as 'the law') and enjoy only a limited discretion to make innovative policy choices on behalf of the community.

Dworkin presents another argument for embracing a constraint of this kind, allowing that the conventionalist could claim that respect for conventions ('the law' as defined by legal positivists) helps to achieve the benefits of coordinated private and commercial activity. If people and corporations are to plan their lives and make sound investments they need to make reliable predictions about what their legal rights are.[12] More significant, legislators need to know that they can trust judges to honour their intentions. Why draft statutes and consider constitutional proposals carefully if you know that the chosen words will not bind anyone? Another consideration that has been used to justify conventionalism relates to the difficulties judges face when they make policy judgments. They are often poorly suited to the task because they lack time and relevant expertise; nor do they enjoy the necessary support from suitably trained staff. Yet another consideration relates to the fact that they are not accountable to the people who may be effected by their decisions. Thus, it is foolhardy for them to attempt to second-guess those who are better placed to assess the many complex issues that must be considered when important policy choices are made.

These are not legal arguments and they do not necessarily feature in the kind of scrutiny that even Dworkin's fictional Justice Hercules brings to his task. He is certainly not humble and never seems to consider whether he or anyone else elevated to the bench is suited to the task he sets himself. But actual judges are unlikely to share Hercules' energy or his intellectual skills. Even Hercules, as we shall see, is unable to consider all the relevant issues in dealing with particular cases.

Consider his treatment of *Tennessee Valley Authority* v. *Hill* (the Snail Darter case) that Dworkin analyses in great detail.[13] The case involves conflict over the Endangered Species Act that empowers the Secretary of the Interior to designate species that would be endangered by the destruction of some habitat that he or she considers crucial to its survival. If a designated species is deemed threatened, federal agencies are required to ensure that 'actions authorised, funded, or carried out by them do not jeopardise the continued existence of such endangered species'. Conservationists complained that a dam being built by the Tennessee Valley Authority was going to destroy the only habitat of a 3-inch fish (the Snail Darter) that the Secretary had designated as endangered. The Authority was reluctant to cease building a dam for which it had already committed $110 million. It responded to the demands of the conservationists by arguing that the Endangered Species Act should not be construed to prevent the completion or operation of any project substantially completed when the Secretary made his-or-her designation order. Its legal argument seemed weak, however, because it is difficult to construe 'carried out' as not embracing a project already under construction. The drafters of the Endangered Species Act would surely have anticipated that 'carried out' could be construed as referring to projects already under way, yet they did nothing to signal that they meant to allow for an exception.

After agonizing at great length, Hercules reaches the following conclusion about what to do in dealing with this seemingly straight forward case, as reported by Dworkin:

> He thinks reading the statute to save the dam would make it better from the point of view of sound policy. He has no reason of textual integrity arguing against that reading, nor any reason of fairness, because nothing suggests that the public would be outraged or offended by that decision. Nothing in the legislative history of the bill itself, properly understood and taken as the record of public decision, argues the other way, and later legislative decisions of the same character argue strongly for the reading he himself thinks best. He joins the justices who dissented in the case.[14]

The first thing that should be said about this Alice-in-Wonderland world where plain words have little force is that it gives rise to a great deal of litigation. Lawyers thrive in such a world and a good deal of public money would be wasted in fruitless legal dispute. If the Tennessee Valley Authority had known, by previous signals from the Court, that it would not normally contemplate ignoring the common understanding of the phrases included in statutes – that it was likely to read 'carried out' to mean 'carried out' – there would have been no legal controversy for Hercules to consider. The Authority would have gone straight to Congress to secure the necessary amendment to the legislation, saving everyone a good deal of time, trouble and money.[15] When lawyers can agree about what the law requires, they do not need to resort to the courts. This is one very important reason why judges should value objectivity – it is a good thing for a society to discourage pointless litigation. This is why it matters when people perceive that the courts are prepared to reconsider every policy issue on its merits, no matter how carefully a contract or a statute may have been drafted or how clear the relevant constitutional precedents seem to be. If courts send a signal that judges are prepared to listen to any line of argument, skilled advocates will appeal to what they take to be the prejudices of various judges; and will do this in every case they think important. As the Snail Darter controversy shows, American litigators do not think it a waste of money or time to go to court even when their case requires judges to ignore the plain meaning of a statute.

This is not the only consideration. The conservationists who were dragged through the courts by the Tennessee Valley Authority lost a good deal of money – wasted on legal fees. But they were encouraged to pursue their case by the plain meaning of the words included in the Endangered Species Act. Is this fair? Dworkin argues that surprise in a case like this is unfair only when a prediction has been specifically encouraged by those who deliberately defeat it.

Thus, if federal courts in the United States had not signalled that they are going to be bound by the plain meaning of statutes, plaintiffs who rely on phrases in a statute to secure their claims have no grounds for complaint when courts rule against them.[16] But this seems to belittle the costs that the conservationists must have suffered because of the refusal of the judiciary to try and secure greater certainty about outcomes.

Political life relies on trust and the meaning of words matters in establishing this. Many people would have supported the Endangered Species Act, and some would have spent money and time securing such a firm commitment from the Congress and President. What other words could they have included in the Bill to make the final protection of designated species absolute? Their efforts, time and money, and the votes of those in Congress who supported their views matter. Yet Hercules does not think this is important because he does not value certainty in law very highly as an ideal. Had his penchant for reading plain words to mean what they are not normally understood to mean prevailed, the conservationists would have been very surprised and extremely angry. The Court would have told them, in effect, that what they had accomplished in securing the Endangered Species Act – an achievement they must have regarded as an important political victory – was not exactly what, in good faith, they took it to be. Thus, they are likely to have seen the process of judicial invalidation as totally unfair. It is one thing to lose a political battle in Congress after the votes are counted, quite another to lose the opportunity to contest the issue because the Supreme Court has imposed an amendment to a statute acting on its own authority.

A breach of trust of this kind is not a trivial issue, as illustrated in the United States by the controversy over the meaning of the Civil Rights Act, 1964, which was read in a quite unusual way by the Supreme Court to virtually require companies to make use of racial quotas when recruiting employees, even though the words of the statute did not entail this result and despite the fact that efforts were made to include phrases in the civil rights statute that would ensure that this outcome did not happen.[17] This intervention by the Court (ignoring legislative history and plain meaning) caused a lot of anger at the time but it also left a legacy that made it extremely difficult to reach agreement about future proposed amendments to the Act, as in 1990 and 1992. Nobody in the United States now believes that the words that legislators and executive officials embrace, especially after extensive negotiations involving a lot of conflict, will be proof against judicial innovations. With regard to the Civil Rights Act, President Bush was also able to gain political advantage by declaring that proposed amendments would require racial quotas – even though, on a plain reading, none of the phrases proposed for inclusion in the statute actually required this outcome. But most people believed him because they had come to suspect that the judiciary in the United States is full of judges like Hercules.[18]

A related problem with Hercules' opinion in the Snail Darter case is that he overlooks the fact that the executive shares legislative authority in the United States so that, unless Congress has marshalled a two-thirds majority to overrule a presidential veto, statutes are a contract between President and Congress. This is why the plain meaning of the phrases agreed to should matter more in the United States than in other democracies. Both President and Congress employ very skilled advisers to help in the legislative process which is usually painfully slow and tortuous. Each side will consider how they are likely to be frustrated by every proposed term. Unless circumstances at a future time are of a kind that could not have been contemplated, judges would be wise to act as though they had been foreseen and considered by these experts. In the Snail Darter case we must surely allow that those who drafted the Endangered Species Act must have foreseen the possibility that some project already undertaken could be placed in jeopardy. It is also relevant that a senior executive official (the Secretary of the Interior) had thought it necessary to designate the Snail Darter as an endangered species. This judgment should have carried some weight with Hercules because the Secretary is the relevant agent of the President. Presumably, the Secretary was informed that this action would place the completion of the $110 million dam in jeopardy and he or she is likely to have evaluated the competing interests of the public. If this is so, it is surely not for Hercules to ignore this opinion (considering that the Secretary is also advised by a large number of highly qualified staff and is designated in the Endangered Species Act as the relevant executive official for making important judgments that impact on the agreed goal of preserving endangered species).

Yet another problem of some significance concerns the signals that courts send to the public. Here, we must consider the role of the judiciary in securing democratic accountability. In the Snail Darter case, for example, many members of the Congress would have been embarrassed politically. They would have acknowledged the importance of the dam – $110 million is not an insignificant loss – and appreciated the political influence of the Tennessee Valley Authority, yet they may have sympathized with conservationists. These legislators would have been pulled in two different directions. It would have been difficult to vote against the influential Tennessee Valley Authority; but many would have known that a large number of voters are very influenced by conservationists and many of these would have opposed the building of the dam whether or not the

Snail Darter was threatened by the construction. Some of the legislators who experienced these conflicting loyalties may even have been regarded as leading conservationists, and they may have been reluctant to jeopardize this reputation. If they voted for the continuation of the dam, as the Authority requested, their credibility as conservationists would have been badly damaged. On the other hand, if they voted as the conservationists requested, that is, against the construction of the dam, they may have been regarded by their colleagues in Congress as unreasonable, possibly losing influence. These kinds of dilemmas that elected officials sometimes face are the substance of political life. For a democracy to work effectively, accountable leaders must declare their policy preferences by taking sides, even when this causes pain to a section of the electorate. But politicians do not like doing this. This is why the members of Congress associated with the conservation groups (who had helped to secure the Endangered Species Act in the first place) would have been delighted had Hercules managed to persuade the Supreme Court to allow the Authority to proceed with the dam. In this circumstance, they would not have had to face angry conservationists – people who had previously been supporters and friends.

Conventionalists argue that those who are elected to public office should be required to make the kinds of policy decisions that divide the community and they disapprove when activist judges allow them to avoid this responsibility. This is not a trivial concern in the United States because it is a very common tactic for Congress to legislate in a way that allows broad discretion to administrators, independent agencies, commissioners or judges. Congress has even embraced a strategy, adopted in circumstances where its members distrust executive officials or independent agencies, of empowering Congressional committees to exercise discretion (making public policy in secret). Hercules does not seem to be concerned about the damage this kind of practice has done to the political system.

The Embrace of Communitarianism

Dworkin may allow that the arguments conventionalists might use to justify judicial restraint do carry some force. For example, he concedes that procedural fairness and social co-ordination are facilitated when the law is predictable. But he argues that these goals are insufficient to secure a plausible 'constructive interpretation' of legal practices in the United States because, in his view, the strategies and arguments used by conventionalists do not offer any adequate justification for the use of coercion.

Conventionalists can respond that they are reformers, not philosophers, and that it is sufficient for them to show that their strategies will make the political system work better regardless of whether they can present their rulings as a 'constructive interpretation'. They may even believe that the kind of justification that Dworkin seeks is not possible. In any event, it is not implausible to view justification of this broad kind as lying beyond the brief allocated to the judiciary. They can also remind Dworkin that judges are inclined to make bad policy decisions and may be very poor philosophers. Thus, more good than harm is likely to follow, in the longer term, if judges assume that they are generally required to respect conventions and accept a more modest role than that taken on by Hercules.

It is at this point in the dispute that Dworkin has to rely on arguments about the most adequate conception of American democracy. According to him, it is not enough for a judge to be a reformer – she must help to construct the prevailing system by offering a comprehensive interpretation of its practices. According to him, a judge must assume responsibility for conceptualizing what it means to be a citizen in the United States offering an explanation of how what she takes to be law provides a general justification for the exercise of coercive power by the state.[19] On this view, then, every judge must identify the purposes that display the system in the most defensible way. The ultimate goal is to show that the use of coercion in the society is legitimate. Dworkin criticizes judges who embrace legal positivism for avoiding this responsibility, and he explains that this is why they accomplish their judicial tasks badly. Even if we recast positivism as a constructive interpretation, endorsing the position he describes as conventionalism, he claims we will find no good reasons for supposing that certainty about the law is a sufficiently worthy purpose to serve as a guide as to what judges *should* be doing in the United States. Such a limited ideal for law is insufficient to explain why Americans should suppose that the use of coercion on behalf of the State is legitimate.

But what can count as an adequate justification in this context? Surely it matters to whom you are talking?

Suppose that after a long period of negotiations between South Africans a federal system is agreed to by the people of that country that includes provisions that are designed to allow Afrikaners and Zulus regional autonomy and some hope of sharing power, even as minorities.[20] Let us allow that most people are persuaded by retired general Constand Viljoen that the Afrikaners need a homeland to serve as a halfway house for at least 25 years, after which they may then elect to renegotiate their relationship with the rest of South Africa; let us suppose also that Mangosuthu Buthelezi's claim that the KwaZulu–Natal region should be a base for Zulus is eventually agreed to. Suppose that the Afrikaners are allocated part of the present capital, Pretoria, and an area that stretches to include part of what is

now the Orange Free State.[21] Suppose further that responsibility for
the conduct of elections is allocated to the various state governments
and that it is understood that both the Afrikaners and Zulus will
proceed to entrench the power of their ethnic communities in their
respective regions through policies that involve discrimination. For
example, they may decide to draw district boundaries in such a way
that their ethnic groups are able to dominate or they may seek to
regulate the flow of ethnic groups into the two regions to encourage
what they regard as an appropriate mix (to prevent themselves from
being swamped by people who are not members of their respective
ethnic communities). Suppose these developments are anticipated
and come as no surprise to anyone because Buthelezi and General
Viljoen (speaking with authority on behalf of their ethnic communities) had demanded ethnic self-government and had threatened civil
war if these conditions were not met.

Let us suppose the Constitution was framed specifically to avoid
civil war, that the framers had agreed to regional autonomy on terms
that made it possible for regionally dominant ethnic groups
(Afrikaners and Zulus) to secure their power, reasoning that it is
better to proceed towards democracy on the terms demanded by
ethnic groups than to risk the prospect of war and the dissolution of
the union.

Now consider a possible constitutional challenge that is launched
by aggrieved citizens who complain that they are being discriminated against. Advocates speaking on behalf of these citizens argue
that the newly constituted Constitutional Court is entitled to rule
that there is an implied right to political equality in the new South
African Constitution (because it describes the state as a 'democracy'
at various points) and that: (a) citizens have an inherent right to
settle in any area of the nation by virtue of the fact that they are
citizens of one single democratic state; and (b) to have their votes
counted equally in allocating executive authority (disallowing the
power-sharing arrangements). Accordingly, they ask the Court to
rule that discrimination on the basis of ethnic membership in delineating district boundaries and in allocating residential rights is constitutionally forbidden, as is the practice of favouring small parties in
allocating positions in the Cabinet. Should the Constitutional Court
embrace this reasoning?

According to Dworkin's analysis it should because this reading of
the new Constitution provides the best 'constructive interpretation'
of the legal materials. This strategy would provide a better justification for the use of coercion within the South African state as a whole
because it recognizes each individual citizen as enjoying equal political rights. This basic principle is reflected in much of what was
included in the Constitution by the framers and in the rhetoric of

leading politicians (such as Nelson Mandela, Thabo Mbeki and even F.W. de Klerk) who negotiated its terms on behalf of the majority of the people. This interpretation would also be approved by most South Africans who (opinion polls show) are eager to embrace principles that are widely associated with the ideals of democracy in the rest of the world. But some Zulus and most Afrikaners are unlikely to accept this reasoning as offering any legitimation. Indeed, a few are likely to resist the intrusion of federal troops into their regions and any other efforts to enforce the Court's ruling. In their view, coercion against them to uphold the ruling of a Court that blatantly ignored the constitutional terms agreed to at the time of ratification is a violation of the 'rule of law', denying them a legal right to ensure the political control within their respective states that they regard as essential in sustaining their ethnic identity. Thus, Viljoen and Buthelezi prepare their people for war.[22]

Dworkin allows constitutional judges to abandon interpretivism in some circumstances of this kind. Discussing a hypothetical case of a judge he calls Siegfried who despises the system in which he adjudicates, he writes:

> We might decide that the interpretive attitude is wholly inappropriate there, that the practice, in the shape it has reached, can never provide any justification at all, even a weak one, for state coercion. Then we will think that in every case Siegfried should simply ignore legislation and precedent altogether, if he can get away with it, or otherwise do the best he can to limit injustice through whatever means are available to him.[23]

But this is not the situation that the new South African Constitutional Court, in our example, faces. There are materials at hand that allow an acceptable interpretation. The problem the judges face is that significant sections of the political community are unwilling to accept 'the best' interpretation as binding. They view the Constitution as a kind of contract and believe that social order should be guaranteed only if the terms agreed to are honoured.

Surely legal positivists are more clear-headed when they describe this situation as one where the law of this system is bad and should be changed, rather than as one where there is no law. According to the conventionalist approach, the Court would uphold provisions in the Constitution that the negotiators had thought expedient to accept (for example, the provisions in the interim South African Constitution that allow for power-sharing). The judges may each declare their moral commitment to political equality as a basic principle, but each would nevertheless recognize that there is a necessary distinction to be made between 'law' and 'morality'.

Let us now suppose that some years have passed and that South Africa has emerged as a successful multi-ethnic democracy in which a number of different political parties successfully compete. We may speculate that neither the Zulus nor the Afrikaners feel so alienated that they are prepared to go to war if the constitutional law affording privileges to them was to be changed, and that the initial African National Congress coalition that established a dominant one-party system is no longer so cohesive. Now a conventionalist judge may contemplate imposing a revolutionary change. She may decide to declare that the circumstances in which the Constitution had been negotiated had been coercive (the threat of war) and that, now that this threat is no longer serious and a genuine multi-party democracy is in place, the nation should declare its commitment to the elimination of ethnic privileges. A decision in this context would be openly political and would reflect an assessment of the balance of power and the salience of moral principles, rather than any scrutiny of the sources of law. This is why a constitutional court, according to conventionalists, should be extremely cautious about departing from conventions. The judges in South Africa will know that Zulus, Afrikaners, Coloureds and Indians had been led to expect a different outcome (for example, power-sharing) and they would assume that the judgment of politicians about what is feasible in the new circumstances must be afforded more authority than their own. Thus, the judges should not initiate any changes unilaterally but should wait until they are sure that there is a secure national consensus supporting their initiative.

The positivist account of revolutionary change has another advantage. It does not require the Constitutional Court to denounce the judges who had previously upheld the Constitution (probably themselves). The earlier judges can be described as having upheld the Constitution. In contrast, when judges impose changes in the Dworkinian manner they must assert that earlier judges had failed in their duty to honour fundamental political principles and had ignored their duty to find an adequate 'constructive interpretation' of the Constitution. This process of denunciation serves to discredit the judiciary, when blame is more realistically directed at forces in the community such as ethnic nationalism and at various political leaders who abuse it (like Buthelezi and Viljoen).

We have been discussing an extreme situation when a breakdown of consensus could lead to civil war. In the United States the consequences of departures from legal conventions are not likely to be so serious. But the situation is not so different that it requires reconceptualization. What some members of the American community accept as a legitimate reason for coercion will be unacceptable to others. Those who hold expectations that they believe to be secured in law will offer a good deal of resistance if the Supreme Court chooses to deny what they take to be their constitutional rights. If they enjoy political power or other sources of influence, they may secure a great deal of harm in trying to reverse the Court's ruling. As communitarian theorists persuasively argue, normative arguments are best understood in a given context. We understand their salience only when we understand to whom they are directed.

Consider some examples from the United States. In November 1991, the world watched four white Los Angeles police officers use their batons against Rodney King, an African American who had been speeding and refused to respond to police instructions, as other officers stood by. Many people in Los Angeles (and other cities in the United States) apparently accept that when law enforcement officials confront a person like King who is resisting arrest, the police are justified in acting decisively. In their view, the police must show that they are prepared to use coercion without hesitation and need not restrain themselves until their instructions are followed without question. This strategy is said to be necessary in the hostile terrain, for police, of places like South Central Los Angeles. Understandably, Dworkin cannot accept this view of justified coercion as representing the best that the American community can aspire to – in the light of his conception of adequate justification, the opinions of these citizens of Los Angeles represent the worst side of America's political culture. Thus, their preferences should not be regarded as capable of supporting democratic authority and the Supreme Court – acting in the name of the Bill of Rights – should overrule any legislators who respond to them by allowing this kind of police discretion.

Consider some other groups that Dworkin would like the Court to disqualify from citizenship. What about religious fundamentalists and Catholics who think that abortions involve a form of murder? In their view, the United States Constitution was initially agreed to by deeply religious people and cannot plausibly be interpreted as securing an unfettered liberty to perform abortions. Dworkin also denies that this interpretation of the Constitution represents America at its best. In his view, a better interpretation of the Constitution's implied principles would allow women to terminate unwanted pregnancies within the first six months.[24] So religious groups are disqualified by Dworkin, to the extent that they try to influence policy on abortion. What about the many millions who think that courts generally offer criminals too many opportunities for avoiding conviction and that those who commit three serious crimes should be put away for life? What about those who think that anyone who murders where there are no mitigating circumstances should receive a death sentence? Dworkin tells us that these preferences should also be disqualified. What about conservatives who think that welfare programmes often harm the very communities they are attempting to help?[25] Dworkin has little time for the assumption reflected in this view about what Americans owe to one another as a matter of justice. What about those who accept that state governments ought to be allowed to set community standards on matters relating to morals? Dworkin also disqualifies them. According to him, their views are inconsistent with the foundational principles, reflected in the Bill of Rights, to which the American people are actually committed.

Given all these disqualifications, it is difficult to identify the section of the American people Dworkin is referring to when he talks about 'the community's values'. Why should we allow that Dworkin is entitled to disqualify certain points of view even when we know that the people who espouse them have significant political influence? Dworkin would even disqualify presidents when they advocate policies that violate fundamental principles of justice (Nixon, Reagan and Bush on abortion; even Clinton on capital punishment and the three convictions rule). Isn't this very like the South African Constitutional Court ruling as though Afrikaners and Zulus are of no significance in the scenario imagined in earlier paragraphs? In the end, the disqualified groups we have mentioned, in the United States, will come to view all references to the Constitution as a liberal confidence trick to disqualify their preferences.

When we examine Dworkin's approach, we find that the only views that count for Dworkin are those of the liberal elite. It is very fortunate for Hercules (and Dworkin) that some vague phrases were included in the Constitution, allowing him to claim that his unrepresentative conceptions of 'freedom of speech', 'due process of law' and 'the equal protection of the laws' have some source of authority other than philosophy; otherwise, he would have had to embrace legal scepticism.

An illusion that Dworkin seems to share in allowing Hercules this licence to read his own values into the Constitution is a misconception that the United States is essentially a liberal society. Thus, it is important to keep in mind when reading Hercules's opinions that most people in the United States are not liberal and never have been. Indeed, if we look at practices in the various states we often find politicians in power who are openly contemptuous of liberal ideals. Consider the Establishment Clause of the First Amendment. This provision was originally understood as applying only to the Congress (apparently it was included as part of the listed liberties because Thomas Jefferson feared that the Church of England would otherwise become the official church in Virginia[26]). But it was not only in eighteenth-century Virginia that religion was taken very seriously by governments – almost all public figures in American history have declared their faith, and most contemporary leaders continue to

do so. Besides embracing religion, many people in the United States
are deeply conservative; they seem to be influenced by various com-
binations of crudely defined ethnic loyalties, regionalism and nationalism. Although liberal individualist values do have some salience as
a rationalization for selfishness when Americans think about economic relationships or when they contemplate the fact that the taxes
they pay may be used to benefit others, the pervasive attitudes displayed reflect a rejection of liberal universalism (the idea that all
individuals should be treated as equals) as well as a rejection of
neutrality (the notion that the government should not favour one
conception of the good over others).[27]

For most Americans, the federal government often seems remote
and, when it has chosen to dominate the states in the name of liberal
ideals, its interventions have been resented. Indeed, a difficulty that
we all experience in trying to comprehend the political culture of the
United States is the antinomy that exists between the prevailing
social values in regional communities and the public philosophy that
informs debates among elites in the federal arena. Liberalism is perceived as the national ideology only because the Madisonian framework is accepted by most contributors to public debate within universities and the bureaucracies. On their home turf, however, federal
politicians must communicate to people who are uncomfortable with
the abstractions that make neutrality possible and usually resort to
quite different, more populist idioms.[28] This is one reason why
people in the United States are obsessed with issues such as school
prayer, abortion and obscenity.

How liberalism has managed to survive – even flourish – in the
United States for 200 years is something of a puzzle. The fact that
representatives from the various states used liberal ideas to keep the
federal government at arms length is one explanation. But this *modus
vivendi* broke down after World War II when, for various reasons,
there was consensus among the elite to impose liberal values nationally. This change has not proved popular or successful. Today, as
Robert Hughes has noted in his recent lectures, hostility to liberal
values is manifest on both the left and right of the political spectrum.[29] Given the passions now in contention within the federal arena,
the prevalence of ethnic politics at every level of society, and the
growing hostility to liberalism even within the elite, it is questionable whether liberalism will survive as the public ideology in the
United States into the twenty-first century.

One reason why liberalism is under threat in the United States
today may be the fact that it has presented itself as a countermajoritarian philosophy of the kind that Dworkin recommends. From
Madison to Dworkin, the leading legal philosophers have aspired to
more than they have thought it is possible to realize through the

democratic processes, trying to achieve progressive changes despite significant opposition within the electorate. This persistent practice has resulted in a perception of the legal arena as merely another site for interest groups to pursue their objectives and there is a pervasive distrust of the judiciary. Madison's strategy for securing liberty – using one group of elites to restrain another – ensured a great deal of autonomy at the state level. With the abandonment of a strict division of powers between state and federal authorities in the modern period, however, serious institutional problems have begun to emerge because liberals are no longer willing to allow more traditional communities to exercise autonomy on matters of importance to them. For Dworkin and many other contemporary American liberals equality is the fundamental value that the judiciary should seek to realize as a first priority, even when non-liberal forces oppose this. In terms of this view, nobody should have authority to oppose liberalism. But their strategy of enlightened judicial leadership – using judicial authority to impose solutions that cannot be realized through the political process – has resulted in a weakening of the bonds that tie the society together and in a resurgence of claims to local autonomy.

This desire for self-government at the local and state levels was acceptable in the eighteenth and early nineteenth centuries (and provisions in the Constitution allow for it) but a modern society requires a more effective central government. Indeed, Franklin Roosevelt's New Deal revolution can be seen as an attempt to correct the antinomies within the system that resulted from its Madisonian design. If Roosevelt had not succeeded and all the divisions Madison envisaged prevailed today, the political system in the United States would have collapsed; as it is, the system is failing badly precisely because power is divided between President and Congress and because people are no longer satisfied with the performance of federal institutions and politicians. Judicial activism has also given rise to problems. For 40 years judges have attempted to impose enlightened values but the country remains bitterly divided along lines of race, gender and class.

In summary, we can say that liberalism is resented in the United States today because:

1   'gridlock' in the system brought about by the Madisonian divisions means that national leadership is often too weak to deal with serious problems;
2   reliance on executive authority often involves conflict with constitutional provisions that specifically allocate authority to Congress (although the system has been changed to allow the President to claim democratic authority in providing national leadership, as the only official apart from the Vice-President who must contest a nation-wide election); and

3   the Supreme Court has acted as a countermajoritarian institution, creating hostility towards liberal values.

Although Dworkin's jurisprudence is derived from a very appealing political philosophy, one we should all embrace, he fails to understand why liberals should resist the temptations of elitism in securing its objectives.[30]

The Historical Argument

At one point in his book Dworkin embraces a utilitarian justification for his countermajoritarian conception of law. Reflecting on Chief Justice John Marshall's judgment in *Marbury* v. *Madison*, he tells us that:

> The United States is a more just society than it would have been had its constitutional rights been left to the conscience of majoritarian institutions.[31]

But he admits that he has not provided convincing evidence for this claim.

He does, however, make a number of observations about the historical record, comparing the consequences during times when the Court acted in a deferential manner with the record in its active periods. Although he concedes that *Lochner* v. *New York*, and other cases he does not cite, show how a Court upholding abstract rights can cause serious harm by preventing legislators from implementing useful programmes to address serious social problems, he writes:

> But we would have more to regret if the court had accepted passivism wholeheartedly: southern schools might still be segregated, for example. Indeed, if we were to collect the court's decisions most generally regretted over the course of constitutional history, we would find more in which its mistake lay in failing to intervene when, as we now think, constitutional principles of justice required intervention. Americans would be prouder of their political record if it did not include, for example, *Plessy* or *Korematsu*. In both these cases a decision of a majoritarian legislature was seriously unjust, and also, as most lawyers now believe, unconstitutional; we regret that the Supreme Court did not intervene for justice in the Constitution's name.[32]

These claims are highly speculative. Can anyone know what would have happened if the Supreme Court had refused to allow the relocation and internment of citizens of Japanese ancestry after the bombing of Pearl Harbor? Would Governor Earl Warren and the military have obeyed the Court? The justices thought it prudent to go along with the military, a majority of the politicians and public opinion in allowing the perpetration of a grave injustice in this instance. We cannot infer from this that their judgment was wrong as a matter of expediency – only as a matter of justice.

Nor can we say that activist judges would have behaved in a different manner in dealing with *Korematsu* v. *U.S.* To claim this we must assume that they share our concern that the internment of the Japanese–Americans was an injustice in the circumstances of a war and that they would have known, as we know (thanks to the advantage of hindsight), that the danger posed by the presence of Japanese Americans in California at that time was exaggerated by the military. Dworkin implies that activist judges would have had cooler heads than military leaders and politicians after the bombing of Pearl Harbour. But there are no reasons for assuming this. In fact, the presiding Supreme Court justices shared the very policy preferences that Dworkin wishes had been frustrated by the Court! The justices found that racial animus against the Japanese was absent and that the public interest in safety was compelling (the problem with their ruling is not that they misunderstood the claims of justice in the circumstances but that, like the military leaders of the day, they grossly exaggerated the dangers that the nation faced).[33]

The same problem arises when we consider Dworkin's view of *Plessy* v. *Ferguson*. He seems to assume that because most people agree today that racial segregation is unjust, activist judges in the nineteenth century would also have regarded the practice as unjust. But segregation was practiced throughout the British Empire at the time of *Plessy*, as well as in most of the United States, and very few people thought the practice improper or immoral. Even if we are to suppose that all the justices on the Supreme Court considering *Plessy* thought that they were entitled to impose any conception of justice they thought 'the best' in the light of a 'constructive interpretation', we cannot conclude that a majority of them would have viewed racially segregated railway carriages in the same manner as Dworkin's Justice Hercules.

We must conclude that the reasons why the Supreme Court upheld the military order in *Korematsu* and the Louisiana statute challenged in *Plessy* probably reflected the values and assumptions of the presiding justices. There is no reason for thinking, as Dworkin claims, that these outcomes resulted from judicial scruples about the impropriety of overruling legislators.

Another problem with Dworkin's claim is that he seems to share the widespread view that very few progressive changes would have occurred in the United States had the Warren Court chosen to be deferential. But this underestimates the importance of the Civil Rights Movement – the willingness of people to confront police batons and dogs and to engage in sustained boycotts – and discounts the change in values that occurred after World War II. For all we know, there may have been more changes had the Court refrained from provoking conservative communities. In any event, as Gerald Rosenberg has persuasively shown, Dworkin's judgments greatly exaggerate the beneficial effects of the actual judicial interventions.[34]

Cass Sunstein and the Rehnquist Conservatives

Cass Sunstein shares Dworkin's social democratic values but the two writers disagree over the importance of liberty in a democracy and about the value of democratic participation and consultation. Sunstein is a liberal republican who would like to see the media regulated to facilitate greater fairness in the political system. He would also censor hate speech and pornography because they pose impediments to the participation of women and minorities in social and political life. Dworkin cautions against imposing fairness standards on the media, and would not allow states to regulate pornography and hate speech. Partly because of this conflict over how to interpret a fundamental political principle, Sunstein makes very different recommendations about how judges should approach their task. Indeed, he confronts Dworkin from the left, warning, in effect, that the institutional device of allocating power to the judiciary does not necessarily ensure power for judges like 'Hercules' or for someone like himself but power for Rehnquist, Scalia, Thomas, O'Connor, Souter and Kennedy. This is why he thinks progressive Americans should be more wary about investing too much of their energy in securing judicial authority.

In reflecting upon the present composition of the Supreme Court, Sunstein thinks that we have now come full circle because we face circumstances when conservatives are again dominant. Moreover, legislators are often more progressive than federal judges. In his view, the Rehnquist Court has been unjustifiably frustrating well-intentioned legislators who have been making good faith efforts in dealing with problems over which judges have no special competence. He is particularly angry about the Court's use of its power to frustrate 'programs developed by the president, the Congress, and hundreds of state and local governments' in addressing the crisis in race relations. According to him:

> [d]emocratic considerations strongly argue against an aggressive judicial role in this setting. In general, courts ought not to intrude into state and federal legislative processes where the text and history are ambiguous and where the arguments from basic principle are so unclear.[35]

As we have seen, this statement could have been taken from Judge Robert Bork! The central point that conservatives such as Bork, Scalia and Rehnquist have made about the activism of the Supreme Court under Warren and Burger is that too many of the justices have been willing to impose policies even when they acknowledge 'text and history ' offer no clear guidance.

Sunstein gains credibility by conceding that the conservatives have been right to question judicial activism when this is not supported by objective legal sources (he cites structure, text and history as the sources of law); indeed, there is a heavy irony in his charge that conservatives are inconsistent in securing their favoured agenda through the judiciary while overruling liberal precedents they dislike. This charge hits the target squarely because it makes use of arguments that the conservatives themselves acknowledge as relevant. The conservatives need to avoid this charge (that they make use of the judiciary to secure a conservative agenda that is not supported by the people) precisely because they claim to be motivated by a desire to remove the Court out of the political arena.

If they are to change the United States political system, the conservatives must convince both political parties that the judiciary is now more confined. They must so dominate public debate and perceptions that even future Democratic Party presidents will not wish to nominate judges who are going to reinstate the liberal practice of judicial policymaking that characterized the 1960s and 1970s. But the conservatives are unlikely to succeed if Sunstein is correct in charging that their own use of judicial authority is blatantly political. They must meet his challenge by showing that they are themselves willing to be bound by the text and the actual traditions of the American people in sustaining liberties and in recognizing rights.

Like the conservatives, Sunstein does not argue that judicial review has no proper place in the United States system or that the Bill of Rights should be interpreted so narrowly that it becomes little more than a symbolic affirmation of the society's good intentions. But Sunstein does not want the Court to continue along the path chosen by the Rehnquist majority because he thinks they are wrong in their reading of the First Amendment (forbidding hate speech codes and resisting campaign finance reform), and wrong to read the Fourteenth Amendment as prohibiting affirmative action plans that use racial quotas or set-asides. He most certainly does not think that the protection of rights should be justified by a backward-looking rationale – these are our traditions, this is what we have agreed to in the past, this is what can be recognized by the Court. According to Sunstein past agreements and traditions offer little legitimation because they were often entered into by a select section of the population (for example, the Constitution was negotiated without the participation of African Americans and women). Nor does he think the actual traditions of the American people are always a good guide for these include lynching, segregation and the confining paternalism towards women that has prevented their participation in public life as equals. He tells us that what we learn from history about ourselves must be guided by critical reason to distinguish those elements from the past that must be discarded. Had the Supreme Court merely deferred to past prejudices, he tells us, Roosevelt's New Deal would not have been possible and women and minorities would remain more vulnerable than they are today. This is why he advocates that the justices make substantive judgments about whether past principles ought to continue to have salience. His positive agenda is forward-looking and he argues passionately against the Rehnquist Court's judicial conservatism, which he claims is implicated in the injustices that, although constituted in the past, continue to be reflected in the status quo.

A forward looking Court will still uphold some constitutional rights even unenumerated ones, according to Sunstein, and will sometimes act in a countermajoritarian manner (for example, when a majority of the people in a state think that abortion is a violation of God's will, Sunstein thinks the Court should not allow legislators to respect this fundamental religious belief). In his view, some rights that are listed in the Bill of Rights should be read so that they are no longer constraining (the Takings Clause of the Fifth Amendment) whereas others should be read to legitimate aggressive judicial review (the Establishment Clause of the First Amendment).

These judgments are supported by the use he makes of the 'representation reinforcing' rationale that we explored in considering the work of Ackerman, Meiklejohn and Ely. Sunstein differs from Ely and Meiklejohn in that he claims that a distinctive republican tradition that reflects a commitment 'to deliberation, citizenship, agreement as a regulative ideal, and political equality' can be identified if we look carefully at American history.[36] He argues that the Supreme Court, together with the other branches of government and all citizens, is a guardian of this tradition. It has a responsibility to secure the necessary conditions for effective deliberative democracy. Thus, unlike Ely and Meiklejohn who confine themselves by embracing a Schumpetarian conception of democracy in developing the representation-reinforcing rationale, Sunstein embraces a positive agenda. His Supreme Court would be concerned with substance, not merely with procedure. Indeed, his democracy has the noble purpose of advancing widespread participation by the citizenry and approximate equality of political resources. Ultimately, the purpose of political life is to transform the citizens so that they 'develop salutary human characters';[37] their participation in the system should eventu-

ally change their existing preferences so that they choose liberal policies as their own.[38]

In embracing the notion of 'deliberation' as a laundering mechanism distinguishing 'higher', deliberative lawmaking from the ordinary processes of struggle for power between well-organized interest groups, Sunstein is influenced by Ackerman. For Sunstein, the
relevant consideration is whether the preferences that are counted
have been subjected to critical scrutiny through a process of democratic dialogue in which everyone participates as an equal, and in
which reasons have to be provided to support beliefs. Thus, he dis-
tinguishes 'democracy' conceived as a process for implementing existing desires into law from 'political deliberation', a conception that
embraces a process of preference-laundering so that unacceptable
points of view are disqualified simply on the grounds that the
reasons provided to support them are inadequate. He writes:

> The status quo, too, may be accepted only on the basis of the reasons
> that can be brought forward on its behalf. In this respect, the New
> Dealers subjected the status quo to a version of the impartiality prin-
> ciple, on the antiauthoritarian ground that the distribution of social
> benefits and social burdens must always be defended by reference to
> reasons.[39]

What this means, in effect, is that the New Deal Supreme Court was
justified in questioning the way that the Supreme Court had read the
Due Process Clause of the Fifth Amendment in *Lochner* v. *New York*. It
also means that many assumptions about the importance of rights in
the United States Constitution simply have to be abandoned as indefensible. Like Dworkin, Sunstein is out to disqualify from having
their preferences counted anyone whose views seem to reflect an ill-
considered acceptance of the status quo – for example, those who
support the 'Women Who Want to be Women' movement rather than
feminists.

According to Sunstein, the genius of United States constitutional
democracy lies in the fact that all the different branches of government have an important part to contribute in securing rights, liberties and justice to all. He challenges what he calls the 'court-
centredness' of recent liberal jurisprudence which he believes has
been too focused on experiences under the Warren Court. What he
wishes to see is a new emphasis on the fact that the Constitution is
addressed to everyone, including legislators, executive officials and
ordinary citizens. But Sunstein reassures us that the liberal republican framework is not hostile to the idea of rights. Far from it. According to him, we must read the Constitution as though it were designed to facilitate genuine deliberation because, in this way, we

reconcile the national commitment to rights with its commitment to democracy. In this endeavour, rights will often be justifiable as 'preconditions for the deliberative process itself'. Here Sunstein draws attention to free speech (which must now be read to allow what he wants, namely, rules that regulate political campaigns and advertising in the name of fairness, rules that prohibit hate speech and pornography), privacy (to allow 'a large degree of security and independence from the state' and freedom from 'unreasonable searches and seizures'), and equality (as a defence against political exclusion, racial discrimination, and servitude).[40]

Sunstein's desire to identify some rights that are worthy of the Court's protection, regardless of the political balance of forces, is in conflict with his understanding of the place of the Court as one of the many institutional mechanisms designed to secure rights within the United States political system.[41] More significantly, in making his own selection of what liberties and entitlements are fundamental, Sunstein exhibits a sensitivity that many conservatives in the United States would describe as 'politically correct' (the interests of minorities, women, gay men and lesbians count; the interests of Christian religious communities and white males do not). Thus, he is vulnerable to the very charge he levels at the conservatives: exhibiting a selectivity that is biased by political prejudices. To give one example, the reasons he gives for suggesting that the Court should continue to insist on a principled separation between Church and State in reading the Establishment Clause are totally unsympathetic to religious communities who are told that they may not receive a single dollar from the state to help them educate their children – money that is available to everyone else – and that they may not pray in public schools or decorate their city buildings at Christmas. These restraints on religious communities are imposed even though many American citizens clearly regard religion as central to their identity and social lives, and despite the fact that religious practices have been a part of life in American communities for most of their history.[42] Yet Sunstein encourages the Court to renege on longstanding traditions protecting freedom of speech in order to please feminists or those who advocate hate speech codes.

We see from this that Sunstein's reliance on liberal republican democratic theory serves in a similar way to Dworkin's reliance on egalitarian liberal theory – it enables him to launder the Constitution so that it is coloured the way he likes, eliminating all the stains he regards as nasty. When push comes to shove, the rights that are conceptually derived from Sunstein's commitment to equality/democracy must be afforded priority, according to him, 'trumping' other political considerations that have been historically important. Sunstein criticizes Dworkin for placing too much reliance on the

Supreme Court, allowing that the judiciary is not necessarily the best branch of government for securing rights. But it is difficult to see why a Supreme Court justice who accepts her liberal republican outlook should hold back from imposing the outcomes she desires. Thus, despite the reservations Sunstein articulates about the limitations of the court-centred system in the United States, he is faced by many of the same problems that beset dualist constitutional theories. Indeed, we must suspect that his deliberative approach will not prove successful in practice because he aims to eliminate ordinary people's preferences from the democratic system, declaring them unreasonable.

Political judgment cannot be avoided so long as the Supreme Court in the United States is expected to secure some rights and liberties. So the differences between the conservatives and Sunstein come down, in the end, to a matter of evaluating different strategies. Is the Court wise to frustrate governments who are addressing a particular policy problem? Is the Court wise to ignore tradition? Is the Court wise to depart too far from the Constitution's text in delineating legal rights? Is the court wise to ignore people's actual wishes? Choices of this kind should be evaluated in the light of the shared understanding (between Sunstein and the conservatives) of the constraints on the judiciary in the United States system. But when this is done, we find that Sunstein's judgment is the more vulnerable.

Notes

1 Ronald Dworkin, *Law's Empire*, (London: Fontana Press, 1986), 96. One response to this has been to accuse Dworkin of being an apologist for capitalism! If the political system in the United States does not promote equality or fairness and the coercion used by officials is often outrageous, then anyone who chooses to interpret its institutions as though these ideals are realized simply propagates a misleading description, according to one critic. See Allan C. Hutchinson 'Indiana Dworkin and Law's Empire', *The Yale Law Journal*, vol. 96 (1987), 637–65. But this reading rests on a misunderstanding of what Dworkin is trying to accomplish.

2 Dworkin, op. cit., 52.

3 Ibid., 66.

4 Ibid., 80.

5 Ibid., 93.

6 Dworkin's views about constructive interpretation are crucial to his theory. He develops them at great length and has engaged in an on-going debate with literary critics and philosophers about the nature of interpretation. His views are presented in ibid.

7 Dworkin associates utilitarianism with a different theory of law that he describes as pragmatism. He can dismiss 'pragmatism' because its commitment to 'law' is purely strategic; and he dismisses 'conventionalism' because it cannot make use of arguments available to the 'pragmatist'. But this overlooks the possibility that the two positions may be brought together if more sophisticated versions of

utilitarianism, distinguished by philosophers as 'indirect utilitarianism' or 'rule utilitarianism' are embraced. Most legal positivists in Europe are indirect utilitarians, so there is no reason why the same line of argument cannot be made use of in North America.

8   To maximize certainty, according to Dworkin, conventionalists would have to adopt a mechanical rule for resolving difficult cases. He suggests a position he calls 'unilateral conventionalism' that endorses the rule 'that the plaintiff must win if he or she has a right to win established in the explicit extension of some legal convention, but that otherwise the defendant must win' (ibid., 142). But the opportunities for securing other desirable goals beyond certainty, if such a rule were followed, would be high.

9   See Silas Wasserstrom, 'The Empire's New Clothes', *The Georgetown Law Journal*, vol. 75 (1986), 233.

10   This point is made by Silas Wasserstrom, ibid., 237.

11   Hercules features throughout the second-half of *Law's Empire*, op. cit. (introduced on 239), as well as in earlier essays by Dworkin. See his essay 'Hard Cases' in *Taking Rights Seriously* (Cambridge, Mass.: Harvard University Press, 1977), 105–30.

12   Dworkin, *Law's Empire*, 144–7.

13   437 U.S. 153 (1978). Discussed by Dworkin, ibid., 20–3, 330–47.

14   Ibid., 347.

15   The Act was eventually amended to allow the construction of the dam. Fortunately, the snail darter was not made extinct as a species because it was later discovered to be living in a number of other areas.

16   Dworkin, ibid., 141.

17   *Griggs* v. *Duke Power Co.* 401 U.S 424 (1971); on the legislative history, see Rehnquist's dissenting opinion in *United Steelworkers of America* v. *Weber* 47 L.W. 4851 (1979); also Hugh Graham, *The Civil Rights Era: Origins and Development of National Policy, 1960–72* (NY: Oxford University Press), 383–90; and Robert Fullinwider, *The Reverse Discrimination Controversy: a Moral and Legal Analysis* (Totowa, NJ: Rowman & Allanheld, 1980), 258–61.

18   The Rehnquist conservatives will control how the new amendments are read by the Supreme Court and they are likely to give 'plain meaning' significant weight. Unless Congress actually orders that racial quotas be implemented, the use of quotas or set-asides is unlikely to be tolerated by the Court (except, possibly, in the area of college admissions under the rationale provided by Justice Powell in *Bakke*). The notion that conventional rules do not bind has now penetrated the practice within subordinate courts in the United States who sometimes disregard the rulings of the Supreme Court when they think this expedient or when they believe that they can offer a better interpretation that shows the legal system in a better light. Judges seem to make predictions about how the changing composition of the Supreme Court impacts on a precedent. If they think that a previous ruling of the Supreme Court will no longer be supported by five justices, they sometimes choose to ignore it. For example, Clarence Thomas, writing for the DC Appeals Court before his elevation as an Associate Justice of the Supreme Court, clearly thought that Justice Brennan's opinion for the majority in *Metro Broadcasting* is unlikely to be supported by five votes, given the present composition of the Court; thus he seems to have considered himself free to follow the reasoning of the four dissenting justices, largely ignoring Brennan's opinion. See his opinion for the Court in *Lamprecht* v. *F.C.C.* 958 F. 2d 382 (D.C. Cir. 1992), 390–98. But why not? If Brennan does not regard himself as bound by conventions, by the phrases included in statutes or the Constitution, or by traditions, why should subordinate judges feel that they need to follow his rulings in circumstances when they believe (a) the public would be better served by ignoring them or by placing a different interpreta-

tion upon them, and (b) that there are no longer five justices on the Court who are prepared to stand by them?

19   Dworkin, *Law's Empire*, 190.

20   South Africans have agreed to embrace some forms of positive discrimination, favouring minorities. Thus the interim Constitution (Act No. 200, 1993) provides: (1) that the Senate will be composed of ten senators from each of the nine provinces, regardless of population, # 48; (2) that every party holding at least 80 seats in the 400 seat National Assembly shall be entitled to designate an Executive Deputy President, # 84; and (3) that a party holding at least 20 seats in the National Assembly, and that has decided to participate in the government of national unity, shall be entitled to be allocated one or more of the Cabinet portfolios, # 88.

21   General Viljoen has proposed this. He also demands that the boundaries of the autonomous area must be drawn in such a way that Afrikaners emerge as the dominant ethnic group. See the report by Ross Dunn, 'Double Trouble' in the *Age*, Melbourne, 12 Jan. 1994. Buthelezi also assumes that his ethnic group will be dominant in Kwa-Zulu-Natal but, in his case, it is also clear that he hopes to sustain dominance for the Inkatha Freedom Party through the barrel of a gun.

22   At the time of writing this example is somewhat dated. The Afrikaner nationalists seem to have lost any resolve to continue to fight for a homeland. More significantly, Buthelezi's Inkatha Freedom Party has lost a good deal of its support. Few people wish to fight wars that they are clearly going to lose.

23   Dworkin, ibid., 105.

24   Ronald Dworkin, *Life's Dominion: an Argument about Abortion, Euthanasia, and Individual Freedom* (NY: Alfred A. Knopf, 1993) (defending the trimester framework endorsed in *Roe* v. *Wade*).

25   See Charles Murray, *Losing Ground* (NY Basic Books, 1984); Richard E. Wagner, *To Promote the General Welfare: Market Processes* vs. *Political Transfers* (San Francisco, Calif.: Pacific Research Institute for Public Policy, 1989). Cf. Christopher Jencks, *Rethinking Social Policy: Race, Poverty and the Underclass* (Cambridge, Mass.: Harvard University Press, 1992), ch. 2.

26   As Stephen Carter explains, for Jefferson and other members of the founding generation, 'the idea of separating church from state meant protecting the church from the state – not the state from the church'. See, Stephen L. Carter, *The Culture of Disbelief: How American Law and Politics Trivialise Religious Devotion* (NY: Basic Books, 1993), 115–20.

27   The evidence for these claims provided by Herbert McClosky and Alida Brill, in *Dimensions of Tolerance: What Americans Believe about Civil Liberties* (NY: Russell Sage Foundation, 1983), is quite conclusive. See my discussion in Chapter 2.

28   In making this claim, I have been influenced by the political scientist Theodore Lowi. He gave a lecture at Melbourne University during his visit to Australia in 1991.

29   Robert Hughes, *The Culture of Complaint* (NY: Oxford University Press, 1993); See also David English (editor of London's *Daily Mail* from 1971 to 1992), 'The Greatest Madhouse' (syndicated from *The Spectator*) published in the Melbourne *Age* (Tuesday, 2 Nov. 1993, 11).

30   Cf. John Rawls whose political morality is very similar to Dworkin's. Rawls observes that 'judged by the values of a reasonable political conception of justice', a regime based on parliamentary supremacy with no bill of rights may be thought by some people to be superior. In responding to this claim and others that might be made about other kinds of system, he allows: 'Political liberalism, as such, it should be stressed, does not assert or deny any of these claims and so we need not discuss them' (*Political Liberalism*, NY: Columbia University Press, 1993, 235). In a footnote he also says that he agrees with Robert Dahl who argues that specific solutions to the problem of how to protect rights 'need to be adapted to the historical conditions

and experiences, political culture, and concrete political institutions of a particular country' (citing *Democracy and Its Critics*, New Haven, Conn.: Yale University Press, 1989, 192).

31   Dworkin, *Law's Empire*, 356.

32   Quoted by Silas Wasserstrom, loc. cit., 302 whose discussion of the issues discussed in the text I found very useful. The selection is taken from Dworkin, *Law's Empire*, 375–6.

33   Wasserstrom, loc. cit., 302.

34   See Gerald N. Rosenberg, *The Hollow Hope: Can Courts Bring About Social Change?* (Chicago: Chicago University Press, 1991). I discuss his evidence in Chapter 2. This point is also made by Wasserstrom, ibid.

35   Cass Sunstein, *The Partial Constitution* (Cambridge, Mass.: Harvard University Press, 1993), 150.

36   Ibid., 141 for the definition of liberal republican quoted. Sunstein tells us the notion of deliberative democracy should be understood with reference to three conspicuous sources. The first is the liberal republicanism that has characterised American public law since the founding period. The second is the Civil War and its aftermath. The third is the New Deal reformation of the constitutional system. He also cites political theorists Mill, Rawls and Dewey as exponents of this tradition.

37   Ibid., 141.

38   Ibid., 135.

39   Id., 135.

40   Ibid., 136.

41   Cf. Sunstein on abortion funding with the political pragmatism of O'Connor, Souter and Kennedy. See Nancy Kassop, 'From Arguments to Supreme Court Opinions in *Planned Parenthood* v. *Casey*', *PS: Political Science & Politics*, vol. XXVI, no. 1 (Mar. 1993), 51–9, esp. her section 'Standard of Review', 54–5. The three conservatives understand that *Roe* v. *Wade* impacts on very fundamental values, placing the Court between a rock and a hard place. Thus the pragmatic 'reasonable restraint' test recommended by O'Connor allows the religious communities who object to abortion some opportunity to use the legislative process, without requiring the Court to overrule *Roe* v. *Wade* (as opposed to the normal 'strict scrutiny test' or the alternative 'undue burden standard').

42   See Steven Carter, op. cit.

9   Tribe and Dorf: On How to Read the Constitution

In a recent book, Laurence Tribe and Michael Dorf have been highly critical of Scalia's jurisprudence. Their essay is more interesting than most attempts to diminish Scalia's influence, however, because they take trouble to articulate and contrast their own understanding of how to read the Constitution of the United States. In this chapter I will explore their arguments for it is a major challenge to the conservative resolve to place less reliance on the judiciary in securing rights.[1]

Following James Madison, whom they cite as an authority for the kind of approach they advocate, Tribe and Dorf are convinced that 'judicially enforceable rights are among the necessary "auxiliary precautions" against tyranny';[2] and they view the work of the Warren Court with enormous enthusiasm, also praising Justice William Brennan for sustaining its legacy during the Burger years. Like Brennan, Tribe and Dorf tell us that the Court will need to identify unenumerated rights when they are instrumentally required (for example, the right to own a typewriter or word processor is instrumentally required for free speech to flourish); and they also argue that the Court must identify some liberties (like the right to obtain contraceptives or the right to control the nature of our intimate associations with others) which 'are logically presupposed if those specified are to make much sense'.[3]

As Brennan's successful career demonstrates, these are the guiding assumptions which have prevailed on the Supreme Court through the 1950s, until quite recently. Indeed Tribe and Dorf's book is an attempt to sustain this 'liberal' orthodoxy against the challenge of more conservative approaches of the kind I have delineated in earlier chapters that are now prevailing.

As I have said, my purpose is to consider their arguments. Why do they reject judicial restraint as an ideal? What strategies do they recommend for the Supreme Court in honouring its obligation to uphold the Constitution? How plausible are their criticisms of Scalia?

I show their arguments are compromised by the many problems that characterize earlier attempts to defend judicial activism in the United States. I shall also suggest that Tribe and Dorf exhibit poor political judgment when advocating their brand of activist jurisprudence. In their effort to take rights seriously, they fail to take the democratic processes and traditions in the United States seriously enough; yet it is crucial to seek to secure liberties through the political system for the hope that justice will be secured through the judiciary is a hollow one.[4]

What We Wish It Says and What It Actually Requires

Tribe and Dorf begin by distancing themselves from those who treat the open-ended nature of the Constitution's text as an invitation to make it exactly what they wish it to be. They cite Ronald Dworkin as someone who is guilty of this kind of wishful jurisprudence because he recommends that the justices impose their own vision of what a good constitution should require. For Tribe and Dorf, in contrast:

> The authority of the Constitution, its claim to obedience and the force that we permit it to exercise in our law and over our lives, would lose all legitimacy if it really were only a mirror for the readers' ideas and ideals.[5]

According to them, a line between what we wish the text would say and what it actually requires must be maintained. It is in this spirit that they seek to articulate 'principles of interpretation that can anchor the Constitution in some more secure, determinate, and external reality'.[6]

As we have seen, this point of departure is shared by Justice Scalia. According to him, competent legal advisers should be able to know roughly where to look in establishing the law. If they do not, there is something wrong with the judicial theory the Supreme Court is employing. In his view, the Court should recognize that indeterminacy in law, although sometimes inevitable, is not a good thing and should be avoided when this is possible. Thus, Scalia argues that the Supreme Court has a responsibility to read the Constitution in a manner that indicates that it will strive to cite objective sources and it should articulate clear rules even if this narrows its own discretion.

In a footnote attached to his judgment in *Michael H.* v. *Gerald D.* Scalia adds an important clarification of his method. He tells us the Court must be backward-looking not forward-looking; its responsibility 'is to prevent future generations from lightly casting aside important traditional values – not to ... invent new ones'.[7] Thus,

historical evidence such as the ratification of the Civil War Amendments will sometimes establish the importance of a liberty but historical evidence may also count against the existence of a right which
individuals assert in asking for the Court's protection. Scalia argues
that it is always impermissible for the Court to ignore 'a long-standing and still extant societal tradition withholding the very right pronounced to be the subject of a liberty interest'.[8] This is why Scalia
regards the *Roe* v. *Wade* abortion decision as such a serious abuse of
judicial discretion. The majority ignored historical evidence that
showed conclusively that the American people did not share an
understanding that the liberty in question was fundamental. To prevent itself from simply deciding to do what it thinks without regard
to text or tradition, as happened in *Roe*, Scalia suggests that the
Supreme Court would be wise to test any claim by reference 'to the
most specific level at which a relevant tradition protecting, or denying a protection to, the asserted right can be identified'.[9] If a practice
is well known but has never been protected, it cannot be presumed
that there is a fundamental liberty to engage in it. In his view, judges
are bound by the laws and traditions of their own society and are not
free to invent law so as to make it into the kind of society they wish it
to be.

Reading the Ninth Amendment

Tribe and Dorf wish to reject Scalia's positivism without embracing
philosophical jurisprudence. But it is not easy to see how this is
possible. If they allow that judges are free to make use of subjective
sources in determining the law, it is difficult to see how this discretion will be restrained. A judge's interpretation of the open-ended
constitutional phrases will empower him or her in just the way that
Dworkin envisages.

One way of rejecting Dworkin's approach without embracing
Scalia's is to show that the Constitution mandates judicial activism.
Tribe and Dorf attempt to persuade us that the Ninth Amendment
(which states: 'The enumeration in the Constitution of certain rights
shall not be construed to deny or disparage others retained by the
people') should be read as a broad mandate for the making of 'constitutional choices'. They argue, then, that there is an 'objective source
for the kind of innovations initiated by Brennan and other activist
justices during the Warren–Burger period'.

But this seems wrong as a matter of law, for the Supreme Court
has been cautious about reading the Ninth Amendment as an open-
ended mandate to discover rights. Restraint is necessary in reading
the Ninth Amendment because the justices must balance the ideal of

fidelity to the Constitution against other important ideals and objectives, such as, democratic accountability, 'certainty' in the law, and the need for public sources. Modern judges are also wise to be cautious about commitments made in the eighteenth century because these are usually informed by a discredited natural law philosophy or by reflections that presume a much simpler society and level of technology. This is especially the case when the liberties in question are in conflict with other important political principles.

Although Tribe and Dorf are happy to dispose of the right to acquire and use weapons, citing original intent as a good justification for reading out the Second Amendment,[10] and they favour restricting the Lockean property right protected under the Fifth Amendment, also approving *West Coast Hotel* v. *Parrish* in which the Court refused to secure the liberty to enter into economic contracts,[11] they advocate a broad reading of the Ninth Amendment. Indeed, as I have noted, its open-ended invitation provides the key with which they hope to reconcile their fidelity to the Constitution as the foundation of law in the United States and their activist jurisprudence. According to them, the Constitution's text advocates activism in the Ninth Amendment! For Tribe and Dorf, the justices of the Supreme Court should view the Ninth Amendment's instruction 'not to disparage unenumerated rights' in the way that a dutiful son who is told 'always do the right thing' by his mother might view her advice. They write:

> The dutiful son would strive to do the right thing, knowing that he will sometimes falter, but knowing that if he simply abandons the effort to implement his mother's wishes he will surely fail. So too, judges, legislators and other officials sworn to uphold the Constitution would be derelict in their duty if they were simply to ignore those parts of the document whose meaning is not crystal-clear to them. ...
> You may not *like* the Ninth Amendment, but it is undeniably part of the Constitution.[12]

According to Tribe and Dorf, then, the justices may not ignore the instruction of the Ninth Amendment even though it seems to blur the distinction between what they think the Constitution says and what they wish it would say.[13] They write:

> The Ninth Amendment creates and confers no rights; it is a rule of interpretation. In fact it is the *only* rule of interpretation *explicitly* stated in the Constitution. It tells each reader: whatever else you're going to say to conclude [that a claimed right is not protected] ... you cannot advance the argument that those rights are not there just because they are not enumerated in the Bill of Rights.

The Constitution does not mention identity cards, compulsory seat belts in vehicles, helmets for cyclists, topless dancing, electronic lie detectors, sophisticated surveillance equipment, the right to die, surrogacy arrangements for childbearing, political advertising, commercial speech, cable television, family life in prisons, modern pornography or social security entitlements. Nevertheless, according to Tribe and Dorf, the Supreme Court must find a way of reviewing policies dealing with all these matters. Not only must it detect the circumstance when government policies violate the enumerated rights, it must protect unenumerated rights.

But there is no objective way of doing this, nor does the Court have the resources or the time to undertake the necessary research and to consider all the implications of the many policy choices it needs to make. For example, if a future United States government decided that the present Social Security Number was not serving as an adequate tool in preventing tax evasion, financial frauds, money laundering, immigration fraud and abuse of the welfare system, it could not contemplate introducing a more comprehensive identity system without considering how the Supreme Court is likely to view its initiative. Otherwise it would find that after spending millions of dollars in consulting, planning and introducing a modern Identity Card, it is faced by a judicial ruling that a protected liberty had been implicated. It would not matter that years of discussion and planning had been undertaken involving more than one administration or even that the proposals were supported by both parties in the Congress. Nor could the government planners resolve the civil rights issue in advance for it is not possible (thanks to the jurisprudence recommended by Tribe and Dorf!) to identify the protected liberties simply by reading the Constitution carefully or looking at past cases. Good lawyers are likely to find arguments supporting a variety of solutions precisely because, in their view, the sources of law in the United States sometimes includes philosophical arguments and assumptions. In the end, the government's lawyers will have to guess which arguments are the most likely to influence the various members of the Court. Because the Constitution says nothing about identity cards or the problems of regulating financial transactions or delivering health and other services in a complex society, the justices will make the final judgment and the government must abide by it. Rightly so, according to Tribe and Dorf, because the Court is responsible for protecting unenumerated liberties. Indeed, they cite the Ninth Amendment to challenge Justice Scalia's more modest judicial scepticism that views this kind of broad-ranging scrutiny as a form of countermajoritarian hubris.

The Framers and the Ninth Amendment

But the framers did not intend the Ninth Amendment to be read this way. The Ninth and Tenth Amendments were inserted to make clear that the framers had no intention of granting unenumerated powers to the federal government.[14] The Anti-Federalists who demanded this reassurance were very concerned to ensure that the newly created federal government should not usurp the authority of the states. None of the framers seems to have been preoccupied with crafting a document that would allow future generations an easy means of amendment through unbridled judicial interpretation. Policymaking powers were placed in the hands of state governments and Congress, as was the power to amend the Constitution. The framers simply had no conception of the kind of judicial review that was to be exercised by the Supreme Court in the twentieth century; indeed Article III of the Constitution, which spells out judicial power, is among the least informative of the sections delineating the separation of powers.

Even if we concede that Tribe and Dorf are correct in thinking that the framers deliberately instructed future Supreme Courts to identify unenumerated rights, they never question whether this is a satisfactory arrangement. For them, judicial activism is a part of the constitutional plan that all Supreme Court justices have sworn to honour. In terms of this view, any justice who does not acknowledge this responsibility fails to uphold the Constitution's promise. Thus, when considering the death penalty in *Furman* v. *Georgia* (see p. 139–41 above), Chief Justice Burger should have decided what is to count as 'cruel and unusual'. This is what he is sworn to do, according to Tribe and Dorf, and he is wrong to claim that this choice was not his to make. Indeed, they seem to regard a judge who is reluctant to address 'constitutional choices' on behalf of the nation as a dissembler – in their view, he usually has a hidden political agenda.[15] Why Supreme Court justices are bound by the framers' undemocratic instruction to overrule policy-judgments made by legislators but may ignore all of the framers' other intentions (substituting their own, better conceptions) is a puzzle.

Drawing a Line Between Philosophy and Law

Tribe and Dorf characterize their dispute with Justice Scalia and other conservatives as involving a disagreement over the level of abstraction at which legal reasoning should proceed. But this is misleading because Scalia's point is that the appeal by judges to abstract general principles illegitimately dislodges law from its more traditional sources in text and history. Scalia worries that if legal reasoning should proceed through an appeal to abstract general principles, law reduces to applied political philosophy.

This is a problem for Tribe and Dorf because, as we have seen, they concede that 'law' should not be reduced to philosophy. They seek to disclose the difference that the Constitution makes. Thus, they think it important to identify objective sources for only in this way can they effectively distance themselves from the philosophical jurisprudence advocated by Ronald Dworkin. But their attempt to secure an objective source for legal activism by citing the Ninth Amendment is an unsatisfactory way of achieving this goal. When we examine their arguments, we find that they do not depart very far from a philosophical approach in practice, as is shown when we review what Tribe and Dorf tell us about the importance of general principles in their account of the privacy cases.

Consider the subordinate principles that various judges and scholars make use of: 'the right to be let alone', 'the right to control the nature of intimate associations with others', 'the right to decide whether or not to beget or bear a child', 'the right to make decisions about family, marriage and conduct'. Tribe and Dorf argue that appeals to these kinds of principles help various justices connect cases that the Court had resolved or was considering and they characterize divisions on the Court as involving disputes about which abstract principle is the most appropriate in the circumstances of a particular case.[16] Following what they take to be the second Justice Harlan's method in *Poe* v. *Ullman*, they write:

> To the extent that it coheres with our experience to view decisions about childrearing and family, decisions about marriage, and decisions about procreation as concerning completely isolated areas of life … we will not seek an underlying unifying principle. However, if presumptively excluding government from these areas of life appears to be a connected project – if these freedoms appear to be different manifestations of the same underlying liberty to control the nature of one's intimate associations – then we might well connect the 'points' of liberty …[17]

As we have seen, Tribe and Dorf do not recommend that we model legal reasoning in the hierarchical manner recommended by those who embrace philosophical approaches. This kind of reasoning, while perfectly legitimate among political philosophers, reduces law to philosophy and we end up with an ever diminishing Constitution as text and history become less and less relevant. The method completely obscures the relationship between law and politics. Power relations which secure unfair benefits are simply deemed illegitimate – indeed, any traditional practice in conflict with liberal principles is deemed to be a violation of fundamental interests that are held to be constitutionally protected.

If power and public sentiment did not matter, substituting philosophy for law would be a good thing. As Plato argued, the best possible society is one in which the philosopher imposes his or her conception of justice. But Tribe and Dorf have conceded that it is essential to maintain a stance 'in which reading the Constitution differs from writing one'.[18] Thus they need to provide an account of philosophical jurisprudence that avoids this consequence.

Restraining Philosophical Jurisprudence

One way they explore possibilities for restraining philosophical jurisprudence is by considering what would happen if the Constitution were to be amended so that its core provisions were incompatible with one another. For example, suppose the Constitution is changed to frustrate the protection of the First Amendment by a duly ratified amendment allowing Congress to prohibit burning or otherwise desecrating the national flag. What should the Supreme Court do if it were forced to evaluate a flag-desecration statute in this circumstance? What we face here, according to Tribe and Dorf, is a conflict between the abstract principle of free speech presupposed in the First Amendment and the new Flag-Desecration Amendment. If the Court appeals to abstract principles, it must find this incompatibility intolerable. This is because flag-burning at public demonstrations is a means whereby very angry citizens express deep dissatisfaction with government policies – a liberty which lies at the core of the First Amendment. If we seek coherence in constitutional adjudication and are inclined to generalize across cases in the light of abstract principles without noting the actual understandings that people have articulated and embraced, we may argue that attempted constitutional amendments that conflict with the core of the First Amendment are simply unacceptable and should be ignored.[19]

Tribe and Dorf think that such a cavalier attitude would violate legal norms. In their view, such disregard for the Constitution would take abstract theorizing too far. To illustrate why this is so, they ask us to consider another hypothetical set of circumstances. Suppose that a group of law professors get together to write their own version of the Constitution. Let us say they dislike the arrangements embodied in the actual Constitution proposed at the Philadelphia Convention and ratified by the American people, believing that their own proposed document offers better prospects for justice and liberty. Tribe and Dorf comment as follows:

What makes the former the actual supreme law of the land and the law professors' effort a mere conceit are certain beliefs about political theory and history ... readers of the Constitution agree that sovereignty derives from the people; that one generation may bind another; and that the Philadelphia Convention of 1787 and subsequent ratification process were in fact expressions of the national will to create a lasting government. [20]

This is mostly right. Resilient liberty must reflect some shared understanding about the national will even when it is not what we wish it to be. The professors' constitution is worthless to the extent that it fails to embody the political will necessary to secure it as the basis of public life.

But Tribe and Dorf also mention political theory. Why do they suppose that the professors' Constitution is less adequate when viewed in the light of philosophy? After all, the whole point of the professors' enterprise is to secure a constitution which is easier to justify than the present one in the light of the best available theory of justice. Let us suppose the leader in the group is Professor Ronald Dworkin and that he recruits distinguished political philosophers to provide additional support and advice. Even so, Tribe and Dorf are correct to see that constitutional law is not a story these academics are able to make up in the light of abstract principles of justice; its substance must be rooted in the actual traditions and understandings that inform social life – and this includes reverence for the phrases of the Constitution actually ratified by the people, as well as for longstanding conventions and practices.

Let us change the hypothetical case. Suppose that Professor Dworkin and members of his group are suddenly called upon to serve on the Supreme Court. Imagine that some terrorist has blown-up the Supreme Court building killing all nine justices and that President Clinton unwisely recruits Professor Tribe to help him nominate the nine most reliable liberals in the land. Suppose, in the crisis, the Senate confirms all these unlikely candidates. Would they now be entitled to implement their plans?

The nomination and confirmation process is no substitute for the actual processes by means of which the national will has manifested itself over the years. It contributes by securing justices who reflect prevailing opinions at the time of their appointment, of course, and the selection of the justices is an important manifestation of the national will. The nine justices in our scenario are recently appointed by one president and cannot presume to enjoy a mandate to rewrite the Constitution. If they do choose to embrace their abstract ideals, disregarding the actual Constitution and the conventions and understandings that have prevailed in the United States, they will discredit their role as justices.

But why is this behaviour – in such a good cause – so different from Justice William Brennan's practice (recommended by Tribe and Dorf) of ignoring longstanding traditions that he dislikes (such as the persistent attempts by state governments to impose regulations that make it difficult for women to secure abortions, individuals to commit suicide, or the terminally ill to refuse life-sustaining treatment) simply because they are incompatible with the rights that he believes, in the light of the abstract philosophical principles that seem to have most relevance, ought to be protected? If abstract philosophical principles should not prevail in dealing with constitutional amendments, such as the proposed Flag Desecration Amendment, why should they prevail in the face of a conflicting 'long-standing and still extant tradition' when expounding the unwritten 'text'? Isn't Scalia right to treat a tradition 'withholding the very right pronounced to be the subject of a liberty interest' as analogous to a discordant constitutional amendment? Why are Tribe and Dorf entitled to ignore political reality and public understandings (signalled by persistent patterns of behaviour on the part of governments) when they cite abstract principles to pick out the unenumerated rights enjoyed by citizens; yet they concede that they are not entitled to make use of these abstract principles when the understandings in question are listed in the text? The liberal practice exemplified by Brennan's record and supported by Tribe and Dorf – of selecting only what is in accordance with the best philosophical understanding of a just society – is in conflict with their scrupulous fidelity to illiberal terms set out in the Constitution that render the document incoherent.

Let us assume that activist justices come to dominate on the Supreme Court in less dramatic ways. Suppose President Clinton makes four appointments (choosing activist judges) and that he is followed by another Democrat who also appoints two justices. In this circumstance, it is plausible to argue that there is now a mandate for the Court to impose a liberal agenda. But it would be wiser for them to try to keep the Supreme Court out of the political arena by citing objective sources for their rulings. The justices will know that the role of the Supreme Court will not be critical in securing progressive changes for the other branches of government, now dominated by the liberals who appointed them, will be better placed to act; and they will also know that serious damage to the integrity of the Court will follow if appointments are viewed as a crucial means for achieving political goals. To put the point bluntly: when the Court acts with a genuine mandate, its activist role will be unnecessary; when it acts without a mandate, it is likely to be ineffective in securing the implementation of its rulings and will likely provoke a significant backlash, empowering conservative politicians who are hostile to liberal ideals. These politicians will promise to pack the Court to undo the work of the liberals.

Conclusion

What is troubling about Tribe and Dorf's account is that they do not see why any solution to what we might call the 'tyranny' of abstraction must not only appeal to the text of the Constitution (their own solution), but to the traditions and practices of the American people. The sources of law (text, tradition and precedent), as Scalia recognizes, reflect a prevailing consensus. It may be desirable to go beyond this consensus and, as policy advocates, we may hope for progressive changes. But if judges act to frustrate democratically elected politicians who are deemed too slow in securing these desired outcomes (presumably, because they sense that influential groups in the community are not willing to accept the change in question) unexpected and undesirable consequences are likely to follow. This is why leadership for securing liberal objectives in a democracy is best left to politicians who are accountable to the people for what they do. Without consensus in the community, judicial rulings are impotent and usually self-defeating; when there is a consensus that change is necessary, the judges can afford to defer. Because liberals like Tribe and Dorf seem unaware of this, it is conservatives, like Justices Rehnquist and Scalia, who see the relationship between law, politics, and philosophy more clearly.

Notes

1   Laurence H. Tribe and Michael C. Dorf, *On Reading the Constitution* (Cambridge, Mass.: Harvard University Press, 1991).
2   Ibid., 6.
3   Ibid., 77.
4   See Gerald N. Rosenberg *The Hollow Hope: Can Courts Bring About Social Change?* (Chicago: University of Chicago Press, 1991) who demonstrates the dependence of the judiciary on the other branches of government.
5   Tribe and Dorf, op. cit., 14.
6   Ibid., 15.
7   105 L Ed 2d 91, 105, n. 2.
8   Id.
9   Id.
10   Tribe and Dorf, op cit., 11.
11   Ibid., 65.
12   Ibid., 53–4. This statement is similar to the analogy that Dworkin uses in *Taking Rights Seriously* (Cambridge, Mass.: Harvard University Press, 1977), 134–6. His position is closer to their own than they seem to think because, like them, Dworkin claims that the Constitution requires a form of interpretation that requires the articulation of a theory. Cf. my discussion of Dworkin, (see 79–80).
13   Tribe and Dorf, op cit., 17.
14   James H. Hutson, 'The Bill of Rights and the American Revolutionary Experience' in M. Lacey and K. Haakonssen (eds), *A Culture of Rights: the Bill of Rights in*

Philosophy, Politics and Law – 1792 and 1991 (NY: Cambridge University Press, 1991) 88–96.

15   See Tribe and Dorf, op. cit., 109-110.
16   Ibid., 73ff.
17   Ibid., 78.
18   Ibid., 17.
19   Tribe and Dorf cite W. Murphy, 'An Ordering of Constitutional Values' in *Southern California Law Review* (53), (1980) 703, 755–6, as someone who has defended this view. The position has recently been defended by John Rawls who tells us, 'The successful practice of its ideas and principles over two centuries place restrictions on what can now count as an amendment, whatever was true at the beginning' (*Political Liberalism*, NY: Columbia University Press, 1993, 235) This would be plausible if the historical claim was persuasive, but we know that the First Amendment principles that Rawls defends have not been broadly endorsed by the American people for 200 years. Far from it. They have been endorsed by a few of the justices over a period of two or three decades. Even the Court has been fundamentally divided about which free speech principles to apply in difficult cases, see D.F.B. Tucker, *Law, Liberalism and Free Speech* (Totowa, NJ: Rowman & Allanheld, 1985).
20   Tribe and Dorf, op. cit., 83.

10 Bringing it all Together: The Affirmative Action Controversy

In this chapter I will try to illustrate many of the perspectives I have outlined in earlier chapters by showing them at work. No issue has divided conservatives and liberals more than the debate about affirmative action. Although there is consensus in the United States that it is appropriate for judges and administrators to remedy past injustice when this can be attributed to the actions of identifiable agents, there is a heated controversy over whether any agency of government may use legal instruments to change the distribution of resources in society between racial groups when no prior acts of discrimination (giving rise to undesirable inequalities) have been identified. Suppose that legislators think the United States would be a better community if there were more African Americans in positions of power and leadership so they favour this group in allocating university scholarships. In this circumstance, they do not accuse the nation's universities of discriminating on the basis of race. Rather they choose to discriminate in order to ensure that more African Americans are assisted than other Americans who would otherwise be eligible for the scholarship. This widespread practice of advantaging specifically designated ethnic groups is known as 'forward-looking affirmative action'. This chapter will be concerned with the debate about forward-looking affirmative action, both among conservatives and between them and liberals. The orientation that I will delineate and assess will serve to illustrate some of the strengths and weaknesses of the various approaches that I have already identified in earlier chapters.

The issue of forward-looking affirmative action is especially difficult for conservatives because they wish to exercise judicial power to disallow the initiatives of various levels of government in addressing

187

the problem of racism in the United States. Significantly, their treatment of the issue is quite different from their treatment of privacy problems. In the latter case, as we have seen, they argue that the judiciary has no authority to exercise judicial review and try to show why liberal claims that this is justified are unpersuasive. In the former case, in contrast, the positions are reversed – it is liberals who require courts to defer to legislators, whereas the conservatives wish to exercise judicial review. Because of this reversal, it is necessary for the conservatives to explain why they think it is appropriate for judges to defer to legislators who violate the privacy of individuals but argue that it is legitimate to overrule their initiatives when they seek to pursue policies to increase minority participation as business people, in the professions or to help them gain positions of power.

In analyzing this debate, I will explore disputes relating to the appropriate interpretation of the Civil Rights Act (1964), focusing on *Griggs* v. *Duke Power Co.* and *United Steelworkers of America* v. *Weber*, and cases that involve competing interpretations of the Fourteenth Amendment, focusing on *City of Richmond* v. *Croson* and *Metro Broadcasting* v. *FCC*. The two constitutional cases differ in that the forward-looking affirmative action programme in *Croson* is authorized by a local council whereas the Federal Communications Commission (responsible for the programme at issue in *Metro Broadcasting*) is supervized by the United States Congress. Nevertheless, the circumstances giving rise to the cases are similar for they concern the efforts of various, governmental agencies to secure the greater participation of African Americans and other minorities in American society. For example, in Richmond, Virginia, the City Council wished to change a situation in which minority businesses receive only 0.67 per cent of prime municipal contracts to one in which they must receive 30 per cent. Similarly, the Federal Communications Commission aimed at achieving broadcasting diversity through its discriminatory policies favouring minorities and women. These important objectives are not remedial in the sense of compensating particular individuals who have suffered because of past discrimination; rather, the beneficiaries are businesspeople who may not be particularly deserving in their own right.

Affirmative Action

The foundations of affirmative action programmes resulting from the Fourteenth Amendment go back to the school desegregation cases, beginning with the landmark decision *Brown* v. *Board of Education*.[1] When the Supreme Court ordered the dismantling of segregation in southern school districts, reasoning that African–American children could not be offered an equal education as long as they were taught in separate schools, it was found that the use of racial quotas in allocating school placements was sometimes necessary. Thus, to eliminate one harmful effect of past racism the Court accepted the use of race as a basis for discriminating between individuals.

School desegregation poses enormous ethical and legal difficulties that have not yet been fully resolved. In many respects, however, the problems are easier to deal with than those that arise in other affirmative-action cases. For one thing, the harm addressed is clearly identifiable – the inferior, educational opportunities offered in some public schools. Moreover, this could be easily remedied by desegregating the schools. Unless the schools were reorganized (so that they were no longer predominantly white or black), the lives of the disadvantaged African–American children would have continued to be deleteriously affected. Thus, to prevent harm to African–American children, the southern school districts had to integrate the previously segregated schools and this often required them to make use of racial quotas. The use of race as one basis for discrimination in allocating school placements is benign in this context because it does not (in theory at least) harm any individual or group selectively. The purpose is to offer the same educational opportunities to everyone by ensuring that any school is as good as any other within the districts implementing the plans.[2] No child can complain that he or she is asked to carry a heavier burden than any of the others. (I leave out of account here the burden of having to travel to a distant school on a bus.)

It is understandable that minority leaders in the United States demand more in challenging the effects of racism. Their over-representation in remedial or punitive institutions and under-representation within the professions and business are partly a result of past deprivation and discrimination. Not surprisingly, then, civil rights advocates concerned about addressing the continuing effects of past illegal discrimination, hope the implementation of affirmative action will prove useful. But many of the programmes they recommend impact on innocent individuals in harmful ways. Thus, in the programmes under review in *Croson* and *Metro Broadcasting*, business people who might otherwise qualify for government contracts or for a broadcasting licence are disqualified on the basis of their race. Moreover the persons who stand to benefit from this have no personal claim to this favourable treatment, serving as representatives for their group. The kind of harm addressed by these more forward-looking programmes is also, often, significantly different to the harm alleged to be caused by segregated schools. What does it matter to a poor, unemployed person whether a few select members of his-or-her minority group get into graduate, business or professional degree programmes at elite universities? Why should it matter to such an individual if prosperous business people are given a greater share of government contracts or are privileged in obtaining broadcasting licences? He or she is not affected directly but may only benefit indirectly, if at all; whereas, in the case of school desegregation, African–American children benefit directly by the outcome and they would have suffered serious harm if the schools had been allowed to remain segregated.

In fact, most affirmative action programmes aim to achieve collective goals (such as improved social harmony through the elimination of prejudice or greater diversity in broadcasting). Indeed, many are forward-looking rather than remedial in orientation and no specific individuals are the intended beneficiaries. We all benefit when society is improved by having more African Americans and other minorities in the police or working as school teachers, competing in business, or practicing as lawyers and doctors.[3]

From a legal point of view the problem which forward-looking affirmative action programmes present arises largely from the fact that they invariably involve a harmful discrimination against some innocent, identifiable party. The Court must then decide whether this harm is legitimate, given the important societal concerns that often motivate the programmes. Moreover, the Court must come to terms with its own past declarations that the use of race as a basis for classifying individuals in allocating burdens violates the Fifth and Fourteenth Amendments of the Constitution.[4] It has also had to face the fact that the Civil Rights Act 1964 (as Amended by the Equal Employment Act of 1972) provides that it is unlawful for an employer to discriminate on the basis of an individual's race, colour, sex or national origin.[5] If the Court chooses to tolerate any affirmative action programme, then, it must explain why it is making an exception to its previous holding that discrimination by race is constitutionally proscribed in most circumstances; and it must explain how the use of race-conscious quotas can be reconciled with the Civil Rights Act.

Affirmative Action and the Civil Rights Act: *Griggs* and *Weber*

Those who believe that constitutional protections are more potent than statutory protections will be surprised to learn that the Civil Rights Act has proved more enduring in establishing the 'equal protection of the laws' for minorities in the United States than the Fourteenth Amendment.

As Charles Fried explains in *Order & Law*, the Civil Rights Act had resulted in the widespread resort to racial quotas by employers who sought to demonstrate their willingness to comply with the Act's provision in the most convincing way possible. To avoid the charge that they discriminate, many companies ensure that the number of employees they recruit from minority communities reflects the number of the minorities among the pool of qualified applicants. They achieve this by imposing racial quotas or (until this practice was forbidden) by the 'race norming' of aptitude and other tests.[6] These practices violate the traditional 'merit' system in terms of which individual applicants are recruited or promoted on the basis of their achieved score in tests, on the basis of their past experience and on their demonstrated capacity to perform various tasks.

The Reagan administration opposed the use of quotas and 'race norming' as a matter of political principle (because it discriminated against white applicants), as a matter of economic rationalism (because managers must enjoy a prerogative to hire the best possible labour force if American industry is to compete effectively in world markets) and as a matter of political expediency (because any president who was seen to support racial preferences for minorities would lose significant electoral support). But the President was not supported by the Congress. Indeed, the issue of preferences for minorities goes to the heart of one of the many battles between the United States Congress and the presidency.

Republicans who have dominated in recent presidential elections view the Democratic Party controlled Congress as a problem institution that operates in a manner largely indifferent to the wishes of the electorate. What often happens when Congress is forced to address politically sensitive issues, according to the Republicans, is that it tries to please every side and often succeeds in doing this by delegating its constitutional authority to administrative agencies or to the federal courts. Thus, deliberately vague statutes are enacted so that the members of Congress on either side of an issue are free to claim victory. Resolution of ambiguity takes place later, at the time of implementation, when bureaucrats must interpret the statute or when disputes over the significance of the sometimes meaningless phrases are brought before the federal courts and specialist tribunals. Republicans are frustrated because legislating seems to be a process that often takes place at one remove from Congress, avoiding the possibility of a presidential veto. They argue that this delegation of authority is undesirable because it encourages politicians to lead from behind without exposing the policymaking process to the scrutiny of the electorate.

Griggs v. *Duke Power Co.* and *United Steelworkers of America* v. *Weber* were particularly troubling to most Republicans because these rulings transformed the Civil Rights Act from what was publicly heralded as a statute that prohibits the use of sexual or racial categories into one that mandates the use of racial and sexual quotas in hiring, firing and promotion decisions. The cases illustrate the Democrat's strategy of rule by indirect control, according to Republicans, and allowed politicians to take credit for opposing discrimination while avoiding responsibility for imposing quotas.

Most Americans dislike racism and do not think that a person's race should determine whether they are employed or promoted. This is why pressure built for the enactment of the Civil Rights Act in 1964. But most Americans also dislike the use of racial and sexual quotas to help minorities (which they take to be a form of reverse racism) and, to placate them, the Civil Rights Act included a clause stating that the Act should not be interpreted to require preferential treatment because of race or 'on account of an imbalance which may exist with respect to the total number or percentage of persons of any race ... employed'. The Democrats, who sponsored the Bill called the quota-hiring fear a 'nonexistent ... bugaboo' but there were many who suspected that the, then, liberal Supreme Court would regard the use of racial quotas as the only effective, feasible, means for addressing the entrenched, racially motivated, exclusion of vulnerable groups. Those Democrats who agreed with this view were prepared to personally disown any ambition for promoting quotas – they wanted to be re-elected – but they secretly hoped or even suspected that a likely result of the Act's anti-discrimination requirement would be that some companies that persistently excluded minorities or employed them only in low-paying menial capacities would be ordered to implement remedial, affirmative-action programmes.

This anticipated result underestimated the degree to which the Supreme Court had moved toward egalitarianism during the 1960s. The Court's reading of the Act in *Griggs* and *Weber* went beyond the imposition of remedial quotas on those who persistently discriminated (against the express wishes of Congress), for the Court took the Act to be addressing the problem which has come to be known as 'structural discrimination' – inequalities between races that make the prospects for advancement of some groups better than for others.[7] In *Griggs* the Court ruled that so long as an employer's practices had a 'disparate impact' on minority employment, racial discrimination would be presumed; so, if a company is to avoid having to pay compensation it must ensure that its work force is racially representative in the required manner or it must explain why its failure to hire enough minorities is justified by 'business necessity'. This 1971 ruling left employers exposed for they could (a) abandon testing potential employees and ensure that they recruit sufficient employees from the designated minorities (b) test applicants to select the most capable but adjust the test results so that they do not produce a 'disparate impact' or (c) show that a given test is required by 'business necessity'. The last requirement is a difficult burden to meet and the first two strategies require the employer to use racial quotas.

Griggs is blatantly hypocritical – allowing the screening of applicants by tests deemed to be inappropriate (insufficient to establish the business-necessity justification) yet allowing companies to require different levels of competence in those same tests for various racial groups (white workers who did not achieve a minimum score were deemed unemployable, whereas minorities with much lower scores were employed).[8] The ruling also places employers between a rock and a hard place: if they wish to avoid vulnerability under *Griggs*, they need to discriminate in favour of minorities; but whites, who lose out, can then claim that this racial discrimination violates the anti-discrimination requirement of the Civil Rights Act. This conflict is resolved in *Weber* when, in 1979, the Court ruled that private companies which voluntarily embrace racial quotas in affirmative action programmes to remedy 'traditional patterns of racial segregation and hierarchy' are entitled to do this.

Weber completed the transformation of a statute introduced as a remedy for harms suffered by individuals because of subjective discrimination into one primarily concerned to rectify structural inequalities between racial groups in the United States. What is remarkable is how this judicial usurpation of the legislative role proceeded without provoking a response from the legislators. It provoked the public and the various Republican presidents;[9] but Congress has been disinclined to express itself on the issue of quotas and, until 1991 when it enacted a new Civil Rights Act that includes a clause forbidding race-norming, it preferred to leave leadership on civil rights matters with the Supreme Court.[10]

Conservative Response to the Liberal Reading of the Civil Rights Act 1964

Fried is clearly sympathetic to the Republican side of this debate and takes pride in explaining how, under his leadership as Solicitor General, the Reagan administration successfully persuaded the Supreme Court to retreat from *Griggs*. The first part of Fried's strategy involved reminding the justices of their own analysis of the Fourteenth Amendment's Equal Protection Clause. By working through relevant cases (like *Regents of the University of California v. Bakke, United Steelworkers of America v. Weber, Wygant v. Jackson Board of Education, New York Transit Authority v. Beazer, Washington v. Davis*[11]) Fried was able to show that most of the justices had (a) endorsed the view that race quotas should be tolerated only when they are needed to remedy the disabling effects of identified discrimination (or when the state has some other 'compelling' reason);[12] and (b) been willing to take a flexible view of 'business necessity' (for example, ruling that the

New York City Transit Authority may choose not to employ anyone using narcotic drugs and that the D.C. Police Department may use a verbal aptitude test, even though these requirements excluded many African Americans and Hispanics from potential employment[13]).

Fried's second strategy involved finding a suitable case to remind the Court that Congress has no authority to require companies to discriminate in ways that the Constitution forbids. Nor had it intended this in 1964 when the Civil Rights Act was introduced – according to him, the Supreme Court's ruling in *Griggs* was in conflict with the Fourteenth Amendment. Fried believed that once the justices were shown that *Griggs* forced private companies to embrace racial quotas in their employment practices, they would reverse their ruling. What he needed was a case that highlighted the inconsistency between *Griggs* and the Rehnquist Court's understanding of the Equal Protection Clause. It was necessary to persuade the Court that a statistical imbalance in the proportion of racial groups employed by a private company – the so-called 'disparate impact' rule enunciated in *Griggs* – did not amount to sufficient evidence to establish the 'identified discrimination' that is constitutionally required if racial quotas are to be tolerated.

Wards Cove Packing Co. v. *Antonio*,[14] involving a cannery company that employed large numbers of Filipino workers in its cannery plant and very few in higher status positions, provided the perfect opportunity to establish Fried's point. The disparity between the number of Filipinos employed in the cannery and in the company's more general workforce was the result of very unusual circumstances. Indeed, Fried assures us that it was possible to show that (a) the Filipino workers were favoured by the company – it employed a disproportionate number of Filipino cannery workers – and (b) the company had not acted in a prejudiced manner when recruiting for its higher status positions in the non-cannery positions. Once these factual claims were accepted, the Court was forced to reconsider *Griggs* for that ruling specifies that discrimination can be presumed once a statistical disparity is shown. Not surprisingly, the Supreme Court ruled that the *Griggs* burden was excessive and the presumption that the canning company had discriminated could not be accepted in the circumstances. It ruled that plaintiffs, in cases brought under Title VII of the Civil Rights Act, must show that they have suffered from discrimination – the demonstration of a statistical imbalance in a company's workforce cannot be accepted as sufficient evidence. What the Court now requires from plaintiffs is that they identify the specific practices of an employer that produce the forbidden exclusionary effect. Only when this is established, must the employer meet the burden of showing why these requirements are 'reasonably related to his business'.[15] By requiring plaintiffs to establish their claims, rather than rely on a presumption of guilt, as in the past, the Court has signalled its resolve to 'dispose of the interpretations of *Griggs* that had pressured innocent employers to use quotas in order to avoid the expense and uncertainty of litigation'.[16]

Quotas and the Fourteenth Amendment

The Fourteenth Amendment declares a commitment to 'equality' using the words '[any person] is entitled to the equal protection of the laws'; 'race' is not specifically used. Nevertheless, it is clear from the context of the times that the framers had in mind the circumstances of recently emancipated, former slaves when they composed the phrase and it makes good sense to read the Equal Protection Clause as prohibiting racial discrimination. This is the interpretation that Fried defends and he is able to show that it is the settled conventional understanding of the Clause. Importantly, in terms of this understanding, white plaintiffs who complain that they have suffered because of race-conscious affirmative action plans can seek protection from the federal courts. Thus, when the government uses a racial quota for various purposes, however well-intentioned, it has to meet a heavy burden of justification for it must demonstrate that its discriminatory actions are 'narrowly tailored' to secure a *compelling* state interest.

The Liberal Reading of the Fourteenth Amendment, Relating to Affirmative Action

A liberal reading of the Equal Protection Clause has sometimes gained acceptance on the Court. Until recently, this position was articulated by Justices Brennan and Marshall who reject the view that 'race may not be used to classify' because it forecloses responses to the problem of structural discrimination by making it impermissible for governments to use racial classifications affirmatively, even though the framers did not contemplate this possibility. Brennan and Marshall argue that the Equal Protection Clause must not be held restrictive of good public policy if a less-restrictive construction is available. In their view, the Court should not normally frustrate good faith efforts to increase the participation of minorities within the workforce or the professions; thus, on their reading, a racial classification should only be subjected to strict scrutiny when it is used to stigmatize or when it unfairly isolates a politically vulnerable group.[17] When this is not the case, Brennan and Marshall prefer to impose a lower burden of justification, asking whether the reasons the state gives for using a racial classification are 'important and legitimate'. Moreover, they have made clear that they suppose that this burden can be easily met in the United States; indeed, according to them, discrimination can be presumed in most circumstances (such as in Richmond, Virginia); and, even a purely forward-looking rationale will usually be acceptable. (For example, in *Metro Broadcasting*, they held that the FCC's desire to licence more minority owners in order to promote programme diversity was enough, in itself, to satisfy the 'important and legitimate objective' requirement; and neither justice required the Commission to demonstrate any past discrimination against the minorities it was willing to favour in awarding broadcasting licences.)[18] Thus, their standard of review in cases where white males who allegedly have suffered loss because of affirmative action is no more demanding than the normal scrutiny traditionally applied. As their opinions in *Croson* and *Metro Broadcasting* show, even substantial harm to white males as a means for accomplishing the increased participation of minorities and women is acceptable to them. They claim that no protection can be afforded a business person who shows that he or she has lost a lucrative government contract; nor to another who has lost an opportunity to hold a broadcast licence. In their view, these substantial harms must be accepted so long as the discrimination in question is not shown to have been maliciously motivated.

The Positivist Approach: a Conservative Analysis of the Alternatives

Let us first consider the alternatives facing the Supreme Court when confronting constitutional challenges to forward-looking affirmative action plans.

The Court is bound by compelling precedents holding that the Fifth Amendment's due process requirement imposes the same standards on the federal government as the Fourteenth Amendment imposes on the states.[19] Thus, in dealing with all discrimination problems, the justices must decide how to read the constitutional requirement that persons be afforded the 'equal protection of the laws'. Does this requirement mean that all racial discrimination is proscribed, regardless of the motivation of the governmental agency responsible? Are white Americans entitled to the same protection, given that the Amendment was primarily intended to protect African Americans?

In a paper discussing the first affirmative action case, *DeFunis v. Odegaard*,[20] Richard Posner offers some interesting observations about the choices that the justices must make. His analysis has served as the basis for the positivist approach and has been extremely influential.

According to Posner, the need for judicial choice arises because there may have been no settled common understanding about the implications of the Equal Protection Clause at the time that it was debated and ratified; in any event, historians seem unable to agree about what this might be. The Clause is clearly relevant when anyone discriminates against African Americans and it is probably true that the framers also contemplated that some of the individuals who had supported the Union in the Civil War would face discrimination in southern states. But no one, in 1867, could have foreseen that it would be held impermissible to segregate schools on the basis of race; nor the kind of circumstance where white Americans would ask for protection against racial discrimination; and they certainly would not have thought about the propriety or impropriety of recognizing group rights. Thus, Posner concludes, the Supreme Court cannot easily establish limits on its own discretion by trying to determine the original understanding and specific intentions of the framers.

Because of this, Posner suggests that the Court has only two further alternatives when racial quotas are imposed. It can:

(1)   Claim that the Fourteenth Amendment authorizes the justices to enact into constitutional doctrine their own values.

This strategy is unacceptable, according to him, because the nine justices on the Supreme Court have no special claim to legislate in this way. But, Posner tells us, the conclusion is difficult to avoid as long as the wording of the Amendment is accepted on its face.[21] What is required to afford persons 'the equal protection of the laws'? Does this mean that all legislation that discriminates between the rich and poor, the elderly and the young, men and women, those who live in the country and those in the cities, must be subjected to close scrutiny by courts and held invalid, depending on the dispositions of various judges? Because the Constitution places no restraints on what can count as 'equality' in this context, we face a situation where judges are required to place any meaning they choose on the Equal Protection Clause – it is completely open-ended. The Court has never accepted that states are forbidden to make discriminations between persons or that it should treat all classes equally; on the other hand, it has not been prepared to defer to legislative judgments in all circumstances. What we need, then, is clarification about how the Court ought to proceed in distinguishing illegitimate discrimination.

Posner prefers a clear rule that limits the discretion of the judges who are required to apply it and recommends that we:

(2)   Understand the Constitution's promised protection as prohibiting all classifications on the basis of race.

Strategy (2) is in accordance with the interpretation advocated by Justice Scalia and may be defended in the following way. Although the precise intentions of the framers are indeterminate or inconclusive, we do know that they had not contemplated preventing legislators from enacting laws distinguishing women, children, farmers or the elderly for special treatment. Thus, we are justified in rejecting any literal reading of the Equal Protection Clause. Because the framers were concerned primarily about the problems of the recently emancipated, former slaves we would also be justified in limiting the scope of the Clause to that clear purpose only. But the Amendment does not refer to former slaves and their descendants specifically; rather, it uses the words 'any person' to designate the protected class. Thus, option (2) is the construction that best fits the known intentions of the framers and the actual words that they use. Posner believes that only this interpretation offers any possibility of precision and objectivity.

Anyone who adopts option (2) forecloses other possibilities. Indeed, in a more recent essay, Posner warns, 'Even the decision to read the Constitution narrowly, and thereby "restrain" judicial interpretation, is not a decision that can be read directly from the text. The Constitution does not say, "Read me broadly", or, "Read me narrowly". That decision must be made as a matter of political theory.'[22] By selecting option (2), we embrace an absolute rule ('race may not be used to classify') that forecloses the Court's responses in various complex circumstances. In particular, we use our jurisprudential preference for precise definition to make it impossible for governments to use racial classifications affirmatively, even though the framers did not contemplate this possibility.

But if a provision is vague, surely the courts are justified in supposing that policymaking ought to be left to the political branches. As we have seen, Judge Robert Bork actually suggests such a strategy, arguing that courts should restrict themselves to the kernel of clear meaning, when interpreting vague constitutional provisions, leaving further elaboration of the rights in question to the more responsive, political branches.[23] This alternative is not analysed by Posner but, as we have seen, the liberal justices, Brennan and Marshall, develop their interpretation along these lines.

Of course, the Brennan–Marshall strategy depends on presenting a clear delineation between 'benign' and unacceptable cases of discrimination for, otherwise, all protection afforded by the Amendment may be undermined (as is seen in the *Plessy* v. *Ferguson* judgment where the Court accepted the state government's alleged 'benign' purposes in segregating railway carriages).[24] We can see, then, that the choice facing the Court is between (2) and variations on the liberal position summarized above that we can state succinctly, as requiring the justices to:

(3)   Defer to co-equal branches of government (that is, accept *Plessy*);

This result should not necessarily trouble anyone with a strong commitment to judicial passivity for, after all, when public opinion shifts, bad laws can be repealed by legislators. On the other hand, if the Court makes a bad policy choice when interpreting the Constitution's provisions broadly, it cannot easily be changed.[25]

or

(4)   Defer to co-equal branches of government unless the discrimination in question is clearly malicious (Brennan and Marshall).

The Rehnquist–Scalia Approach to Forward-looking Affirmative Action

Consider, first, the position of the more conservative justices in the landmark cases, *Bakke*, *Weber* and *Fullilove* v. *Klutznick*.[26]

In *Bakke* and *Weber*, they had been able to avoid choosing between options (2), (3) or (4) by arguing that the discrimination complained of, in the disputed affirmative action plans, be dealt with under Titles VI or VII of the Civil Rights Act 1964. They held that the statute unambiguously proscribes racial discrimination, regardless of motive.[27] By refusing to subordinate the Civil Rights Act to constitutional analysis, the justices signal that they are prepared to accept Congress's leadership. In their view the Congress did not wish to allow for any benign racial discriminations. Thus, Rehnquist joins Justice Steven's opinion in the *Bakke* case, arguing that the minority preference admissions programme (which reserved 16 places for minority group members at the medical school of the University of California, Davis) violates Title VI. And in the *Weber* case, which requires the Court to decide whether a policy reserving 50 per cent of openings for blacks in a craft training programme violates Title VII, he takes issue with Brennan's judgment that race-conscious affirmative action plans are not necessarily inconsistent with the underlying purpose of Title VII and may sometimes be regarded as 'benign'. Indeed, Rehnquist goes so far as to accuse Brennan of intellectual dishonesty for refusing to accept the plain meaning of the legislation. He argues persuasively that the debate in the Congress offers no licence for Brennan to tolerate 'benign' racial discrimination; rather, the legislative history of the provision indicates an intention to outlaw all racial discrimination, including preferential treatment in employment and training practices.[28]

Fullilove presents circumstances where it is not possible to avoid a choice between options (2) and (3) or (4). This is because the affirmative action in question results from an initiative of the Congress and must, consequently, be dealt with under the Fifth Amendment's Due Process Clause. The Court must decide whether a provision in the Public Works Employment Act of 1977 (requiring that at least 10 per cent of the federal funds granted for local public works projects be used by the state or local grantee to procure services or supplies from businesses owned by minority group members, defined as United States citizens 'who are Negroes, Spanish-speaking, Orientals, Indians, Eskimos and Aleuts') violates the Fifth and Fourteenth Amendments. Again, the Court upholds well-meaning affirmative action, continuing the liberal strategy of deference by choosing (4). Indeed, in the principal opinion for a plurality, Chief Justice Burger notes that Section 5 of the Fourteenth Amendment requires Congress to enforce the equal protection guarantee by 'appropriate legislation' and he concludes that 'in no organ of government, state or federal, does there repose a more comprehensive remedial power'.[29] It is clear, then, that Burger (and he is joined by White) believes that the Congress must provide leadership in dealing with the legacy of segregation and slavery and that it is constitutionally empowered to do so.

But Rehnquist dissents. Rather than concede any Congressional prerogative, he joins an opinion which argues that the Constitution requires an absolute prohibition of racial classifications, that is, Posner's own preferred position (2). According to this view, the Court should take its orientation from the first Justice Harlan's declaration, dissenting in *Plessy* v. *Ferguson*, 'Our Constitution is colour-blind, and neither knows nor tolerates classes among citizens. ... The law regards man as man, and takes no account of his surroundings or of his colour.'[30]

It is interesting to observe that Charles Fried also defends this interpretation. As Solicitor General, acting for Reagan, he tried to show that it is the settled conventional understanding of the Clause. Importantly, in terms of this understanding, white plaintiffs who complain that they have suffered because of race-conscious affirmative action plans can also seek protection from the federal courts. Thus, when the government uses a racial quota for various purposes, however well-intentioned, it has to meet a heavy burden of justification for it must demonstrate that its discriminatory actions are 'narrowly tailored' to secure a *compelling* state interest.

Fried's response to the Court's inconsistency in dealing with racial quotas involved three strategies. First, he provided legal argument, closely examining the relevant cases and debates about the Fourteenth Amendment to demonstrate that a majority of the members of the Supreme Court share his view that racial quotas may only be resorted to if the state has a 'compelling' reason; second, he articulated philosophical grounds for preferring his individualist political morality to one in which group rights are recognized; third, he concentrated on finding a favourable case in which he could persuade the Court to finally choose between the competing interpretations of the Fourteenth Amendment, so as to bring to an end the present ambiguity about the Court's position.

City of Richmond v. *Croson*

The issue of minority-business-enterprise set-asides (MBEs) provided the perfect vehicle for Fried. As he points out, these programmes were not actually remedial in intent but represented a blatant attempt at social engineering. Moreover, the benefits are directed towards individuals who are wealthy, rather than towards those in need; and the burdens placed on those who suffer the discrimination (the businesses that lose potential contracts) are very heavy. Perhaps the most distressing aspect of MBEs from the point of view of those who are wary of racial politics is that they encourage wealthy groups to compete in the political arena for spoils allocated on the basis of ethnicity. To get contracts for their most powerful supporters minority leaders must mobilize anger and resentment about the past, trying to secure the majorities needed to privilege their group; to protect the businesses that feel threatened, other politicians will resist. If there was any affirmative action practice, which was more likely to encourage the Court to act against racial quotas, the MBE was it.

The case Fried chose for focus involves dispute over an unusually high (30 per cent) set-aside established by the Richmond Council. He regarded the case as favourable because (a) the city's lawyers defended the programme 'as broadly remedial on a formula that differed in name only from societal discrimination', (b) the set-aside was by no means 'narrowly tailored' and the 30 per cent figure seemed totally arbitrary, and (c) the designated minority contractors who were favoured by the set-aside were not required to have been resident in Richmond. Fried asked the Court to distinguish affirmative action programmes of this kind from those in which the state adopts a programme to remedy identified instances of discrimination. He argued that the Richmond Council must meet the 'compelling' interest standard by (a) identifying the specific acts of discrimination against minority contractors alleged to be occurring or to have occurred within its jurisdiction – the city needed to show that some minority contractors were being denied work in Richmond even though their bids were competitive – and (b) showing that the 30 per cent set-aside is a suitable remedy. The fact that there were very few minority contractors in Richmond or that African Americans and other designated minorities were less well-off than whites, was insufficient to establish that minority businesses were suffering from discrimination or that the city was somehow responsible for this.

Justice O'Connor's opinion for the Court gave Fried everything he had asked for, providing 'a firm and eloquent statement for the proposition that the constitution protects all alike, and protects them as individuals, not as members of groups'.[31] Although she allows that the Richmond Council could take action 'to rectify the effects of identified discrimination within its jurisdiction' and that 'some form of narrowly tailored racial preference might be necessary to break down patterns of deliberate exclusion', she finds that no serious effort was made by the Council to establish that racial discrimination had been occurring in Richmond. In her view, the fact that discrimination probably occurred in the distant past and prejudice against African Americans remains as a general, social problem in Virginia is not sufficient to justify the use of a specific race-conscious remedy. O'Connor requires a showing that local minority contractors have been harmed by persistent discrimination if they are to benefit from targeted government contracts.[32]

The other Reagan appointees (Scalia and Kennedy) also seem to be unremittingly hostile to forward-looking affirmative action. They certainly reject strategy (4), favoured by Brennan and Marshall, and while they concede that Congress has a unique remedial power under Section 5 of the Fourteenth Amendment, they do not regard this as a broad grant of authority.

As O'Connor explains their view in *Metro Broadcasting*, the 'Constitution's guarantee of equal protection binds the Federal Government as it does the states, and no lower level of scrutiny applies to the Federal Government's use of race classifications'.[33] She concedes that the Congress's unique, remedial authority empowers it to initiate programmes designed to remedy the result of past discrimination by state governments and to ensure that none of them continues to discriminate. Yet the means that the Congress employs in achieving these legitimate goals must be subjected to very close scrutiny in order to ensure that they are tailored precisely to the stated goals. The scrutiny demanded here is in no way different from the care that the Court would have to take if a state government voluntarily imposes racial quotas (for example, to remedy the under-representation of minorities in the faculty of many of its schools). Thus, for the Reagan justices the Congress's unique authority under Section 5 of the Fourteenth Amendment reflects a distrust of certain state governments in dealing with matters pertaining to race. Section 5 changes the relationship between the state governments and the federal government but it provides no licence for Congress to advance the general good by the illicit means of racial classification.

All four Reagan appointees impose a strict scrutiny test in all cases, whether or not the stated purpose is remedial. Scalia seems to be the most demanding of the four (although I suspect that Kennedy and Rehnquist agree with him).[34] In his view, the only circumstance in which a state government may use a racial classification is to undo the effects of its own past discrimination. Moreover, the remedial power 'extends no further than the scope of the continuing violation'.[35] Thus, it was necessary to force school districts who had discriminated in the past to desegregate schools even when this required allocating children to particular schools on the basis of their race. But it would be wrong to allow tertiary colleges to favour minorities in allocating places in order to increase their participation because, in this circumstance, the under-representation (although it may result from a deprived schooling for which the state may have been responsible) does not constitute a discrimination against them or affect the quality of education offered to them. Of course, it matters that they are not able to make use of opportunities if they cannot get qualified but while it makes sense to compensate any particular person who has suffered harmful discrimination, we should not suppose that racial preferences favouring minorities in general somehow evens the score. If we do, Scalia warns, we are prepared to embrace the 'proposition that our society is appropriately divided into races, making it right that an injustice rendered in the past to a black man should be compensated for by discriminating against a white'. According to him, 'Nothing is worth that embrace'.[36] In any case, he tells us, this is precisely what the Constitution forbids.

O'Connor offers a more complex response but it is also fatal to most forward-looking, affirmative action plans. As we have seen, she accepted Fried's recommendation agreeing that racial classifications should be confined to remedial purposes only. Thus, she insists that clear evidence of past discrimination must be shown before any governmental authority makes use of a race-conscious classification.[37] She also agrees that any affirmative action programme must be narrowly tailored and should extend no further than its stated remedial purposes.[38] The two requirements are linked. In her view, the evils resulting from the identified discrimination must be specifically stated so that the remedies are not 'ageless in their reach into the past, and timeless in their ability to affect the future'. O'Connor's position is similar to Rehnquist's view, in dealing with busing cases, that school districts should not be required to embrace system-wide integration strategies when they are guilty of discriminating in only one part of their district or when the illicit discrimination took place many years in the past. Like O'Connor, he supposes that remedial measures should narrowly address only the actual harm that is shown to have resulted from the discrimination in question. O'Connor is even more demanding, not only does she require that affirmative action plans be restricted narrowly but she is also reluctant to approve them if the goals they seek to realize can be achieved in other race-neutral ways.

Unlike Scalia, O'Connor accepts that racial quotas (as long as they are not rigid) may be used to address cases of persistent and clear discrimination. Moreover, she makes it clear that employers need not admit to actual cases of past discrimination when establishing that they have a firm basis for believing that remedial action is necessary. (This is because such a requirement could discourage voluntary efforts to eliminate discrimination by placing the employer in a vulnerable position *vis-à-vis* those who had been harmed by the past illegal acts.) What they must provide, however, is evidence that discrimination is still a problem. For example, they could show an anomalous, statistical imbalance in the relevant workforce that cannot be explained by general, societal discrimination alone or in some other plausible way. In her view, then, a governmental agency or private company that recognizes that the composition of its own work-force indicates that it is recruiting or promoting with a racial bias, may impose race-conscious numerical targets to ensure that the discrimination no longer continues. Also, as O'Connor notes with reference to the activities of the Richmond Council in *Croson*, nothing 'precludes a state or local entity from taking action to rectify the effects of identified discrimination within its jurisdiction' and in the extreme case, 'some form of narrowly tailored racial preference might be necessary to break down patterns of deliberate exclusion'. What she finds objectionable about the set-aside for minority businesses established by the Richmond Council is that no effort is made to establish that discrimination, against the cited minorities, is a problem. In her view, the fact that discrimination probably occurred in the distant past or that prejudice against African Americans remains as a general, social problem in Virginia is not sufficient to justify the use of a specific race-conscious remedy. If minority businesses are to be benefited by targeting government contracts, O'Connor requires a showing that local minority contractors are harmed by persistent discrimination. Scalia would restrict race-conscious remedies much more narrowly and would disallow even the flexible quotas that O'Connor believes may sometimes be necessary.

Despite this difference, there is no substantial conflict between Scalia's absolutist approach and O'Connor's rigorous scrutiny rule. Both clearly mark a shift in the Court's approach because they reject the idea that racial discrimination can be benign. Both justices are against purely, forward-looking affirmative action and are also determined to eliminate the prophylactic strategy, often resorted to by larger companies and government bureaucracies, of adopting racial and sexual quotas to avoid litigation by minorities or women who allege discrimination. Those who adopt such strategies will now be vulnerable to litigation by the individual whites or males who suffer the exclusion. Unlike Scalia, however, O'Connor does not recommend a clean break with the past, preferring a narrowing and confining of earlier holdings. She would protect the business people who complain about the FCC's minority preference policies, Croson and perhaps Bakke; but not Weber or Johnson. As her citations show, her orientation is compatible with most of the Court's holdings in *Bakke* and *Fullilove* – probably also with *Weber*.

Individualism and the Rehnquist Court

Apart from Rehnquist, whose motives for opposing affirmative action are often difficult to fathom (and whose point of view I consider separately below), the conservative justices cite other, normative, individualist concerns when justifying their application of the Court's prerogative to review the activities of Congress. This creates a difficulty because it would seem that they are inconsistent; approving libertarian values in some instances but embracing positivism as a general orientation. Do they feel that the imposition of individualist values by the Court is somehow less problematical because of their central place within the American legal and political tradition? If so, their position would seem to be similar to that of many liberal constitutional theorists; only the values that they embrace would be different.

Another interpretation is available. We may view the appeal to individualist values as part of the arguments conservatives provide to challenge the prevailing liberal view that the Court can identify cases of benign discrimination. In particular the conservatives address the Brennan–Marshall arguments for supporting this claim. On this interpretation, which I believe to be the most plausible, the conservatives enter into a dialogue with liberals about the individualist values and concerns that call collective categories such as race into question; their purpose is to persuade us (and Brennan/Marshall) that the Court should not try to identify benign cases of racial discrimination. This reading allows us to judge the conservatives less harshly for we need not suppose that they depart from their positivist commitment to distinguish law from political morality. Their analysis of the underlying values in the debate about positive discrimination is put forward to advance their view that Brennan and Marshall are often inconsistent when they exclude white individuals from the protection of the Fourteenth Amendment, not to establish their own interpretations of the Amendment's abiding significance.

In any event, it is interesting to observe that many of the conservative justices are quite happy to draw on a tradition of liberal jurisprudence that requires that legislators refrain from casually using a 'suspect' collective category, such as race, as a basis for distinguishing individuals for special treatment. One claim is that group categories often distinguish sections of the community who are particularly vulnerable as a 'discreet insular minority', excluded from the normal protections afforded by the political process; another is that misconceptions and traditional associations often manifest themselves in prejudicial treatment. Racial classifications also conflict with other core individualist principles, for example, the notion that people should be able to enjoy freedom of association and the ideal that allocations approximate merit. We clearly have no control over our race, yet it is fundamental to the notion of a free society that people should not be penalized for immutable qualities. Of course, group categories such as race are also suspect because they are invariably over- and under-inclusive.

Interestingly, the conservatives make use of these rationales in unusual ways. Let me consider some of these briefly.

Individualism and Constitutional Theory

The 'discreet insular minority' rationale is used to justify affirmative action in addressing the special problems of the African–American community in the United States. This line of argument has been especially relevant in the past because African Americans were effectively disenfranchised in many southern states. Thus, they were clearly vulnerable and could not easily resort to the political system to protect themselves. The rationale is also given a special twist by John Ely who uses it to establish when racial classifications can be regarded as benign. In his view, a white male (such as DeFunnis, Bakke, Johnson or Croson) need not be protected by the Supreme Court because the group to which he belongs is not politically vulnerable.

O'Connor does not draw this conclusion. In her view, the emergence of minorities into positions of power should caution against a new kind of racial politics in which whites are vulnerable and discriminated against. This is clearly what she believes happened in Richmond, Virginia, where 50 per cent of the city's population are African American and five of the nine seats in the Council are held by politicians who are responsive to the interests of this community. Thus, she tells us that the set-aside (in the *Croson* case) was probably the result of racial politics as those with political strength struggle for a piece of the action. Scalia strongly agrees, holding that the enactment of a 30 per cent set-aside was clearly and directly beneficial to the dominant racial group in Richmond. But he adds a further refinement to O'Connor's analysis: he thinks it sound to distinguish between federal and state (or local) action. As he explains, the struggle for racial justice has been a struggle by the national society in the United States against oppression in the smaller political units where racially based factions are often able to dominate. Scalia approvingly quotes James Madison on this very point:

> The smaller the society, the fewer probably will be the distinct parties and interests composing it; the fewer the distinct parties and interests, the more frequently will a majority be found of the same party; and the smaller the number of individuals composing a majority, and the smaller the compass within which they are placed, the more easily will they concert and execute their plan of oppression.

It is for this reason that Scalia believes the dispassionate objectivity needed to mould a benign race-conscious remedy (that is, one narrowly tailored to the specific purpose of eliminating the past effects of discrimination) are unlikely to be found at the state or local levels. Here, only the strictest scrutiny will prevent the politics of racial spoils in jobs and contracts from arising.

The notion that racial classifications are associated with unsubstantiated assumptions and prejudice is also put to a special use by the conservatives. In the past it was feared that stereotyped assumptions could disadvantage a group; now Scalia and O'Connor claim minorities benefit in some circumstances because policymakers rely on false generalizations. Thus, O'Connor takes issue with the FCC because it assumes that minority owners are likely to possess unique experiences and backgrounds that make it likely that they will behave differently from whites. As she points out, even if minority individuals are more likely to express distinctive viewpoints, there is no reason to suppose that minority business managers will. Like white owners, O'Connor tells us, they must respond to the marketplace and are likely to disseminate programmes that attract and retain audiences.

Generalizations and stereotypes are especially misleading when quantitative data are presented to show that some groups have been systematically awarded less than a fair share of positions or promotions, for it is easy to assume that the disparities reflect a pattern of discrimination, even when this is not the case. As O'Connor points out, the plausibility of statistical evidence depends to a large extent on the assumptions we start with about who is eligible or qualified for various positions (and this is often a matter of subjective judgment, to say the least). Although she is prepared to concede that significant disparities between the racial composition of a workforce and the 'per centages of qualified minorities in the relevant labour

pool' may show the existence of past discrimination warranting remedial affirmative action, what O'Connor requires is a careful and
sceptical scrutiny of all statistical evidence. For example, when she
comes to analyze the situation in Richmond where minority businesses received 0.67 per cent of the prime contracts from the city,
while minorities constitute 50 per cent of the city's population,
O'Connor is unwilling to accept that racial discrimination is necessarily the cause of this disparity. Although she admits 'the sorry
history of both private and public discrimination' in Virginia, she
claims that it is 'sheer speculation how many minority firms there
would be in Richmond absent past societal discrimination'. And because the city does not know how many minority businesses are
actually qualified and bidding in the relevant market or how well
they do (in comparison to other firms), she believes there is no basis
for deducing that there is racial discrimination – the idea is a totally
unsupported assumption.

One final observation about stereotyping is worth noting. In most
traditional approaches the concern is that deeply imbedded, racial or
sexual prejudice will come to be reflected in stereotypical but misleading opinions about a group. The argument is expressed most forcefully
by Justice Brennan in *Frontiero* v. *Richardson* in which he draws attention to the fact that sexual stereotypes are often a problem. It is interesting that Justice White joins Brennan's opinion in this case. He clearly
accepts that the Court has a responsibility to ensure that discrimination in the law is rationally related to legitimate purposes and that
sexual distinctions are inherently suspect because they frequently bear
no relationship to a person's ability to perform various societal roles.
This opinion by White can be compared to his reasoning in *Griswold*
(the privacy case we examined earlier). It would seem that White is
prepared to subject legislation, which implicates liberties, to quite a
demanding level of scrutiny; but the test he applies demands that a
'rational relationship' be demonstrated and does not require him to
recognize novel rights not found in the Constitution's text.

Apart from Rehnquist who dissented in *Frontiero*, most of the other
conservatives are also concerned about stereotyping, but they seem
more worried about the origins of prejudice than its current manifes-
tations. In their view, false generalizations about a group are likely to
arise whenever it is distinguished for special treatment, whether or
not the motives for this selection are malicious. Thus, in a case involving a challenge to the existence of a state-sponsored, all-female
nursing school, O'Connor warns that the exclusion of men 'tends
to perpetuate the stereotyped view of nursing as an exclusively
woman's job'. And we find Scalia using a similar argument in responding to the *Bakke* case, explaining how affirmative action in the allocation of college places establishes a racial stereotype. In his view the

process mirrors the situation that occurred when baseball was segregated for racist reasons: quotas establish 'a separate "league" for minority students, which makes it difficult for the true excellence of the minority star to receive his or her deserved acknowledgment'. The problem, for Scalia, is that all the members of the racial group will suffer the stereotype. He claims that so long as an affirmative action graduate is not an equal graduate, he or she will never acquire the status of those who are forced to compete equally. More significantly, Scalia worries that if members of a racial group are promoted too rapidly because of affirmative action (above their level of competence) or are forced to compete with others who are very much better equipped by their past experiences and training, negative stereotypes will come to be accepted.

The most serious problem about affirmative action programmes for the individualist is that they are unfair. The allocation of burdens is the disturbing problem here for those who are excluded from a benefit, promotion or position because of their race may not have been responsible for any of the past mistreatment (cited as warranting remedial action). As Scalia puts the point, 'even "benign" racial quotas have victims, whose very real injustices we ignore whenever we deny them enforcement of their right not to be disadvantaged on the basis of race'. As for those who gain, some of the individuals selected on the basis of their race may have less need than others who are equally deserving. Related to these problems is the subjective assessment that is so often required in determining the groups deserving remedial action; and who, out of many applicants, is genuinely a member of such a group.

The over-inclusiveness of racial classification is an issue raised in one way or another by all the dissenting (conservative) justices in *Metro Broadcasting*.[39] In responding to the FCC's policy, favouring minority businesses, they also seem to be influenced by social science research which documents a growing split within the African–American community between those who are making it - an upwardly mobile and expanding middle-class – and those who are not.[40] The finding calls into question the assumption that the African–American population can be treated as one community, as well as the use of racial classifications to identify people who have suffered special deprivation requiring remedial attention. African Americans clearly do not all suffer the same disadvantages. Thus, Kennedy questions the assumption that minority entrepreneurs who are wealthy enough to purchase broadcasting stations share views or interests with people whose background is very different, just because they are of the same race.

As I have said, the fact that the conservatives get into a debate about values when considering the propriety of affirmative action plans does not mean that they abandon their resolve to distinguish legal from moral arguments. Their concerns about the Court's departures from American individualist assumptions are used to respond to the Brennan–Marshall view that discriminations can be benign. They are used, then, to show why the option I earlier identified as (4) [defer to co-equal branches of government unless the discrimination in question is clearly malicious] is unacceptable. In the conservatives's view, arguments about when racial discriminations are benign are inherently speculative and inconclusive and have no legitimate place in the law. Thus, the only choice for them is between option (2) [understand the Constitution's promised protection as prohibiting all classification on the basis of race] and option (3) [defer to co-equal branches of government, that is, accept *Plessy* v. *Ferguson*]. I have shown why Posner's judgment in favour of (2) would recommend itself to those who are influenced by the kind of positivism advocated by Scalia.

Finally, a word about Rehnquist.

Although Rehnquist joins O'Connor's opinions in *Croson* and *Metro Broadcasting* and obviously feels comfortable with the values articulated by her, it is very unlikely that he approves her manner of reaching legal conclusions in these cases. As we have seen, Rehnquist considers John Marshall's defence of judicial review in *Marbury* v. *Madison* to find the correct answer, which, he claims, is that judicial authority in the United States is derived from the people: '[T]hey have parceled out the authority that originally resided entirely with them by adopting the original Constitution and by later amending it.' Thus, the Court should overrule other branches of government only when they 'overstep the authority given to them by the Constitution ... or invade protected individual rights'.[41] As we have seen, however, it is not always easy to comprehend the precise meaning of the Constitution and there are phrases that are so general that they will inevitably be applied differently, depending on the philosophical views of justices. Rehnquist tells us that to the extent that the language in the Constitution is general, 'the courts are of course warranted in giving them an application coextensive with their language'; but, he warns, justices should act with caution, acknowledging that the framers deliberately placed responsibility with the popularly elected branches of government to make the appropriate policy responses in facing the challenges of the future. In his view, the framers certainly did not intend to bind later generations by suggesting the 'correct' answers to unknown problems.

In applying the Civil War Amendments, Rehnquist warns us not to read them as though they are designed 'to solve problems that society might confront a century later'; rather, they were 'designed to prevent from ever recurring abuses in which the states had engaged in prior to that time'.[42] Thus, Rehnquist feels that the Equal Protection Clause of the Fourteenth Amendment should not be taken to establish a broad-ranging judicial power. The implication of this line of argument is that the Court should embrace option (3) [defer to co-equal branches of government]. Indeed, Rehnquist has been accused of supporting the ruling in *Plessy* v. *Ferguson* and he did express such sentiments in a memo while he was a law clerk, working for Justice Jackson. Whether he genuinely held the views developed in that memo is beside the point, however, because it is clear that he now accepts that the Court was correct to overrule *Plessy*, even though he can offer no good reasons, apart from political expediency, to support this view. In any event, like Judge Richard Posner, he now holds that the Court should not prevent legislators from discriminating, except when they do so on the basis of a person's race or act irrationally.[43]

Conclusion

The conservative majority on the Supreme Court is seeking to implement an enormous change in the United States institutional system in the name of norms that are linked with the ideal of lawful, accountable government. Their goal is to justify their resolve to abandon the conception of the role of the Court as a legitimate policymaker that they inherited from the Warren and Burger eras.

My purpose in this chapter has been to set out some of the reasons that the various justices who make up the conservative group have provided for advocating this kind of change in dealing with affirmative action problems. I was interested in the fact that the conservative justices were willing to protect white business people when local governments adopt affirmative action programmes yet refuse to intervene to help individuals whose privacy is threatened. Through my analysis of the leading cases and exposition of the jurisprudential orientation that informs the conservative approach, I have shown that they provide good reasons for distinguishing the two kinds of problem and cannot plausibly be accused of playing fast and loose with the Bill of Rights to suit a conservative agenda.

Notes

1   347 U.S. 483 (1954).
2   As Justice Douglas puts the point: '[the] policy would impinge on no person's constitutional rights, because no one would be excluded from a public school and

no one has a right to attend a segregated school'. (Dissenting in *DeFunnis* v. *Odegaard*, 416 U.S. 336, n. 18).

3   Kenneth L. Karst, 'Private Discrimination and Public Responsibility: *Patterson* in Context' *The Supreme Court Review* (1989), 50–1; also Robert Fullinwider, *The Reverse Discrimination Controversy* (Totowa, NJ: Rowman & Allanheld, 1980).

4   The most important declaration is found in *Brown* v. *Topeka Board of Education* (1954) (announcing that racial discrimination in public education is unconstitutional) in which the plaintiffs persuaded the Court to overturn *Plessy* v. *Ferguson* (1896). The notion that race is an impermissible classification is also implied in the companion case *Bolling* v. *Sharp*, 347 U.S. 497 (1954) (in which the Court held that racial classifications were so arbitrary and unfair as to amount to a denial of due process of law). See also *Korematsu* v. *United States* 323 U.S. 214 (1944) (race is a suspect classification). Gender discrimination has never been regarded with the same caution. However, the Court has applied an intermediate standard of scrutiny, see *Craig* v. *Boren* 429 U.S. 190 (1976) (ruling that classifications based on gender must be carefully scrutinized).

5   In Section 703(a) of Title VII, Public Law 92-261, 86 State. 103 (1972).

6   This is the practice of adjusting scores so that people from different ethnic groups are not compared.

7   The economic prospects for the various ethnic groups in the United States today are mostly determined by their economic and cultural circumstances and this is what those who refer to 'structural discrimination' wish to make more equal. But, the notion that federal courts have the authority to order the redistribution of resources from one section of the community to another, however desirable such transfers might seem in the light of egalitarian political theory, is quite novel.

8   Many companies choose to select the 'best' minority applicants competitively, using tests that they have not proved to be required by 'business necessity' (for example, taking aptitude test scores and school certificates into account) and, under *Griggs*, they are entitled to do this so long as a sufficient number of individuals from the designated minority groups are employed or promoted. When the racial quota is filled, other applicants are required to meet more stringent requirements (for example, a designated aptitude score or a higher grade in a school diploma). See *Griggs* v. *Duke Power Company*, 401 U.S. 424 (1971).

9   The most recent Democrat president, Jimmy Carter, strongly supported racial quotas and 'race norming' and Reagan and Bush have not been able to fully reverse his legacy.

10   The Civil Rights Act 1991 overrules *Griggs* in two important ways: (a) it requires plaintiffs to show 'that an employer uses a particular practice that causes a disparate impact ...' and (b) bars employers from 'adjusting the scores of, using different cut off scores for, or otherwise altering the results of employment-related test on the basis of race, colour, religion, sex or national origin' (*Congressional Quarterly* 7 Dec. 1991, 3621). In these changes, it follows the lead of the conservative Supreme Court in *Wards Cove Packing Co.* v. *Antonio* 490 U.S. 642 (1989) that I discuss in the text (see the next Section). But the new Civil Rights Act also departs from the conservative position, attempting to reverse some elements of the ruling in *Wards Cove* v. *Antonio*. Before an accusation about discrimination that is supported by nothing more than a showing of a statistical imbalance in an employer's workforce can be dismissed as unwarranted, the new civil rights statute requires employers to establish that this result is required by 'business necessity'. This specific allocation of the burden of proof in the new Civil Rights Act may, however, be in conflict with the Fourteenth Amendment (as interpreted by the Rehnquist Court). I suspect that the conservative justices will agree that Congress may not set the burden of proof in a manner that may force employers to make use of quotas to avoid litigation.

11   *New York Transit Authority* v. *Beazer,* 440 U.S. 568 (1979) and *Washington* v. *Davis* 426 U.S. 229 (1976).

12   Fried cites Justice Powell's judgment in *Bakke* who describes this limited goal as 'far more focused than the remedying of the effects of "societal discrimination" an amorphous concept of injury that may be ageless in its reach into the past', *Order & Law: Arguing the Reagan Revolution* (NY: Simon & Schuster, 1991), 98.

13   *New York Transit Authority* v. *Beazer* and *Washington* v. *Davis.*

14   490 U.S. 642 (1989).

15   This phrase replaces the *Griggs* standard of 'business necessity' and signals that the Court will be willing to accept discriminatory practices so long as they are 'reasonable'. Congress has attempted to reverse this in the Civil Rights Act 1991 by requiring that 'the challenged practice is job-related for the position in question and consistent with business necessity' (*Congressional Quarterly,* 7 Dec. 1991, 3621). But Congress has supported the most important changes enunciated by the Court in *Wards Cove* v. *Antonio* (see note 10 above).

16   Fried, op. cit., 129.

17   This line of argument is defended by Ronald Dworkin (in *Law's Empire,* London: Fontana Press, 1986, 393–7) and John Hart Ely (*Democracy and Distrust: a Theory of Judicial Review* (Cambridge, Mass.: Harvard University Press, 1980, 151–7).

18   As O'Connor notes in her dissenting opinion, the reasoning of Brennan and Marshall in this case is very questionable. For one thing, the minorities favoured in the programme seem to have been selected because they are the usual list (included for remedial purposes because of past discrimination against them) but if the Federal Communications Commission genuinely wished to increase the diversity of viewpoints, these are not the only minorities who have a claim to a preference. More importantly, she complains that they do not require the FCC to demonstrate that the programmes put to air would be more diverse when more stations are owned by the favoured minorities (*Metro Broadcasting,* 11 L Ed 2d at 497–8).

19   See *Washington* v. *Davis,* 48 L Ed 2d, 597; *Bolling* v. *Sharp,* 98 L Ed 2d 884 (holding that equal protection analysis in the Fifth Amendment area is the same as that under the Fourteenth Amendment).

20   Richard Posner, 'The DeFunis Case and the Constitutionality of Preferential Treatment of Racial Minorities', *Supreme Court Review* (1974), p. 1.

21   This point is also made by Walter Berns, *Taking the Constitution Seriously* (NY: Simon & Schuster, 1987), 212ff.

22   Posner is commenting on the approach recommended by Walter Berns (1987) which he calls 'strict constructionist'; see Richard Posner, 'What am I? A Potted Plant?', *The New Republic* (28 Sept. 1987), 24.

23   Robert H. Bork, *The Tempting of America: the Political Seduction of the Law* (NY: The Free Press, 1990), 229 where he argues that every expansion of rights diminishes 'the liberty of the individuals who make up a community to regulate their affairs'.

24   41 L Ed 2d, 256.

25   This is why writers who are strongly in favour of judicial passivity prefer to cite *Dred Scott* v. *Sandford* as an example of judicial policy-making. See, Walter Berns, op. cit., 218–9. In a memorandum written in 1952, Rehnquist (who was then a clerk working for Associate Justice Jackson) wrote: 'I think *Plessy* v. *Ferguson* was right and should be re-affirmed'. This statement was fully discussed during the Senate's Judiciary Committee Hearings when he was nominated by President Nixon, but he was able to reassure senators that it did not reflect his considered view. For discussion of this episode see, Sue Davis, *Justice Rehnquist and the Constitution* (Princeton, NJ: Princeton University Press, 1989), 15ff.

26   448 U.S. 448 (1980).

27   Title VI prohibits discrimination in activities or programmes that receive federal assistance; Title VII, Sections 703(a) and 703(c), prohibits discrimination in employment practices and training programmes.

28   This interpretation of the legislative intentions is given substantial support by Hugh Graham in his historical account of the passage of the Act. See Graham, *The Civil Rights Era: Origins and Development of National Policy, 1960–72* (NY: Oxford University Press), 383–90. In his dissenting opinion in *Johnson* v. *Transportation Agency, Santa Clara County, California*, 480 U.S. 616 (1987), Scalia accepts Rehnquist's view of Title VII.

29   65 L Ed 2d 902 (plurality opinion); 448 U.S. (1980) at 483.

30   Stewart (joined by Rehnquist, dissenting) *Fullilove* 65 L Ed 2d 902, at 53; citing *Plessy* v. *Ferguson*, 41 L Ed 256, (Harlan, dissenting).

31   This is the interpretation that Fried defends as Solicitor General acting for Reagan and he is able to show that it is in direct conflict with *Metro Broadcasting*. See Fried, '*Metro Broadcasting* v. *FCC* (110 S. Ct. 2997): Two Concepts of Equality', 107–27. There is little doubt, given the changes to the Court following the departure of Brennan and Marshall and their replacements with the two Bush appointees, Souter and Thomas, that the individualist view of the Fourteenth Amendment recommended by Fried will prevail.

32   Scalia would restrict race-conscious remedies much more narrowly, embracing the doctrine known as a victim specificity (see Fried, *Order & Law*, op. cit., 105–17) and would disallow even the flexible quotas which O'Connor and Fried believe may sometimes be necessary.

33   *Metro Broadcasting* 111 L Ed at 488.

34   Kennedy and Rehnquist join O'Connor's opinion for the Court in *Croson*. They may have acted strategically in this instance, however, to help establish the Court's first majority on the Constitutional issues. Kennedy's separate dissenting opinion in *Metro Broadcasting* makes it clear that he also takes his orientation from Harlan's claim 'Our Constitution is colour-blind' (dissenting) in *Plessy*.

35   *Croson* 102 L Ed, dissenting at 902.

36   Ibid., at 904.

37   Whether this requirement applies to private firms who adopt affirmative action programmes to avoid vulnerability under the Civil Rights Act 1964 is not as clear. See Charles Fried's closing comments in 'Affirmative Action After the *City of Richmond* v. *J.A. Croson Co.*: a Response to the Scholars' Statement', *The Yale Law Journal*, vol. 99 (1989), 161. In my view the conservative justices (including O'Connor) are signalling that a prophylactic use of quotas will not serve as a sufficient justification to meet the strict scrutiny test that they are determined to apply. This is why *Wards Cove Packing Co.* v. *Antonio*, 109 S. Ct. 2155 (1989) (diminishing the vulnerability of employers by narrowing the scope of the 'disparate impact' cause of action under Title VII) is such an important case.

38   O'Connor's opinion in *Ward Cove Packing Co.* v. *Antonio*, 109 S. Ct. 2115 (1989) is relevant here for it is clear that she will review the use of statistical measures very closely. A simple showing of under-representation, comparing the numbers of the minority in the general population with the numbers employed or awarded contracts, will not be accepted as evidence of persistent discrimination. Analysis will have to begin with a clear delineation of the minority members who are qualified for various positions. Evidence of general societal discrimination against a group will not be accepted as sufficient in establishing any claim that discrimination has taken place. (See *Croson*, 102 L Ed 2d at 889).

39   Of the conservatives, only White voted to sustain the Federal Communications Commission's affirmative action plan in *Metro Broadcasting*. He cites the Section 5 provision of the Fourteenth Amendment (see above, p. 200) and believes that the ruling in *Fullilove* is applicable.

40 William J. Wilson, *The Declining Significance of Race* (Chicago: University of Chicago Press, 1980); *The Truly Disadvantaged: the Inner City, the Underclass, and Public Policy* (Chicago: University of Chicago Press, 1987).

41 William Rehnquist, 'The Notion of a Living Constitution', *Texas Law Review*, vol. 54, no. 4 (1976), 693–706.

42 Ibid., 699.

43 As far as I am aware, Rehnquist has never stated this view, but we can deduce his commitment from *Fullilove* (joining the dissenting opinion of Stewart). It is also significant that he has been hostile to extending the protection afforded by the Equal Protection Clause, see, *Michael M* v. *Superior Court of Sonoma County* 450 U.S. 464 (1981); nor does he think the Court should second-guess legislators when they make policies relating to groups such as aliens and homosexuals.

11 Conclusions

Citizens are accustomed to judicial interventions in the United States and they often turn to the federal courts, particularly to the Supreme Court, for the preservation of fundamental rights. The Supreme Court enjoys very extensive powers and a high standing in the community. Since Chief Justice John Marshall's controversial judgment in *Marbury v. Madison* (1803), it has successfully asserted its claim to declare legislation unconstitutional. Authority to do this is derived from the Constitution, which is the fundamental source of all law in the United States.

One reason why judicial authority has taken on this expansive meaning (empowering judges to identify and apply fundamental values to counter the initiatives taken by representatives of the people) in the United States is that there has been a history of abuse within a number of the states. Beginning with the compromise over slavery, most progressive people in the United States have been wary about conceding too much authority to the states. It is through intervention by the federal judiciary that supervision has sometimes been possible. Another reason why the judiciary has been more important as a policymaker in the United States, than it is in other democracies, is that the Madisonian system sometimes ensures that an important problem cannot be adequately addressed by other branches of government or by the states. This is because the arrangements ensure that the officials elected by the people represent different constituencies so that the system can be incoherent – in that different sections of the electorate inevitably demand different responses. When this occurs, the Supreme Court has sometimes decided to intervene. For example, the Supreme Court has sometimes found it necessary to set national standards when the states cannot agree in policy area where national consistency is required for practical purposes (for example, in dealing with libel and obscenity); and they have also interfered when inconsistency is manifest in resolving moral issues of fundamental importance (such as the right to die or the right to reproductive autonomy). Nor has the Court always acted in the name of the majority (by adopting the position that has most support in the various states); far from it, it has often acted to impose solutions that have not been endorsed by many state governments. Of course it seems anomalous that a practice widely prevalent and tolerated in one state should be regarded as a serious criminal offence in another; nevertheless, the possibility of this kind of outcome was part of the compromise that made the union of the states into a single nation possible in the eighteenth century. But the judiciary in the twentieth century are often unwilling to honour this settlement. Indeed, the Warren–Burger Court assumed the power to overrule state governments by treating the Fourteenth Amendment as a warrant for holding that nearly all of the Bill of Rights applies to the states as well as to Congress (even though this was never intended by the framers in 1867).

What is unusual in the United States is that many legal practitioners do not regard the plain meaning of the words of the Constitution or other traditional sources of law, such as the precedents set in previous case law, as confining. For example, Bruce Babbit, who was on President Clinton's short-list to be nominated to replace Justice Byron White, tells us: 'The job of a Justice is justice. That means searching deeply into the aspirations of our Constitution and of the democratic republic it defines ... it means applying enduring values to an evolving society and to circumstances that no eighteenth century author could have foreseen.'[1] We have seen how Babbit's view of the Constitution and his understanding of the judicial role as instrumental in shaping a social agenda is typical within the elite in the United States. For many intellectuals and academics, the primary task of the judiciary should be to uphold a liberal political culture (shared by an enlightened few) by identifying what the listed liberties in the Bill of Rights, together with some unenumerated but implied rights, mean for each generation. On this interpretation the Supreme Court is the institution responsible for upholding countermajoritarian values.

I have argued that this 'dualist' understanding of how the political system in the United States should function rests on poorly supported evidence about the capacities of courts. I claim that dualists show a poor grasp of the actual evidence of judicial behaviour gathered by sociolegal scholars and their position rests on a misunderstanding of the relationship between law and society. We have seen, reviewing the work of Donald Horowitz and Gerald Rosenberg in Chapter 2, how sociolegal evidence places in question the notion that the Supreme Court can serve effectively to counter determined majorities who are effectively led. If we take Rosenberg's research findings as a guide, we must allow that judicial policymaking is unlikely to depart very far from the directions set by other agencies of government. Thus the liberal call for judges to lead in securing social change (exhibited in the work of writers such as Ely, Ackerman and Dworkin) places unjustifiable faith in the efficacy of the United States Supreme Court. If people in the United States wish to secure their rights they must nurture a political culture in which they are taken seriously by most political leaders.[2] But, as we have seen, this is unlikely to occur if issues relating to civil rights are placed prematurely on the political agenda by well-meaning lawyers.

The Political Consequences of Activism

This brings me to speculate about the harm that the persistent embrace of dualism by elites in the United States may have brought about. Consider the following possibilities:

1 Judicial interventions may sometimes impose crucial delays that can be of significance (for example, holding up Roosevelt's New Deal plans).
2 They may impose badly thought out policies that will take years for the other agencies to correct.
3 They may have indirect effects on the political process that are significant and often disabling (for example, encouraging tendencies in the Democratic Party towards ethnic politics; tempting the Republican Party to campaign against liberal values).

I considered all three possibilities but it is the last-mentioned effect that I argued has been the most significant in the United States since the early 1960s. Indeed I suggested that psephological evidence shows how the New Deal coalition – an influential social democratic alliance – disintegrated in the post-World War II period partly because of conflicts about the manner in which liberal values were imposed.

As we have seen in Chapter 2, the alliance of New Deal northerners and southern whites that President Franklin Roosevelt had held together began to disintegrate under President Harold Truman who mistakenly thought that the party could win the presidency without any significant contribution from its traditional southern base. This error of judgment was largely a result of Roosevelt's huge success.[3] Unlike previous Democratic candidates who had needed the South because they campaigned poorly in other parts of the country, Roosevelt managed to win effectively in northern states by appealing to new constituent groups (such as labour unions, ethnic minorities and city-dwellers). Truman thought he could do the same – that the traditional southern support was expendable – this is why he failed to discourage the new Roosevelt constituents from reshaping the party platform to embrace a civil-rights agenda.

When the white South realized that it could no longer rely on the Democratic Party to secure its way of life, its electorate had nowhere to go. This allowed an opening for right-wing Republicans who had been faced by southern resentment against the party of Lincoln for most of the period since the end of the Civil War. Dwight Eisenhower provided them with the perfect candidate to woo the South and his success showed that a change in the traditional party alignment in presidential elections was a possibility. The prize that the Republicans sought after 1948, and continue to seek today, is dominance in southern presidential contests and they were able to secure this from 1964 to 1992 partly because the Democrats allowed them to campaign on issues relating to the role of liberalism in American life.

President Eisenhower got them off to a bad start by appointing Earl Warren and William Brennan to the Supreme Court and he was forced to confront southerners after the *Brown* v. *Board of Education* ruling.[4] All this made the Nixon campaign in 1960 very difficult for most white southerners remained so distrustful of the Republicans that they preferred to waste their votes on an independent candidate who had no chance of winning a national campaign, Governor George Wallace. Despite this handicap, Nixon nearly won in 1960! Indeed, it was partly because of this close contest that the Republicans thought it expedient to elect a genuine candidate of the right – to appeal to southern racial bigotry – selecting Barry Goldwater as the candidate in 1964. But Goldwater did not understand the South at all and he faced a candidate in President Lyndon Johnson who knew it well; moreover, Goldwater's brand of conservatism emphasized free market economics in a region of the country that depended very much on government hand-outs.[5]

When Nixon returned to national politics to contest the presidency in 1968 he had carefully prepared a 'southern strategy'. His idea was simple – capture the Wallace votes he had failed to secure in 1960 by presenting as a viable candidate who understood the concerns of southern whites. Nixon's advantage over southern opponents like Governor Wallace was that he had a capacity to win nationally. Nixon wanted white southerners to understand that although the liberal changes that President Johnson's initiatives had introduced could not be reversed, southern interests and concerns on matters other than segregation had been understood by him and would be carefully considered when policy decisions were made that effected them. What he provided was a campaign that reassured southerners while presenting the Democrats as far to the left of the spectrum on issues such as neighbourhood schools, racial quotas, police powers, capital punishment, and traditional American values relating to the family, pornography and homosexuality. As a Republican, Nixon could also appeal to a shared patriotism and to the prevailing anti-communism in American culture.

The 'southern strategy' was extremely effective and laid the groundwork for a number of impressive victories and a significant realignment (by 1980, 40 per cent of the southern white voters were describing themselves as core Republicans while only 35 per cent still described themselves as core Democrats – a massive shift from the days when the Democrats could rely on winning 80 per cent of the white electorate).[6]

If the Democrats had wished to campaign effectively for southern white votes, they would have needed to take more steps than candidates like Hubert Humphrey, Walter Mondale and Michael Dukakis did to avoid being labelled 'liberal'.[7] There was no need to retreat from the promise of racial equality that the Civil Rights Act and the Voting Rights Act presented (Nixon did not do this and nor did Bush), but they did need to display some moderation in the pace at which they were willing to pursue liberal programmes that most southerners perceived as threatening. They needed to show white southerners that they were sympathetic to their culture and aspirations.

Richard Nixon and Ronald Reagan campaigned promising to change the direction the Supreme Court was leading by appointing conservative justices; and George Bush's campaign in 1988 effectively continued this strategy of blaming the Democrats for the activism of Supreme Court justices. Bush was also able to discredit Michael Dukakis in the eyes of large numbers of Americans by associating him with the ACLU and labelling him a 'liberal'. Indeed, the most effective political advertisement of the 1988 campaign attacked Dukakis for being too 'liberal' on matters relating to law and order in dealing with the rehabilitation of a dangerous criminal.

Conceding that other forces were at work contributing to the difficulties that Democratic candidates have faced in presidential contests, we see from this brief review of recent history how the Supreme Court's role cannot be regarded as insignificant. Although most voters do not follow developments on the Court and display little knowledge of legal matters or of actual cases, we must suppose that the liberal landmark cases that were brought down under Warren and Burger had an important impact, encouraging the Democrats too far to the left to be competitive and tempting the Republicans to pander to the worst instincts at work in United States culture. By projecting issues like quotas, abortion and capital punishment into the political arena at a time when progressive politicians had no capacity to defend the policies endorsed by the Supreme Court, the liberal justices ensured that there would be a backlash that would shift the agenda far to the right of the political spectrum.

Are the Republicans the Problem?

If social-democratic Americans are asked, they tend to blame the social problems in the United States on Republicans. It is all the fault of Nixon, Ford, Reagan and Bush. There is no progress because these leaders have allowed the rich to prosper at the expense of the poor and they are responsible for the backsliding in civil-rights enforcement. But this response simply avoids important questions. Why were these leaders elected? How did they manage to secure a national mandate to govern? Why did they choose to make capital punishment and the criminal justice system an electoral issue? Why did George Bush (who personally strikes one as a not very religious man) campaign so stridently against abortion? Why have the Republicans presented themselves as hostile to liberal values? In answering these questions, we have to recognize that the Supreme Court's activism in the Warren–Burger period helped to polarize the country in very unhelpful ways and that the liberal agenda it set for itself could not be sustained. Justice William Brennan was undoubtedly one of the most politically astute justices; no one could have done better than him in securing five votes on the Court to sustain a principled liberal approach. But five votes are insufficient to prevail in a democracy and not many other people in the United States now agree that liberal principles should override all other policy considerations. In the national contest between Brennan's conception of America and Reagan's – between the 'social agenda' and the 'civil rights agenda' – Reagan's triumphed.

This conflict between the conservative politician and liberal jurist is one important factor that has helped to shape the disastrous history of the last 30 years and its legacy will continue to influence American society in the foreseeable future. The outcome could have been predicted and the lesson this history teaches us should be learned: a society should not rely on the judiciary to provide moral leadership.

I have argued that the conservative justices, now on the Supreme Court, are right to recognize that some of the difficulties that are currently manifest in the American political culture flow from elitism – the attempt to impose values even when the people who are affected by the decisions do not embrace them. In establishing this, I explored policy relating to privacy, abortion and affirmative action. However we regard liberal interpretation of the Constitution relating to these and other issues (for example, whether it is important to read the

Establishment Clause of the First Amendment and the Equal Protection Clause of the Fourteenth Amendment in broad or narrow ways, whether it is legitimate for judges to identify an implied right to privacy), it must be conceded that the conservatives display a better understanding of the United States political system and its society. On each one of these major issues, the liberal position endorsed by the Supreme Court during the Warren–Burger period has been politically unsustainable and the fact that the judiciary went so far out-of-line with the other branches of government, disregarding public opinion, has resulted in the bad consequences I have described.

The Positive Side to the Reagan Era

Many people associate President Reagan with a mean-spirited hostility to minorities and the poor and there is no question that his administration did manifest a lack of sympathy for the circumstances of those dependent on welfare, shifting resources from the poor to the rich by cutting taxes.[8] But Reagan was not perceived by the people of the United States as a reactionary supporter of the rich. Indeed, he served brilliantly as a spokesman for poor and working class whites who turned to him to articulate their well-founded concerns.[9] Many felt that their religious beliefs were regarded as unworthy of respect by policymakers; many felt their patriotism was sneered at by those who were better educated (and often those whose family members usually did not have to serve in the military); many felt threatened by criminal elements in society; many felt economically vulnerable and resented the fact that governments were extending a helping hand to others but not to them; many felt that their children's schooling had been compromised by well-meaning programmes that were unrealistic about the actual burdens placed on some of the schools. This large sector of the American public felt that they were treated badly by the Supreme Court and that they were not well-represented by Democratic presidential candidates such as Walter Mondale, Jimmy Carter and Michael Dukakis who were sympathetic to the liberal agenda; and they detected in Reagan a genuine concern for their predicament – despite his personal wealth, he was perceived as one of them.[10]

When we consider the attitude taken by the Reagan (and other Republican) administrations towards civil rights, we find that there is little to commend. We cannot claim that the Reagan (or Nixon or Bush) presidency was sympathetic to civil rights or that it was worthy of receiving support from anyone who cherished liberal ideals. Indeed, they did all that they could to undermine the progress that had been made during the 1960s under Johnson.

But there are some positive features of the Republican orientation that can be distinguished. This arises because of the more individualist philosophy that some conservative intellectuals share. Many conservatives, including all of those who Nixon, Reagan and Bush advanced to the Supreme Court (with the possible exception of Rehnquist) do display sensitivity to the underlying individualism that makes it possible in a complex pluralist community like the United States to sustain a civilized *modus vivendi*. No writer has more eloquently defended this vision than Reagan's Solicitor General, Charles Fried, whose contribution I reviewed in Chapter 3. Indeed, his recent book outlining the strategies he followed to influence the Supreme Court, *Order & Law*, offers one complex way of reclaiming the liberal individualist legacy in the context of United States constitutional debates. As we have seen, Fried's influence is reflected on the Court by those justices who orientate from the work of the second Justice Harlan (like O'Connor, Kennedy and Souter). Indeed, it would not be exaggerating to claim that Fried has set the new direction the Supreme Court is likely to pursue into the twenty-first century, advocating an orderly withdrawal from the practice of unbridled judicial activism exhibited recently in the United States.

As we have seen, this achievement has not been easy for the dominant legal intellectuals in the United States have enjoyed a long flirtation with a vision of law that requires the identification of fundamental values and even the Supreme Court has been encouraged to explore a new collectivist testament seeking to transform the Constitution and America's traditional commitment to individualism. Fried's contribution has been to help find a strategy for retreating from this damaging development that holds firmly to a more traditional ideal of the rule of law. But he has done so in a distinctive manner. Instead of abandoning *stare decisis* in the name of originalism or embracing legal positivism, as other conservatives have been inclined to, he recommends that courts proceed from case to case, reasoning from analogy. Fried firmly believes that once the Court is faced by the conflict of values that has contributed to its failure to secure clear guide-lines in recent controversial issues (like abortion and affirmative action) it will be forced to rearticulate a commitment to the ideals of certainty, continuity and coherence within law rather than continue unbridled judicial activism.

Fried's vision will be congenial to those who have training in the tradition of the common law and is likely to find more support within Australian and British legal circles than in the United States. On most controversial issues he adopts a moderate position, combining his commitment to individualism and the rule of law with pragmatism. It is not surprising that this position has been endorsed by a number of the conservative justices. David Souter is clearly the most convinced of those who seek to work within the legacy of Justice Harlan that Fried defends; but O'Connor and Kennedy seem to have signed their allegiance. Between the three (perhaps with the help of the two members of the Court appointed by President Clinton, Ruth Bader Ginsberg and Stephen Breyer) they should be able to secure a pragmatic leadership for the Court into the twenty-first century.

Most Americans will be pleased about this. It is, however, clear that very many legal intellectuals remain convinced that the Supreme Court should be much more aggressive in securing rights.

Although Scalia has not managed to secure a leadership position on the Supreme Court his approach (which I find the most intellectually satisfying of those offered by the various Rehnquist conservatives) will remain influential. It is also likely to be adopted in other democracies by judges who are required to uphold liberties. As we have seen, Scalia is much more pragmatic than he is often portrayed. He accepts that the Constitution has been changed over the years by judicial initiatives and he is prepared to work within this legacy. For example, he agrees that *Lochner* v. *New York* and *Plessy* v. *Ferguson* were both questionable judgments, justifiably overruled. According to his understanding of what constitutes good law, there were practical as well as legal reasons for overruling these precedents. Nevertheless, the decision to do so was political. But the existence of these revolutionary moments as a part of American history is not an embarrassment for Scalia. Legal positivists have always allowed that bad laws (or bad precedents) may be ignored by judges when this can be done without causing great harm. However, they caution that a judge who contemplates moving beyond legal sources should know that he or she is *ultra vires*. For a positivist like Scalia, the disadvantages that judges face as policymakers as well as the importance of legal norms that counsel against abandoning precedents and conventions are factors that need to be weighed when a judge considers her options. They are considerations that must count for a great deal in a democracy. But if a desirable change is made successfully and a new rule is acknowledged, the positivist is free to follow it.

The liberal mistake, as Scalia sees it, is that they conclude from the fact that the United States Constitution has changed over the years that judges are free to extend their empire beyond text, history and precedent to include philosophical considerations. They fail to see, as the conservatives do, that the 'rule of law' will become a farce unless judges find ways of constraining their discretion by recognizing clear legal norms as binding in all but the most extraordinary circumstances. Thus, his main concern is that judges should not feel free to redraft the Constitution so that it conforms to their own preferences.

Judges who adopt Scalia's positivist approach will be prepared to uphold rights when these have been endorsed and listed in appropriate charters and they will take the actual traditions of their communities into account. But they will act cautiously, treating certainty in law as a value worth sustaining in its own right. When we consider the volatile nature of political life in most emerging democracies (such as the Ukraine, Poland or South Africa) we can only hope that most judges will be impressed by the rigour with which Scalia has managed to secure some space for 'law' as an independent endeavour – different from politics and intellectually distinguishable from history and philosophy.

Finally a word about values. Both Fried and Scalia are individualists. Their competing visions of how classical liberal ideas should influence constitutional practices in the United States offer viable alternatives. In terms of their liberalism, all individuals should have their interests equally respected and no allocation should be made on the basis of ethnicity or gender without compelling reasons. If two families are in poverty, they should receive the same help; if two students apply for a scholarship or a college place, their applications should be treated without regard to race or gender. It is a simple creed which, despite gross failures of implementation, has enjoyed a secure place within American culture since the *Declaration of Independence* and is likely to endure for many years more. To the extent that Americans depart from it by embracing ethnic and other divisive group identities and by asserting claims to group rights, the United States will become a worse kind of society and is likely to manifest even more virulent conflicts than it does already.

As Thomas Edsell has persuasively argued, Bill Clinton's campaign in 1992 was successful because he embraced this classical liberal vision. This is how he was able to make the case for greater government intervention to secure social justice and to create jobs without leaving the impression that the interests of poor whites would be treated with less concern than those of other disadvantaged groups in the community. Clinton campaigned as the champion of the white working and lower middle classes that had suffered under the Reagan–Bush years; but he did not alienate the African–American community or any other minorities who were looking for support from a more interventionist government. Clinton's victory was precarious in terms of his overall vote (he won only 43 per cent of the popular vote) but he showed that he understood how the Democratic Party must reorientate if it is to be competitive in presidential contests. If the new coalition across the ethnic divide is to hold, Edsell suggests, he needs to neutralize and even counter some of the more divisive aspects of contemporary collectivist programmes in the United States (for example, those that impose racial quotas) and he needs to be more sensitive than previous Democratic leaders have been to the values of the communities whose votes he is seeking, for example, by respecting their deeply felt religious beliefs and their patriotism. To succeed in this, he needs to follow the advice of people like David Gergen who understand why poorer whites have been so angered by liberal elites; but he also needs to return to the kind of political liberalism that is advocated by conservatives.

Lessons for Other Democracies

This book has focused exclusively on the United States. I have not attempted to compare its practices in securing rights with those in other democracies. Rather, I have been concerned to demonstrate, especially to readers who are not familiar with developments in the United States, that there are good reasons for questioning the popular perception that the American system of judicial review by the Supreme Court has always worked well in securing rights, even in the period following World War II. In particular, I have drawn attention to the success of the political backlash against the Warren–Burger justices in transforming the Supreme Court, to the disillusionment about 'law' in the academies and within American political culture generally (in that the legal system is now seen by many as merely another arena for pursuing politics), and to the good reasons conservative theorists have provided for reconsidering the dualist (or court-centred) approach advocated by liberals and some libertarians.

Dualist readings of the United States Constitution remain attractive to many Americans and the orientation prevails as the dominant paradigm within the law schools. As we have seen, many legal intellectuals defend dualism as representing a distinctive American contribution to our understanding of 'democracy'. They present the United States as a model 'constitutional' democracy, and their advocacy on behalf of this kind of system enjoys a wide influence. Indeed, the view that this kind of democracy is superior to parliamentary systems is one of the most successful exports from the United States in recent years, as more and more people in other democracies throughout the world now seek to emulate the United States constitutional system. Even the nations of the European Community are now bound by a charter of rights, the European Convention of Human Rights (adopted in 1950). Under this arrangement, citizens have the right to bring a complaint before the European Commission when they claim that their rights have been violated and, in some circumstances, if the Commission agrees that there has been a violation of protected rights, it may assign the matter to the judges of the European Court of Human Rights in Strasbourg. Indeed, most of the countries in the European Community have made the European Con-

vention of Human Rights part of their domestic law, allowing their
citizens to raise issues relating to these rights in their national courts.
In countries outside the European Community where there may be
no acknowledgment of rights, citizens can often make claims to have
their fundamental liberties recognized by referring to the international commitments made by their nation's representatives and to
actual obligations to uphold rights that may have been entered into
under various treaties.

All over the world, then, thanks to American inspiration, judges
are being tempted to launch forth into activism. Even people who are
critical of the separation of powers that characterizes the American
political system, still praise the role of the Supreme Court in securing
rights.

I have provided reasons for questioning this tendency. Admiration
for the United States Supreme Court usually arises because of a
misunderstanding of its role in recent history. We tend to view the
Supreme Court in a favourable light because we attribute to the
Warren-Court justices some significant role in achieving changes in
the United States that we applaud. Indeed, there is a view of the civil
rights decade that attributes Martin Luther King jr's success partly to
the fact that he was supported by the Supreme Court; whereas, it is
more accurate to hold that the Court was successful in projecting
liberalism because King was able to mobilize African Americans into
a cohesive political movement. The civil rights battle was won in the
streets – ultimately in the hearts and minds of the American people –
not in the courts.

I have claimed that if we are to adequately assess the desirability
of a court-centred system for securing rights, deciding whether parliamentary democracies should be reformed so that they are more
like the United States, we need to focus as much on the indirect
consequences of judicial actions as on the immediate results in particular cases. And we need to rid ourselves of the myth that the
Supreme Court has been such a potent force in American history.

It is easy to be misled about the desirability of empowering the
judiciary because the context in which a court acts will often be
determining. What a constitutional court will do in times of a war or
in confronting a crisis (such as bombing attacks by the Irish Republican Army in London) is difficult to predict. For example, we simply
do not know what American judges are likely to say when confronting the kind of situation that the British have been forced to face
because of the on-going struggle for political dominance in Northern
Ireland. Would the Supreme Court frustrate executive attempts to
deal with a particular crisis (by, say, authorizing the use of wiretap-
ping and other means of secret surveillance to deal with an outbreak
of bombing in New York or Washington) in the name of the abstract

liberties listed in the Bill of Rights? Isn't it more likely that the justices would discover a 'necessary for national security' exemption to
suspend the Bill of Rights? Terrorism is a problem that the British
must face every day and it is not surprising that the Parliament in
Westminster has authorized unrestrained surveillance. Any judgment
about whether the Supreme Court (using the Bill of Rights) would
offer better protection in facing the same circumstances must necessarily be speculative, so there is no way of deciding conclusively
whether American liberties would prove to be more resilient.[11] A fair
comparison requires us to speculate about how each system would
respond if confronted by the problems of the other. If we do try to
make this kind of judgment, however, it is not easy to conclude that
the United States has been better than the British parliamentary system in sustaining rights.[12]

What we can claim is that there are very few grounds for thinking
that judges are more likely to choose principle over policy than legislators have been – history shows us that judges often behave in much
the same way as other public officials when called on by the people
to act expediently.[13]

If we cannot expect much more from judges than from other members of a governing elite, can we expect more from the judicial branch,
as a separate institution sharing power? The answer to this question
seems to be a resounding 'No'. The conservative view of the judiciary as constrained is well-supported by evidence. It is one thing to
have judges deliver inspirational decisions, relying on the most advanced philosophical ideas about justice, quite another to have these
rulings implemented. More significantly, what happens in courts is
very likely to influence what takes place within the executive and in
the various legislative arenas of the nation. Thus, if a constitutional
court advances an agenda that is in conflict with the beliefs of other
elites, especially when this agenda enjoys little support in the community, it is unlikely to prevail. In the end, as the transformation of
the Supreme Court from Warren to Rehnquist shows, the composition of the court will be changed. Unfortunately, in losing the battle
to secure rights that were unsustainable in the first place because of
widespread community opposition, an active constitutional court is
likely to make it more difficult for those politicians who are willing
to advance the agenda of liberty-protection to succeed.

Those who advocate extensive involvement of judges in
policymaking should also be cautioned by Donald Horowitz's evidence (reviewed in Chapter 2) that shows that judges are not usually
good at making well-considered judgments because they must operate from the evidence presented in the case before them; nor are
judges in a position to obtain good advice and they cannot easily
adjust their policies when difficulties emerge.

Even though the considerations I have listed will caution many people against radically restructuring parliamentary systems so that they become more like the United States, the temptation to lists rights in a charter will not be resisted. In most systems today, rights are already recognized (for example, in the European Convention of Human Rights, already mentioned); indeed, only Australia and a few other democracies remain unconvinced of the need for such a list and these systems are likely to change soon, formally committing their nations to upholding fundamental liberties. In the newer democracies there has been no hesitation. All seem to have thought a charter of rights essential. In South Africa, for example, the interim Constitution contains an extensive list of liberties and entitlements that the Constitutional Court is required to uphold, including substantive commitments to, for example, adequate parental care, as well as 'to security, basic nutrition, and basic health and social services' for children.[14]

These developments are understandable and desirable. People value liberties and because it is widely believed that listing rights will help to secure them, it will often seem sensible to do this. No harm will be done if the nations of the world compete to make the most fulsome formal commitment to uphold rights. Indeed, this new fashion in political propaganda should be welcomed. Inspirational statements make a difference in political life and it matters a great deal whether societies try to nurture a respect for liberty.

In most democracies, a list of fundamental rights embodied in a charter will be taken seriously and courts will be expected to uphold them. This will place a burden on the judiciary because it will not be obvious how they ought to read some of the inevitably vague and abstract phrases that will be included in the relevant charter. Here, they will face a choice: they may decide to take the position adopted by Justice Brennan and other members of the Warren–Burger Court in the United States, understanding a charter of rights as an empowerment of the judiciary – as a deliberate and legitimate counter-majoritarian device; or they may follow the conservatives in the United States, trying to reconcile the judicial role in exercising review with a commitment to democratic accountability. If they adopt the latter course, as I recommend, they should be willing to make some advances in the protection of liberty using the representation-reinforcing rationale advocated by John Hart Ely and others, but they will also develop strategies for restraining judicial discretion to secure greater certainty along the lines advocated by Charles Fried or Justice Scalia. This more conservative course will be frustrating to those who think social problems can be solved if intellectuals make strong public statements backed by the authority of the courts. However, those of us who fear that judicial authority will soon lose its value as tender when judges are active may be worried by this kind of development. If we also see the democratic system as a discovery mechanism for finding what is feasible in a given society at a particular time, not merely as a decision procedure, and if we are also committed to the complex processes of accommodation that characterize the formation of consensus in parliamentary systems, we will be happier if judges do not attempt to play the leading role as policymakers.

Notes

1 See *The Washington Post*, 9 June 1993, A7.
2 It is interesting to note that the Rehnquist Court has proved ineffectual in securing some of Reagan's ideals. For example, its ruling in *City of Richmond* v. *Croson* (the 'set-aside' for minority businesses case, discussed in Chapter 10) has not been implemented effectively. This shows the constraints the Supreme Court faces when it acts without the support of Congress. See George LaNove 'Social Science and Minority "Set-asides"', *The Public Interest*, no. 110, (winter 1993), 49–62. Local businesses have every incentive not to complain about racial quotas when they are seeking an on-going relationship with governments that will bring many lucrative contracts. Indeed, they will voluntarily embrace quotas to please politicians who demand them, whether the law requires this or not. It is much easier to discriminate in the required manner than to take a stand on principle.
3 During the New Deal the South gave half of the electoral college votes needed to elect Franklin Roosevelt to four straight terms (Earl Black and Merle Black, *The Vital South: How Presidents Are Elected* (Cambridge, Mass.: Harvard University Press, 1992, 344).
4 We do know that *Brown* v. *Board of Education* served as something of a symbol in the South. Some commentators think that Richard Nixon lost substantial support campaigning against John F. Kennedy and George Wallace in 1960 because he was associated with Eisenhower who had appointed the author of *Brown*, the hated Earl Warren (See, Black and Black, op. cit., p. 190). Certainly Wallace tried to use this association and the fact that Nixon had served as an administration for civil rights under Eisenhower against him. The Eisenhower administration in which Nixon had served as Vice-President was also blamed for sending federal troops to Arkansas to oversee the racial integration of a high school in Little Rock.
5 An explanation of how Lyndon Johnson was able to beat Barry Goldwater in 1964 is provided in ibid., 153–5, 199–203.
6 According to Black and Black the median white Republican vote in the 1972–88 presidential elections was 67 per cent (ibid., 347).
7 No more than 10 per cent of Deep South southern white voters supported Humphrey or McGovern; Mondale and Dukakis attracted respectively 28 per cent and 32 per cent of the total white vote in the South (Black and Black, ibid., 338).
8 See Kevin Phillips, *The Politics of Rich and Poor* (NY: Random House, 1990).
9 In the 1990 Census, 8 per cent of the 213 million whites are classified as living in poverty compared to 29 per cent of the 32 million blacks. Although the proportion of the black community in poverty is higher, the total number of whites and black Americans in poverty is 17 million and 9.28 million respectively.
10 Thomas Edsall and Mary Edsall, *Chain Reaction: The Impact of Race, Rights and Taxes on American Politics*, NY: Norton, 1992, ch. 9, 172–97. As Stanley Greenberg is a

pollster advising President Clinton, it is interesting that they cite his Report on Democratic Defection (DC, Washington: The Analysis Group, 15 April 1985) to support their conclusions.

11   This seems to be the error that Ronald Dworkin makes in his essay *A Bill of Rights for Britain: Why British Liberty Needs Protecting* (London: Chatto & Windus, 1990).

12   A comparative assessment of the two systems is provided in Alan Ryan, 'The British, the Americans, and Rights' in Michael J. Lacey and Knud Haakonssen (eds), *A Culture of Rights* (NY: Cambridge University Press, 1991), 366–440.

13   Ronald Dworkin seems to think that judges are more likely to be principled. See, op. cit., 10–11.

14   Section 30, 1 (c) and (d). On other fundamental rights that are protected, see chapter three of the interim Constitution. But although the framers seem to have tried desperately to establish the new South African Constitutional Court as a countermajoritarian and independent branch of government, and it has been given very significant powers, the Court is unlikely to frustrate a mobilized majority for very long because its members are appointed for a non-renewable period of only seven years (#99).

Bibliography

Ackerman, Bruce, *We the People: Foundations* (Cambridge, Mass.: Harvard University Press, 1991); 'Review of *Takings: Private Property and the Power of Eminent Domain*', *University of Miami Law Review*, vol. 41, no. 1, Nov. 1986.

Barak, Aharon, *Judicial Discretion* (New Haven, Conn.: Yale University Press, 1989).

Berger, Raoul, *Government by Judiciary: the Transformation of the Fourteenth Amendment* (Cambridge, Mass.: Harvard University Press, 1977).

Berns, Walter, *Taking the Constitution Seriously* (NY: Simon & Schuster, 1987).

Bickel, Alexander, *The Least Dangerous Branch* (New Haven, Conn.: Yale University Press, 2nd ed., 1986); 'The Original Understanding and the Segregation Decision', *Harvard Law Review*, vol. 69, 1955, pp. 1ff.

Biskupic, John, 'Bush Treads Well-Worn Path in Building Federal Bench', *Congressional Quarterly* vol. 50, 18 Jan. 1992), p. 111.

Black, Earl (with Black, Merle), *The Vital South: How Presidents Are Elected* (Cambridge, Mass.: Harvard University Press, 1992).

Bork, Robert, *The Tempting of America: the Political Seduction of the Law* (NY: The Free Press, 1990).

Brown, Peter, *Minority Party* (Washington, DC: Regnery Gateway, 1991).

Buchanan, James (with Brennan, Geoffrey), *The Reason of Rules: Constitutional Political Economy* (Cambridge/NY: Cambridge University Press, 1987).

Carter, Stephen, L., *The Culture of Disbelief: How American Law and Politics Trivialise Religious Devotion* (NY: Basic Books, 1993).

Chemerinsky, Erwin, 'The Vanishing Constitution: the Supreme Court 1989 Term', *Harvard Law Review*, vol. 103, 1989.

Dahl, R.A., *Democracy and Its Critics*, (New Haven, Conn.: Yale University Press, 1989) pp. 156–7; 'Decision-making in a Democracy: the Supreme Court as a National Policy Maker', *Journal of Public Law*, vol. 6, 1957, pp. 279–95.

Dworkin, Ronald, *Life's Dominion: an Argument about Abortion, Euthanasia, and Individual Freedom* (NY: Alfred A. Knopf, 1993); 'The Reagan Revolution and the Supreme Court', *New York Review of Books*, vol. XXXVIII, no. 13, 1991; 'Bork's Jurisprudence', *University of Chicago Law Review*, vol. 57, 1990; *A Bill of Rights for Britain; Why British Liberty Needs Protecting* (London: Chatto & Windus, 1990); *Law's Empire* (London: Fontana Press, 1986); *A Matter of Principle* (Cambridge, Mass.: Harvard University Press, 1985); *Taking Rights Seriously* (Cambridge, Mass.: Harvard University Press, 1977).

Edsall, Thomas, 'Clinton, So Far', *New York Review of Books*, vol XL, no. 16, 7 Oct. 1993; [with Edsall, Mary], *Chain Reaction: the Impact of Race, Rights, and Taxes on American Politics* (NY: Norton, 1992).

Ely, John Hart, *Democracy and Distrust: a Theory of Judicial Review* (Cambridge, Mass.: Harvard University Press, 1980).

Epstein, Lee [with Kobylka, Joseph F.], *The Supreme Court and Legal Change: Abortion and the Death Penalty* (Chapel Hill, NC: University of North Carolina Press, 1992).

Epstein, Richard, 'Reply to Critics', *University of Miami Law Review*, vol. 41, no. 1, Nov. 1986; *Takings: Private Property and the Power of Eminent Domain* (Cambridge, Mass.: Harvard University Press, 1985).

Feeley, Malcolm M., 'Hollow Hopes, Flypaper, and Metaphors', *Law and Social Inquiry*, vol. 17, no. 4, 1992, pp. 745–60.

Fried, Charles, *Order & Law: Arguing the Reagan Revolution* (NY: Simon & Schuster, 1991); 'Affirmative Action After the *City of Richmond* v. *J.A. Croson Co.*: a Response to the Scholars' Statement', *Yale Law Journal*, vol. 99, 1989; 'Metro Broadcasting Inc. v. FCC [110 S. Ct. 2997]: Two Concepts of Equality', *Harvard University Law Review*, vol. 104, pp. 107–27.

Fullinwider, Robert, *The Reverse Discrimination Controversy: a Moral and Legal Analysis* (Totowa, NJ: Rowman & Allanheld, 1980).

Glendon, Mary Ann, *Rights Talk: the Impoverishment of Political Discourse* (NY: The Free Press, 1991).

Goldman, Sheldon, 'Reagan's Judicial Legacy: Completing the Puzzle and Summing Up', *Judicature*, vol. 72, no. 6, 1989, pp. 318–30.

Hart, H.L.A., *The Concept of Law* (Oxford: Oxford University Press, 1961).

Horowitz, Donald, *The Courts and Social Policy* (Washington, DC: The Brookings Institute, 1977).

Hughes, Robert, *Culture of Complaint: The Fraying of America* (NY: Oxford University Press, 1993).

Hutchinson, Allan C., 'Indiana Dworkin and Law's Empire', *Yale Law Journal*, vol. 96, 1987, pp. 637–65; (ed.), *Critical Legal Studies* (Totowa, NJ: Rowman & Littlefield, 1989).

Hutson, James H., 'The Bill of Rights in American Revolutionary Experience' in M. Lacey and K. Haakonssen (eds), *A Culture of Rights: the Bill of Rights in Philosophy, Politics and Law – 1792 and 1991* (NY: Cambridge University Press, 1991), pp. 88–96.

Kairy, David, *With Liberty and Justice for Some: a Critique for the Conservative Supreme Court* (NY: The New Press, 1993).

Kassop, Nancy, 'From Arguments to Supreme Court Opinions in Planned Parenthood v. Casey', *PS: Political Science & Politics*, vol. xxvi, no. 1, March 1993, pp. 51–9.

Koh, Harold Hongju, *The National Security Constitution: Sharing Power After the Iran–Contra Affair* (New Haven, Conn.: Yale University Press, 1990).

LaNove, George, 'Social Science and Minority "Set-Asides"', *The Public Interest*, no. 110, winter 1993, pp. 49–62.

Lieberman, Jethro K., *The Evolving Constitution: How the Supreme Court Has Ruled on Issues from Abortion to Zoning* (NY: Random House, 1992).

Macedo, Stephen, 'The Right to Privacy: a Constitutional and Moral Defence', *Political Theory Newsletter* (Canberra, ACT: Australia) vol. 2, no. 2, 1990, pp. 191–9; *The New Right and the Constitution* (Washington, DC: Cato, 1987, 2nd ed.).

McClosky, Herbert (with Brill, Alida), *Dimensions of Tolerance: What Americans Believe about Civil Liberties* (NY: Russell Sage Foundation, 1983).

Meese, Edwin, III, 'Interpreting the Constitution' in Jack N. Rakove (ed.), *Interpreting the Constitution: the Debate Over Original Intent* (Boston, Mass.: Northeastern University Press, 1990), pp. 263–313.

Milner, Henry, *Sweden: Social Democracy in Practice* (NY: Oxford University Press, 1989).

Monaghan, Henry Paul, 'Stare Decisis and Constitutional Adjudication' in Jack N. Rakove (ed.), *Interpreting the Constitution: the Debate Over Original Intent* (Boston, Mass.: Northeastern University Press, 1990), pp. 263–313.

Muravchik, Joshua, 'Why the Democrats Lost Again', in *Commentary*, Feb. 1989, pp. 13–22.

Nozick, Robert, *Anarchy, State, and Utopia* (Oxford: Blackwell, 1974).

Phillips, Kevin, *The Politics of Rich and Poor* (Random House, 1990).

Podhoretz, John, *A Hell of a Ride: Backstage at the White House Follies 1989–1993* (NY: Simon & Schuster, 1993).

Posner, Richard, 'The DeFunis Case and the Constitutionality of Preferrential Treatment of Racial Minorities', *Supreme Court Review 1974*; 'What am I? A Potted Plant', *The New Republic*, 28 Sept. 1987, p. 24.

Rakove, Jack N. (ed.), *Interpreting the Constitution: the Debate Over*

Original Intent (Boston, Mass.: Northeastern University Press, 1990), pp. 263–313.

Rawls, John, *Political Liberalism* (NY: Columbia University Press, 1993).

Rehnquist, William, 'Government by Cliche', *Missouri Law Review*, vol. 45, no. 3, 1980, pp. 379–93; 'The Notion of a Living Constitution', *Texas Law Review*, vol. 54, no. 4, 1976, pp. 693–706.

Riggs, F.W., *Problems of Presidentialism*, (unpublished, available from University of Hawaii, Institute of Government Studies).

Rosen, Jeffrey, 'The Leader of the Opposition', *The New Republic*, 18 Jan. 1993.

Rosenberg, Gerald N., 'Reply to Critics', *Law & Social Inquiry*, vol. 17, no. 4, 1992, pp. 761–78; *The Hollow Hope: Can Courts Brings About Social Change* (Chicago: University of Chicago Press, 1991).

Rossiter, Clinton (ed.), *The Federalist Papers* (NY: New American Library, 1961).

Savage, David G., *Turning Right: the Makings of the Rehnquist Supreme Court* (NY: John Wiley & Sons, 1992).

Scalia, Antonin, 'Originalism', *Cincinnati Law Review*, vol. 57, 1989, pp. 849ff.

Scheingold, Stuart, *The Politics of Rights* (New Haven, Conn.: Yale University Press, 1974).

Schumpeter, Joseph A., *Capitalism, Socialism and Democracy* (London: Allen & Unwin, 1970).

Senate Judiciary Committee, *Report on the Nomination of Clarence Thomas to Be an Associate Justice of the U.S. Supreme Court*, 1 Oct. 1991 (Congressional Session 102–1, CIS No. 91-S524-2).

Stanley, Harold W. (with Niemi, Richard G.), *Vital Statistics on American Politics* (Washington, DC: CQ Press, 1992).

Sundquist, James, *The Decline and Resurgence of Congress*, (Washington, DC: Brookings Institute, 1981).

Sunstein, Cass, *The Partial Constitution* (Cambridge, Mass.: Harvard University Press, 1993).

Thomas, Clarence, 'The Higher Law Background of the Privileges and Immunities Clause of the Fourteenth Amendment', *Harvard Journal of Law and Public Policy*, vol. 12, 1989.

Tribe, Laurence (with Michael Dorf), *How to Read the Constitution* (Cambridge, Mass.: Harvard University Press, 1992); *Abortion: the Clash of Absolutes* (NY: W.W. Norton, 1990); *Constitutional Choice* (Cambridge, Mass.: Harvard University Press, 1985).

Tucker, D.F.B., 'Conservatives on the Supreme Court', *Constitutional Political Economy*, vol. 3, no. 2, 1992, pp. 197–221; *Law, Liberalism and Free Speech* (Totowa, NJ: Rowman & Allanheld, 1985).

Wasserstrom, Silas, 'The Empire's New Clothes', *The Georgetown Law Journal*, vol. 75, 1986.

Wilson, William J., *The Truly Disadvantaged: the Inner City, the Underclass and Public Policy* (Chicago: University of Chicago Press, 1987); *The Declining Significance of Race* (Chicago, Ill.: University of Chicago Press, 1980).

Wolters, Raymond, *The Burden of Brown: Thirty Years of School Desegregation* (Knoxville, T.: University of Tennessee Press, 1984).

Index

abortion; see also, *Roe* v. *Wade* 10–1,
  22 nts. 31 and 32, 40, 160
  public opinion 48 nt. 45
  Clinton 24 nt. 43
Ackerman, Bruce 14, 67 nt. 21, 168,
  219
  'higher lawmaking' 120–27
  'monist' and 'dualist' democracy
  1f., 20 nt. 2
  Bork nomination 126f., 23 nt. 35
  countermajoritarian issue 126
  Reagan revolution 124–7
affirmative action; see also, Equal
  Protection Clause 167, 188–90
  Civil Rights Act 190–95
  Fourteenth Amendment 195–201
  individualism 205–10
  race norming 191, 212 nt. 6

benign discrimination 198
Babbit, Bruce 218
Berns, Walter 20 nt. 3, 56–8, 66 nt. 6,
  61, 81, 213 nt. 21
Bickel, Alexander 27, 46 nt. 3, 86 nt.
  3
Bill of Rights 20 nt. 8, 108f., 167f.,
  173 nt. 30, 178, 218, 229
  and public opinion 5, 21 nt. 13,
  39ff.
Black, Earl and Merle 44, 49 nts. 51
  and 52, 231 nts. 3, 4, 5 and 6
Blackmun, Harry (Justice) 6, 100
Bork, Robert 74–9, 86 nt. 2, 87 nt. 29,
  198
  nomination 126f.
Bowers v. *Hardwick* 96–8, 112, 114f.
Brennan, William (Justice) 3, 19, 66
  nt. 6, 175, 222, 230

affirmative action 195f.
  death penalty 139–41
Brennan, Geoffrey 87 nt. 23
Brill, Alida; see also, McClosky,
  Herbert 21 nt. 13, 38ff., 173 nt.
  27
Brown v. *Board of Education* 18, 24 nt.
  46, 136, 147, 188, 231 nt.4
Buchanan, James; see also, Brennan,
  Geoffrey 87 nt. 23
Burger, Warren (Chief Justice); see
  also, Warren-Burger Court 2, 6,
  141, 180, 200
Bush, George (President) 6, 22 nts.
  27 and 30, 42, 48 nt. 49, 53, 126,
  153

Capital Punishment, see also
  Furman v. *Georgia* 37–40, 139–
  12, 144 nt. 32
  Public opinion 39 (Figure 2.1)
Carter, Jimmy (President) 44, 49 nt.
  55
Carter, Stephen 173 nt. 26
Chemerinsky, Erwin 21 nt. 17, 86 nt.
  1
City of Richmond v. *Croson* 188, 196,
  201–5, 231 nt. 2
Civil Rights Act, see also *Griggs* v.
  Duke Power Co. 153, 172 nt. 18,
  188, 189–91
  business necessity test 192f.
  forward-looking affirmative
  action 199f.
  Wards Cove Packing v. *Antonio* 194
Clinton, William (President) 22 nt.
  27, 24 nt. 43, 42f., 130, 142 nt.
  10, 183f. 218, 225

surburban support 49 nt. 58
communitarianism 155ff., 160
conservative agenda 8ff., 124ff., 167
    Reagan Revolution 69, 74
Constrained Court view; see also,
    Rosenberg, Gerald 25–8, 171,
    229f., 231 nt. 2
conventionalism; see also, Dworkin,
    Ronald 148–51.
    Korematsu v. *U.S.* 164f.
    pragmatism 150
countermajoritarian policymaking
    1, 20 nt. 5, 13ff., 23 nt. 35, 28–36,
    64ff., 78ff., 119, 130, 131–36,
    139ff., 141, 164, 168, 179, 218
Critical Legal Studies 21 nt. 9

Dahl, Robert A. 19 nt. 1, 20 nt. 6, 14–
    5, 46 nt. 6, 173 nt. 30
    countermajoritarian
        policymaking 28–31
DeFunis v. *Odegaard* 196
democracy (various conceptions of)
    1f., 19 nt. 1, 134, 154, 174f.
    dualist 1, 4, 5ff., 20 nts. 3 and 6, 21
        nt. 9, 58, 119f.
    Schumpeter 131
disparate impact rule 194
Dorf, Michael; see also.Tribe 20 nt.
    3, 119, 175, 182
Douglas, William (Justice) 3, 57, 60,
    93, 139f.
Due Process Clause 97, 98, 169, 200
Dukakis, Michael 42, 126, 221, 223
Dworkin, Ronald; 1, 20 nt. 3, 20 nt.
    7, 63, 87 nt. 14, 81, 127, 119,
    145–63, 219, 232 nt. 11
    'concept' and 'conception' 79–82
    concept of law 80
    constructive interpretation 148f.
    conventionalism 148f.
    Fried 80
    Hercules 150, 172 nt. 11
    historical argument 164–6
    legal positivism 146–9, 156
    privacy 98ff., 173 nt. 24
    Tribe and Dorf 176f., 185 nt. 12, 181

Edsell, Thomas 225, 232 nt. 10

Eighth Amendment 140ff., 138–41
Eisenhower, Dwight (President) 220
Ely, John Hart 20 nt. 3, 14, 23 nt. 3,
    87 nt. 16, 119, 168, 219, 230
    capital punishment 138–42
    discrete and insular minority
        rationale 136ff.
    representation-reinforcing ration-
        ale 132–4, 137f.
    Roe v. *Wade* 143 nt. 27
Eminent Domain Clause 57, 60–2
Epstein, Richard 20 nt. 3, 52, 59–64,
    66 nts. 1 and 11
Equal Protection Clause 101, 194f.,
    213 nt. 19, 197–200, 211, 223
Establishment Clause 161, 168, 170,
    223
European Convention of Human
    Rights 227

Feeley, Malcolm 36 nt. 27
Fifth Amendment 169, 177f., 190
First Amendment 167, 182
Fourteenth Amendment 167, 190,
    194, 196, 213 nt. 19, 218
    individualism 205–210
    Racial Quotas 195f., 199–205
    Section 5, 200, 202
Fourth Amendment 43
Fried, Charles 69f., 86 nt. 3, 71–4, 80,
    91, 111f., 116
    abortion 99
    Civil Rights Act 193–95
    Equal Protection Clause 200f.
    minority-business-enterprise set-
        asides 201f., 224
    privacy 97ff.
Frontiero v. *Richardson* 208
Fullilove v. *Klutznick* 199f.
Fullinwider, Robert 172 nt. 17, 212
    nt. 3
Furman v. *Georgia*; see also, capital
    punishment 38, 140–2, 180

Gergen, David 227
Ginsberg, Ruth Bader (Justice) 19,
    225
Goldberg, Arthur (Justice) 93f.
Goldwater, Barry 220

Graham, Hugh 47 nt. 9, 172 nt. 17, 214 nt. 28
Greenberg, Stanley 232 nt. 10
Griggs v. *Duke Power Co.*; see also, racial quotas 29, 32, 153, 172 nt. 17, 188, 191ff., 194
Griswold v. *Connecticut* 57ff., 92f., 96, 98ff., 111, 116
Guinier, Lani 143 nt. 17

Haakonssen, Knud 185 nt. 14
Hamilton, Alexander 13
Harlan, John Marshall (Justice) 69ff., 97f., 111f., 181, 200, 224
Hart, Herbert L. A. 61, 67 nt. 22, 143 nt. 17, 146, 148
Hercules (fictional Justice); see also, Ronald Dworkin 150, 172 nt. 11, 151, 154, 156, 161, 165f.
Horowitz, Donald 10, 22 nt. 29, 23 nt. 37, 31–4, 46 nt. 6, 47 nt. 15, 218f.
Hughes, Robert 24 nt. 41, 162f., 173 nt. 29
Hutchinson, Allan C. 21 nt. 9, 171 nt. 1
Hutson, James H. 185 nt. 14

impartiality principle 169
incorporation doctrine 20 nt. 8, 21 nt. 12
individualism 205–10, 231f.

Jackson, Jesse 42
Jefferson, Thomas (President) 161, 173 nt. 26
Jencks, Christopher 173 nt. 25
Johnson, Lyndon B. (President) 44, 220f., 231 nt. 5
judiciary (conception of its role) 2, 70
   Ackerman's view 127ff.
   Dworkin's view 147ff.
   Ely's view 133
   Sunstein's view 168

Kairy, David 21 nt. 17
Karst, Kenneth L. 212 nt. 3
Kassop, Nancy 174 nt. 41

Kennedy, Anthony (Justice) 5, 72, 92, 97, 113ff., 126, 129, 145, 166, 174 nt. 41
   agreement with (Scalia) 65, (Rehnquist) 90
   forward-looking affirmative action 212f.
   Roe v. *Wade* 111ff.
King, Martin Luther Jr. 228
Korematsu v. *U.S.* 26, 164f.

Lacey, Michael 184 nt. 14
LaNore, George 231 nt. 2
law (concept of) 62, 73, 80, 127, 146f., 149, 150, 164, 171 nt. 7
legal positivism 5, 23 nt. 33, 70, 66 nt. 12, 76, 87, 108, 115, 225
   affirmative action 196ff.
   Dworkin's criticisms 146–55, and communitarianism 156–60
   privacy 96ff., 105ff.
liberalism 162, 163f., 173 nt. 30
   republicanism 174 nt. 36
Liberty Clause 95
Lochner v. *New York* 168, 225
Lowi, Theodore 164 nt. 28
Luban, David ix

Macedo, Stephen 20 nt. 3, 64, 66 nts. 3 and 9, 81, 86 nt. 7, 91
   evolving Constitution 57–8
   Fried 100f.
   privacy 98f.
Madison, James 162f., 175
Marshall, John (Chief Justice) 164, 217
Marshall, Thurgood (Justice) 3, 139ff., 141, 195–6
McClosky, Herbert 21 nt. 13, 39ff., 173 nt. 27
Meese, Edwin III (Attorney General) 53, 66 nt. 2, 86 nt. 2, 143 nt. 20
Meiklejohn, Alexander 131, 168
minority-business-enterprise set-asides 199f.
Metro Broadcasting v. *FCC* 172 nt. 18, 188, 196, 201–4
Monaghan, Henry P. 86 nt. 5

Mondale, Walter 42, 220, 223
Murphy, Walter 186 nt. 19
Murray, Charles 173 nt. 25

natural-law foundationalism 52ff., 56–66
New Deal 146, 163, 168f., 231 nt. 3
Ninth Amendment 82, 93, 96, 110, 177ff., 181
  framers's intentions 180f.
Nixon, Richard (President) 5f., 125, 220f., 222, 231
  capital punishment 38
Nozick, Robert 61–2

O'Connor, Sandra Day (Justice) 145, 166, 213 nt. 18
  'reasonable restraint' standard 113, 174 nt. 41
  affirmative action 202f.
  agreement with (Scalia) 65, (Rehnquist) 90, 86 nt. 1
  City of Richmond v. *Croson* 202
  Metro Broadcasting v. *FCC* 202–5, 208, 223
  Roe v. *Wade* 111ff., 129
  stare decisis 72
  stereotypes 207f.
  suspect category doctrine 206
originalism 53ff., 69f., 72ff.
  Ackerman 128–30
  Bork nomination 126
  Bork-Rehnquist 74ff.
  Scalia's 'fainthearted' 150ff.

Phillips, Kevin 231 nt. 8
philosophical jurisprudence 79f., 94, 98ff., 101, 116, 176–81
  Dworkin 147–9
Planned Parenthood of S.E. Pennsylvania v. *Casey* 105–17, 174 nt. 41
Plessy v. *Ferguson* 164–6, 198, 200, 211, 225
Poe v. *Ullman* 121
Posner, Richard 213 nt. 20, 196ff., 198
Powell, Lewis (Justice) 6, 26, 172 nt. 18
presidential elections 6, 124f., 220f.

1988 contest 22 nt. 27, 126, 143 nt. 15
1992 contest 10, 22 nt. 27, 40–5
privacy 93–102
public opinion 39ff., 48 nt. 45, 128
  death penalty 37–9

quotas (racial), see also affirmative action 47 nt. 9, 153f., 167, 172 nt. 18, 226f., 231 nt. 2
  1992 election 42–3
  and Fourteenth Amendment 195–206
Griggs v. *Duke Power Co.* 29, 189–93

rationality review
  privacy 96f.
  stereotypes 208f.
Rawls, John 20 nt. 3, 24 nt. 45, 63, 173 nt. 30, 186 nt. 19
Reagan, Ronald (President) 6, 53, 69, 78, 181, 124, 128, 129, 142, 191, 221–27
  capital punishment 38
Regents of University of California v. *Bakke* 172 nt. 18, 193, 199f.
Rehnquist, William (Chief Justice) 70f., 74–8, 84f., 91, 94, 166–7, 203f.
  agreement with (Scalia) 65, (other members of the Court) 90
  Equal Protection Clause 211
  Planned Parenthood of S. E. Pennsylvania v. *Casey* 105ff.
  Plessy v. *Ferguson* 210–1
  United Steelworkers of America v. *Weber* 199
representation-reinforcing review; see also, Ely 14, 87 nt. 16, 131ff., 168, 230
  capital punishment 139ff.
  Warren Court 138f.
Republican tradition 168, 174 nt. 36
Riggs, F. W. 21 nt. 11
Roe v. *Wade* 74, 94ff., 100, 103 nt. 26, 107ff., 111, 124, 138, 143 nt. 27, 173 nt. 24, 174 nt. 41, 177
Roosevelt, Franklin D. (President) 146, 163, 168, 219, 231 nt. 3

Rosen, Jeffrey 87 nt. 24
Rosenberg, Gerald 13, 34–5, 46 nt. 6, 166, 174 nt. 34, 185 nt. 4, 218
  indirect impact of Court rulings 36f.
rule of law 3, 60, 71ff., 77, 159
rule of recognition; see also, Hart 143 nts. 17 and 18
  Ackerman 127–9
  Ely 138–41
  Epstein 61f.

Scalia, Antonin (Justice) 70f., 86 nt. 1, 91, 106, 117 nt. 2, 203f., 214 nt. 28, 225f.
  'fainthearted' originalism 78–84
  affirmative action 198f., 206–7, 209
  agreement with (other members of the Court) 65 (Rehnquist) 90
  criticism of liberals 79f., 180ff.
  Dworkin 79–82, 150
  Equal Protection Clause 198f.
  privacy 97
  tradition 175, 177ff.
  Tribe and Dorf 176–80
Scheingold, Stuart 46 nt. 6, 47 nt. 27
school busing 22 nt. 29, 189f., 203
Schumpeter, Joseph 143 nt. 21, 133
Second Amendment 64, 178
Souter, David (Justice) 5, 19, 72, 92, 113ff., 129, 166, 174 nt. 41, 224
  Roe v. *Wade* 111ff.
  agreement with (Scalia) 65 (Rehnquist) 90
South Africa 156–60, 230, 232 nt. 14
  Interim Constitution 173 nt. 20
stare decisis doctrine 91, 106f., 111–5, 117 nt. 6, 129
structural discrimination 192, 195, 212 nt. 7
Sundquist, James 21 nt. 10
Sunstein, Cass 145, 165–71
  First Amendment 167
suspect category doctrine 206
  Caroline Products footnote 132, 136, 143 nt. 25

Takings Clause 60–2, 98, 168
Tennessee Valley Authority v. *Hill* (Snail Darter Case); see also, Dworkin 151–55
Tenth Amendment 180
Thomas, Clarence (Justice) 71, 84f., 106, 143 nt. 18, 145, 166, 172 nt. 18
  natural law 65f.
  agreement with (Scalia) 65 (Rehnquist) 90
Tribe, Laurence 20, nt. 3, 87 nt. 14
  legal positivism 108ff.
  philosophical jurisprudence 66 nt. 5, 182–4
  abortion 22 nt. 32, 102 nt. 6
  criticism of Scalia 176f., 180–2
  Ninth Amendment 177–80

United Steelworkers v. *Weber* 188, 191f., 199
utilitarian arguments 148, 171 nt. 7, 150

Vanberg, Viktor ix

Wagner, Richard E. ix, 173 nt. 25
Wallace, George 220, 231 nt. 4
Wards Cove Packing v. *Antonio* 194
Warren, Earl (Chief Justice) 2, 3, 132, 231 nt. 4
Warren-Burger Court 2–3, 132, 165, 169, 175, 218, 230
  Ackerman 127,
  Ely 132f., 135
Wasserstrom, Silas 172 nt. 9
West Coast Hotel v. *Parrish* 178
White, Byron (Justice) 96f., 106, 117 nt. 6, 139f., 208
William Webster v. *Reproductive Services* 86 nt. 1
Wolters, Raymond 22 nt. 29

Coventry University